Christians, Politics and Violent Revolution

J. G. DAVIES

CHRISTIANS, POLITICS AND VIOLENT REVOLUTION

ORBIS BOOKS

Maryknoll, New York 10545

CONTENTS

PREFATORY NOTE

I am happy to record my thanks to my colleague Neville Brown (Professor of Comparative Law) for reading a preliminary draft of chapter 4, to my former colleague Ninian Smart (now Professor in Lancaster) who read the major part of chapter 6, and to Ronald Preston (Professor in Manchester) who has been through the entire manuscript. I have benefited from their constructive criticism, although the final result is obviously not their responsibility.

The notes and references in this volume are in three forms. First, there are the biblical references which are printed in brackets in the body of the text to allow ease of identification. Second, there are some few notes that add to the text; these are printed at the foot of the appropriate page. Third, there are the sources of quotations and cross references which are printed after the final chapter, where they can be safely ignored by those who do not wish to check them or follow the topics further.

University of Birmingham   J. G. DAVIES

I

INTRODUCTION

This book represents the fulfilment of a promise. To explain this promise is to provide some indication of the scope and intention of this present study. Over the past few years I have been fortunate enough to receive invitations to lecture in both Latin America and South East Asia. These visits brought home to me, far more forcibly than anything had ever done before, the conditions of oppression under which many of my fellow human beings exist and the consequent need for drastic changes in the political, social and economic structures that dominate them. Naturally I had contacts with many students and with theological teachers, and they all raised precisely the same question, somewhat as follows:

> We are Christians living in countries where poverty, exploitation and suffering abound. We are convinced that this is not inevitable, but there seems no other way to alter the situation except by joining in violent revolution. But is it ever possible to do this and remain a Christian?

I found myself incapable of any satisfactory reply, but I promised to reflect upon this and then to attempt to produce a statement that might be helpful. This book is the statement. Sadly some of those who posed the question will never read it. They have been killed by the forces of 'law and order', while others are held in prison without trial. But then this question is wider than the limited sphere of my personal contacts, as evidenced by the opening paragraph of a statement agreed by the Church and Society Working Committee of the World Council of Churches in June 1971.

The Church's increasing awareness of its summons to act in solidarity with the poor and the oppressed has led, in recent years, to a widespread call for clearer thinking about the kinds of action which are appropriate to Christian participation in social conflict and, especially, about the potentialities and problems of violence and non-violence.[1]

The same document traced ecumenical thinking on this subject via the Conference on Church and Society in Geneva (1966) and a meeting at Zagorsk two years later up to the Notting Hill Consultation on Racism of May 1969 which urged the World Council to adopt the position 'that all else failing, the Church and churches support resistance movements, including revolutions, which are aimed at the elimination of political or economic tyranny which makes racism possible'.

The programme to combat racism raised the question of violence and revolution precisely because it led to the recognition of two types of situation and of their interconnection. The first type is one in which the masses are oppressed in terms of economic and political power. The second is one in which the masses are oppressed in terms of a particular racist policy. Their relationship was affirmed in a statement agreed by the Central Committee of the World Council of Churches, meeting in Canterbury in the August of 1969.

> It is no longer sufficient to deal with the race problem at the level of person to person relationships. It is *institutional racism* as reflected in the economic and political power structures which must be challenged. Combating racism must entail a *redistribution* of social, economic, political and cultural *power* from the powerful to the powerless.[2]

Widespread debate was catalyzed within and beyond the churches when, in September 1970, the Executive Committee, at Arnoldshain in Germany, approved the allocation of grants from a special fund to combat racism to nineteen organizations, amongst which were a number of liberation movements. In June 1971, at Addis Ababa, the Central Committee endorsed this disbursement of funds and the issues became and remain matters of intense interest.

There is little to be gained by my reproducing further evidence about the continuing concern with this subject, beyond remarking that it is still very much to the fore, as shown by a debate in the General Synod of the Church of England, as recently as November 1974, when the question of violence was central, and one speaker (Professor J. N. D. Anderson) rightly stressed the importance of further investigating the concept of a just revolution.[3]

Social conflict . . . violence . . . revolution. In a sense these are new themes for Christian concern which indicate a shift in theological thinking. For a long period the church has tended to regard the contemporary world as a threat, and the task of the church was assumed to be the preservation of its faith and life against inroads from the political, scientific and cultural forces shaping the world. Theology was understood as institutional self-understanding. Although this has sometimes been held to involve a redefinition and even transformation of the Christian faith, the aim was primarily to reaffirm its identity. From this standpoint, the questions raised by the contemporary world were seen as questions from outside the fold requiring a Christian answer to be directed outwards from the church to the world. It is now being realized that the questions posed by the world are authentically Christian questions and the interdependence of human, social and political problems with religious problems is seen as an axiom of a theological view of reality. The result has been a loosening up of stereotyped theological ideas and ecclesiastical attitudes. Christians have become involved in the vital problems of the contemporary world. The themes regarded as important are no longer specifically church themes—social conflict, violence and revolution become subjects for theological analysis.[4] So the frame of reference for Christian action changes from church to world and this requires a theological investigation which will go beyond traditional theological views.

Thus, to take one specific example, as the church in Brazil gradually awoke to the extensive suffering around it, many priests underwent a change of direction (*metanoia*) in their thinking and conduct. They 'abandoned the old moralizing standpoint of saving one's own soul and discovered that the political function was an essential component of social life'.[5] In one sense this was to rediscover that social concern that has never been entirely lacking in the church, but it was also to realize that this concern must be directed towards the political and economic spheres. Within this present century in England Archbishop William Temple gave considerable impetus to this growing awareness. In a series of essays on what he called 'Christian politics', published as long ago as 1927, he declared:

There is no doubt that a very widespread public opinion supposes that there is an ascertainable frontier of the Church's legitimate concern; but there is not. No department of human life lies outside the scope of moral principle, and in none are the order of life and the maxims governing public action without influence on character.[6]

In effect, this was to make the same point as Karl Barth when he said of the church that 'there is no problem to which in principle she might not speak'.[7] Violence and revolution then are on the agenda that the world presents to the church, because the twentieth century has witnessed a political awakening of the masses who had hitherto been acquiescent before the existing power structures. These people are demanding a share in power and wealth, even if this involves violent revolution. Theological reflection upon this determination to participate in the shaping of their own future is obviously imperative. This is all the more necessary if theology is to fulfil its task of speaking of God historically and of history eschatologically. After all, the word of God only has active significance if those who accept it also understand it, not in terms of some unreal existence outside history, but in relation to their own authentic experience of life here and now. Moreover the Christian life is a vocation to love and it is love that links the traditional theological concern for redemption with the new theological concern for politicization, liberation and development.[8]

At the same time this fresh orientation carries with it an appreciation of the fact that theology is to be done contextually. This means that theology has not only to be developed within and in relation to a particular situation but it is also to be united with praxis – an idea which has been take over from Karl Marx, who held that practical activity is the very condition of knowledge of the real world. Theory is empty and abstract. Incarnational theology must be action-reflection. So while traditional theology tended to occupy itself with the problem of truth independent of praxis, theology today has to exercise a pragmatic function and understand truth as a sequence of actions for human liberation. If this is so, how can an affluent Western bourgeois, like myself, say anything of value about violence and revolution?

It is as well to be alive to the fact that there are two sorts of revolutionary: those of the drawing room and the real ones. The former talk about it, while the latter make it.[9] So we find bishop Cuthbert Butler, reflecting upon violence in South Africa, asserting that 'light headed academics who ponder the ethics and theology of revolution should think again'.[10] In effect this salutary advice does not preclude theological reflection, but it does mean that no one should recommend *a priori* and in the abstract recourse to either violent or nonviolent resistance in a specific situation. 'Those who stand outside a particular conflict situation,' declared the Cardiff Consultation of September 1972, on 'Violence, Nonviolence and the Struggle for Social Justice', 'do well to be wary of handing out gratuitous advice for which others will be called to pay the price. That is not to say, however, that general evaluations of the efficacy and ethical significance of violent and nonviolent struggle, respectively, are not possible'.[11] It is the latter part of this statement that provides some justification for this present study. In any case to write of violence and revolution outside an advanced revolutionary situation is required because no one in this *one* world can say that he or she is totally unconnected or unaffected by such circumstances.

When the WCC gave grants to certain revolutionary bodies, using money contributed by member churches, including churches in countries where social injustice may still be tackled through constitutional means, these same churches and their members had to face the question whether or not such grants were right and proper. This question cannot be avoided, but to face it requires those in the Western democracies to consider the legitimacy of violent resistance to established governments.[12]

None of this means that we can choose for others. I am not concerned to recommend violent revolution or oppose it in particular situations but to clarify the grounds for possible decisions. Of course while many Christians would not wish to assert that theology should say nothing about the subject, many might assume that any statement must of necessity involve a condemnation, i.e. the view might be taken that a Christian cannot be neutral before the questions. But I cannot accept such a foreclosing of free discussion; rather I hold the view that Christians must be liberated in their thinking in order to exercise freedom of choice. It is in any case impossible to arrive at a general answer valid for all. In this sense I cannot provide a precise reply to my friendly inquisitors, to whom I referred in my opening paragraph. What is possible is to present and illuminate the alternatives. It is possible to analyse the factors involved in revolution and violence. It is possible to set out guide lines which individuals may take into account in making *their own* moral choices. There is no simplistic solution, but if one does not seek to avoid the agony of decision by refusing to face it, it is equally otiose to indulge in generalized and romantic talk about the subject. Unless such spadework is undertaken, Christians will experience a paralysis of conscience. They will become, like Hamlet, 'sicklied o'er with the pale cast of thought . . . and lose the name of action'.

Religion, if it is to be relevant, has to assist the reconciliation of individuals with their acts. If it condemns those acts, and it may be right to do so, then people will either repudiate their religion or give up their actions. Today in many parts of the world revolution seems the only path to liberation. Christians wish to join in, but question if their religion allows them to do so. They appear to be faced with the choice: Christianity *or* revolution. The question I have to investigate is: is this choice a real one?

In Latin America many Christians have already given their answer to this, viz., that Christianity and revolution may go together, and they have developed theologies of revolution or liberation. The emergence of such 'regional' theologies is necessary and to be welcomed if theology is done contextually. But this in itself poses another problem. While it may be a sign of vigour of faith and of theology, the question of communication and understanding looms large. Hence the need, even in Europe, to examine these theologies in order to preserve some appreciation of our Latin American brethren. Conversely no school of theology should be content with a group soliloquy. To talk only to those who belong to the same restricted context can be sterile. While Western theologians need to listen so that their own soliloquy can be opened up and questioned, Latin American theologians and the scholars of Black Theology in their turn need to harken to a sympathetic appraisal of their activities in order that true ecumenism may continue to thrive. This means, for Westerners, a certain kenoticism in relation to their theological understanding, i.e. we have to divest ourselves – and this is difficult – of an élitist and authoritarian stance, fondly believing that we can formulate the ultimate and absolute truth. The day of imperialism in theology, with the domination of the colonized, is over. Dialogue with our fellow believers in the contest of action in the world is the way forward.

Having now given some indication of the scope and limitation of my enterprise and also, I hope, of the justification for undertaking it, it remains to sketch out briefly the logic of the succeeding chapters. This is to provide some guidance about what is being treated, why it is being treated and about the overall sequence of thought.

Revolution, like war according to Clausewitz, is the continuation of politics by other means. Hence the next chapter is devoted to the subject of political involvement. Exploration of this subject is in any case necessary because the questions which the world poses to the Christian community begin here. I can illustrate this from what happened at a symposium in Geneva, some eighteen months ago, on the subject of 'The Theology of Liberation and Black Theology'. The proceedings concluded with a press conference and the questions put by the representatives of the world's press embraced the following:

> As far as I can see, Jesus was not a political figure nor was he at all interested in political questions, so why do you, as Christians, lay such stress upon political involvement?

Other questions point to later chapters in this book, e.g.,

> Did you discuss violence? If so, how can you reconcile engaging in it with the teaching of the Sermon on the Mount?

> What has a violent revolutionary, with a gun in his hand, to do with the Prince of Peace?

The Geneva panel that was to respond to the questions gave no answers and conveyed the impression of evading the issues. In fact its members were concerned with issues far beyond such initial enquiries. In one sense they were right, because the form of the questions, particularly the first, allots to theology its traditional role of self-understanding – and this they were not prepared to accept. Yet, what is the point of a theology if – while not being able to provide simple 'answers' – it does not illuminate the problems that people raise? The following chapter on political involvement is then necessary in order to sketch a response to this first question raised at Geneva. It is also necessary because if one were to decide that Christians should keep apart from the political arena, there would be no point in continuing further. Equally there would be no grounds for extending the analysis as far as violence and revolution, if resistance to the state is always wrong for Christians. So in chapter 3 I examine this matter to see how far obedience is a constant imperative and in what circumstances disobedience may be the right choice.

To resist the state is necessarily to act illegally, for no country's laws allow the possibility of armed insurgency. Consequently the subject of law and order has to be reviewed in chapter 4. What is or should be the Christian attitude to law in general? Is it immoral to act illegally? Must the present order always have priority over the disorder of revolution?

These three chapters, 2 to 4, are to a certain extent theological in the traditional sense. They face questions which Christians put to themselves or have put to them by others. If any reader does not want to tarry with this kind of theological discussion or already accepts that he or she should be politically committed, is free to resist and to act illegally, then it would be better to skip these three chapters and pass on to the discussions successively of revolution and violence. Indeed in chapter 5 we turn directly to the questions raised by the contemporary world in human terms. So revolution is analysed, not in relation to its means but to its character and intention and possible necessity. This includes a description of situations where revolution may be the only way to liberation, a discussion of the relationship between salvation and freedom within history and of the gospel as conscientization. Here in broad outline is set out a theology of revolution or liberation, together with a survey of the criticisms that are sometimes brought against it.

Chapter 6, finally, deals with the means of revolution, with power, force and violence. It looks at the basis of Christian moral choice; it analyses the concept of justifiable force, looks at structural violence and analyses the idea of the just revolution. It concludes with a section on reconciliation and peace.

From this brief introductory resumé of what this book is about, it will also be apparent what it is not about. In particular it is not about nonviolence. There are incidental references to this subject but I have not sought to examine it in depth. The reasons for this are (a) it is not an element essential to this present study; (b) it would require not just an additional short section but at least a chapter to itself and this would make this work over long; (c) there are already available several useful analyses of the problems and techniques of nonviolence, while (d) there are by no means a corresponding number of studies of violent revolution from a Christian perspective and it is precisely this that is my concern.

2

POLITICAL INVOLVEMENT

'No politics from the pulpit . . . No politics in religion and no religion in politics.' These cries have been heard before and, no doubt, they will be heard again. They will go on being heard because the attitude which prompts them is the product of a whole series of firmly held and not lightly discarded convictions. Taken separately, some of these convictions do not have much weight – although some have. Taken together, they represent a comprehensive stance which rests upon an appeal to scripture and is not simply to be dismissed out of hand. A brief summary will indicate both the extent and the coherence of this position.

The church's business – so it is contended – is religion not politics. Just as a bus company deals with transport and the Conservative and Labour parties in Great Britain are devoted to politics, so the church's area of concern is that of religion. Moreover the religion that Christians profess is a private affair; it has to do with face-to-face relations and not with government acts or social structures. The Christians' objective is not this world – certainly not the world of politics – but the Kingdom of God. Christianity is therefore essentially other-worldly. The Kingdom will be established by God upon whom we are totally dependent; activism is not for us but quiet waiting upon the Lord. Jesus himself was entirely apolitical, and we, his followers, must similarly hold aloof from the political arena if we are to be imitators of him. Indeed none of his teaching is applicable to politics, while his emphasis upon love of God placed this above, although not necessarily contrary to, love of neighbour. Certainly he provided no political, social or economic blueprint and we should confine ourselves to general maxims about moral conduct and not attempt to advocate specific policies. Politics, in any case, in most Western countries, means party politics and that leads to conflict. Christians, who are to be one in Christ, cannot pay attention to that which can only produce disunity; their position therefore has to be one of neutrality. Finally, politics requires the use of power and this Christians must repudiate.

It is obvious that if this case were held to be convincing, then there would be no question of Christians and political involvement. On the contrary, they would rather be under an imperative to opt out of politics. But before accepting this, the several arguments have to be set out more fully and their validity tested.

The Arguments against Christian Involvement in Politics

(i) The church's business is religion not politics

I do not intend to dispute the fact that Christianity is a religion.* To those who hold that the church's business is solely religion this means that its adherents share certain beliefs, engage in certain practices, especially worship, and concentrate upon the 'spiritual' side of life. In order to analyse this further it is necessary to distinguish the several dimensions of religiosity and so determine to which type of religious orientation this apolitical stance corresponds.

Dimensions of religiosity, following the American sociologists Charles Glock and Rodney Stark,[1] may be said to be four in number: belief, practice, experience and consequences. It is their contention that these account for all the prescriptions that are required by the various religious bodies. 'Belief' embraces the doctrines and myths which a religion teaches and to which it expects its adherents to subscribe. 'Practice' includes all acts of devotion, whether public or private, such as attendance at church services, fasting or going

---

* It would be possible to present a contrary position along the lines of the Barthian critique of religion. Karl Barth drew a sharp distinction between revelation and religion and maintained that the former abolishes the latter. Religion, in his view, is man made and is a manifestation of human rebellion against God, who by revealing himself denies that any religion, *per se*, is true. To pursue this line here however hardly does justice to those who advance this particular objection to political involvement; they are operating at a different level and with different presuppositions. To carry conviction therefore the subject must be discussed in their terms.

on pilgrimages. 'Experience' refers to the various feelings that are deemed to be religiously desirable, such as seeing visions or undergoing conversion. 'Consequences' entail that which stems from religious motives, e.g. concern with poverty or work done for charitable purposes. Each of these dimensions corresponds with a certain type of religious orientation. Thus, emphasis upon belief is parallel to the gnostic outlook with its claim to esoteric knowledge; practice is to the fore in an introversionist stance that gives priority to devotion and personal holiness; experience is fundamental to the conversionist position, while consequences are prominent in the adventist orientation which places its hope very much in this world. These orientations can be combined with collectivism or with individualism, with other-worldly or this-wordly attitudes, and with the conviction that religion should be either fully integrated with society or entirely differentiated from it.[2]

Those Christians who hold that politics is not the church's business obviously repudiate the adventist type but may combine in different degrees and with varying orders of priority the other three, i.e. they share certain beliefs (gnostic); they engage in certain practices (introversionist) and they tend to be individualistic, other-worldly and to differentiate the church from society.

This short analysis demonstrates that the religion-is-the-church's-sole-business group represents only one form of Christianity among several possible ones. Since it is not the only form of Christianity in existence, the validity of its claim to represent true Christianity has to be investigated. In effect this means considering the biblical basis for such a position, since all Christians, no matter what their religious orientation, appeal to scripture as in some sense authoritative.

Only a cursory glance at the Bible is sufficient to establish two facts: that God is consistently represented as a political God and that he acts in history. To say that, according to the biblical perspective, God is a political being is to recognize that the various writers picture him in political terms. The Hebrews knew God as *lord*, *king* and *ruler*, as the one who sits upon a *throne*. This God has made them a *people*, having delivered them from *slavery*, entered into a *covenant* with them and given them a land or *country*. The covenant itself carried exact requirements of *law* and their life was to be one of *justice* and *peace*. Their affairs were administered by *judges* until, in due season, God raised up *kings* for them and anointed them. In the fullness of time, from David's line, there came the Anointed One or Messiah, the *king* of kings and *lord* of lords, the *ruler* of kings upon earth. He was to give *freedom* to the *captives* and the *oppressed*, to have all things *subject* to himself and he will *reign* as one having supreme *authority*. Everyone of these italicized words are socio-political images, indicating that God is conceived as a political God. But if politics is what God is doing, then equally politics is what people must do in response to God.[3]

Similarly, if God acts in history – and this is so well-worn a theme that it is unnecessary to reproduce the familiar references: to the Exodus, to the Assyrians, the Babylonians, God was in Christ, etc. – then responsibility to the God of history involves taking responsibility for history. Indeed for Christians to arrive at an awareness of the historical dimension of their faith is not to meditate upon eternity but to be concerned with politics. So J. A. T. Robinson can declare that 'right politics *is* religion'.[4] This is his apt comment on Jeremiah 22.13–16 which lists the shortcomings of the ruling class and of the king, demands justice and ends with the question: 'Is this not to know me? says the Lord.' Politics is therefore no distraction from religion but the medium by which both love of neighbour and justice are made effective.

Hence, according to the Bible, religion does not have to do with a specifically religious sphere but with God's dealings with the world. God's activity, so the claim is made, is to be seen in secular phenomena, as much as, or more than, in the explicitly religious sphere of the Hebrews' cultic life or the church's devotional exercises. No wonder that Archbishop William Temple, writing of his hope for a new world, could declare that 'to some people the subjects which I shall deal with seem to fall outside the sphere of religion altogether . . . but . . . God is supreme over all life and at all points we must obey Him if we have faith in Him; and this obedience must in the new world-order take the form of an endeavour to establish international and social justice.'[5]

For Christians this supreme God is both Creator and Redeemer, and as such he is obviously concerned not with one part of human experience but with human beings in their totality. But we share a common nature and we are interdependent, and so the church cannot be just an aggregate of individuals who wish to have their 'religious' needs catered for. The church must be for others; it must serve others, and this immediately brings it into the realm of politics. Jesus too identified himself with humans needs, material as well as spiritual – witness his healing miracles and the feeding of the five thousand – and so 'as the Church preaches and teaches the good news that Christ lived, died and lives again that man may live in proper relation to God and to his neighbour, it creates not only the most basic motivation for social change, but also the most enduring'[6] – politics again.

However, whatever the Christian in the pew may think about Christianity and politics, a theologian has to face the question of the nature of his own task. He must enquire: what is theology? Part of the answer lies in understanding it as critical reflection upon human life in the light of divine revelation, as I have already suggested in my introductory chapter. But this means that theology would 'necessarily be a criticism of society and the Church insofar as they are called and addressed by the Word of God; it would be a critical theory, worked out in the light of the Word accepted in faith and inspired by a practical purpose – and therefore indissolubly linked to historical praxis.'[7] So theology requires reflection upon the presence and activity of Christians in the world and necessitates going beyond the boundaries of the church and facing problems raised by the world and history. It seeks to interpret the meaning of historical and political events in order to make the commitment of Christians within them both more radical and clear. So a theologian cannot accept the view that religion alone is the church's business and not politics. Either we must extend the scope of religion to include political action or we must engage in political action as the working out (consequences) of our faith in history. In either case, politics is seen to be the church's concern. If this is so, why do many people still maintain the contrary?

It would not advance the argument very far to pursue this matter in great detail, but two considerations are germane. Christians should be on their guard against an unthinking acceptance of one aspect of their Platonic legacy, viz., that dualism that divides a person against himself or herself – body versus soul – and emphasizes the importance of the soul to the detriment of the body. This dualism, which has no place in the Hebraic understanding of human nature, leads quite naturally to a dichotomy between the spiritual and the physical, between the sacred and the secular, and so between religion and politics. Those who maintain such a divide have, often unknowingly, a residuum of Platonism affecting their thought.

The second consideration also relates to a legacy – this time from Pietism. There is no doubt that that movement continues to have a profound influence upon people's interpretation of Christianity. To many, being a Christian consists of saying prayers and going to church; it is a matter of individualistic and private devotion. With such a pre-understanding they fail to appreciate the entirely different perspective of the biblical writings where the emphasis is not upon strictly religious acts but upon obedience to God in everyday life. Where there is injustice, there is no knowledge of God (Hos. 4.1); 'I desire steadfast love and not sacrifice' (Hos. 6.6); 'what does the Lord require of you but to do justice, and to love kindness?' (Mic. 6.8). According to James 1.27: 'Religion that is pure and undefiled before God and the Father is this: to visit orphans and widows in their affliction and to keep oneself unstained from the world.' The stress is not upon three of the above mentioned dimensions of religiosity – belief, practice or experience – rather everyday life is the arena of Christian discipleship.

So the Roman Catholic bishops of the Netherlands, in their Lenten Pastoral of 1973, rightly affirm that 'in opposition to those who want to put the centre of gravity of religion in sacred rites and in the sanctuary [the Bible] repeatedly and emphatically points out that liturgy is hypocritical and piety is reprehensible if they do not go hand in hand with active social justice'.[8] They are referring especially to Isaiah 58 which condemns fasting when accompanied by oppression of the workers and declares that true religious observance involves breaking every yoke and sharing bread with the hungry. Similarly a Christian eucharist would lack integrity if it were not understood in part as a political act, referring to the fair distribution of resources, which stands in judgment upon and demands action to change structures of oppression.[9]

Jesus himself appears to have required considerable reticence about religious exercises – prayer is to be away from the public eye and alms giving is not to be ostentatious (Matt. 6.2–6), but his disciples are told: 'Let your light so shine before men, that they may see your good works and give glory to your Father who is in heaven.' (Matt. 5.16). But what are these good works? They cannot be prayer meetings and private devotions; they can only be understood in terms of service to the neighbour and of active concern for the oppressed. And if this is so, is not political involvement a necessary corollary?

(ii) Religion is a private affair

Whether or not religion should be a private affair is what we have to investigate; that there is currently a marked privatizing tendency within Western Christianity is however undeniable. This trend is characterized by an emphasis upon the interpersonal; charity is conceived as a matter of neighbourliness; mutual encounter is the primary category; the proper field of religious experience is held to be the extreme of subjective freedom.[10] Inevitably this outlook is apolitical.

This is all very remarkable when one looks at past history and is compelled to acknowledge time and again the political nature of the church's activity during the centuries gone by, and one is prompted to ask: how has it come about? In part this is to be understood as the working out of Renaissance individualism and of the Reformation stress upon personal commitment. One's relation to God was regarded as a private one and its social content, in the course of the seventeenth century, tended to be lost. Protestantism has encouraged the view that the God-human relationship is vertical and is centred upon the individual rather than upon the community. But the principal influence is to be sought, not in church history or Christian thought but, in the ideology of individualistic liberalism, whence the idea that religion is a private affair was adopted by nineteenth-century social reformers as part of their struggle to free the state from ecclesiastical control. They strove to deny to religion any political function whatsoever. Marx and Engels apart, they were concerned not to attack religion as such but to relegate it to the private sphere, thus establishing the autonomy of politics and removing what was proving to be an obstacle to the emancipation of the workers.

Many Christians, with the exception of such groups as the Christian Socialists, were content to accept this view. It appeared to be consonant with the gospel challenge to the individual and it was a way of accommodating to the socio-economic situation which, especially in large towns, was undermining community and giving prominence to personal choice. Moreover, with the spread of pluralism – each country having citizens adhering to many different faiths or to none – it seemed an entirely reasonable view that the state should be religiously neutral, with religion as a private affair. Granted that some institutions are not all that they might be, then the task of Christianity is to make people good and they will produce a good society. The consequence of all this has been that many Christians 'privatized the message of salvation in a twofold way: by confining it to the private sphere of existence and by rendering it thereby inoffensive and largely meaningless'.[11] With these words of de Clerq we are moving from description to criticism.

The first point of criticism to note is that this conception of a human being as an individual is an abstraction. Human beings only exist in their social reality, and while this does include interpersonal relations, it also refers to co-operative efforts to achieve certain goals that require the creation of institutions – so human social reality embraces institutional life. There can never be such an entity as an entirely private person, for life is not just a private concern. If one has no concern for others, loyalty to religious principles does not mean that one is righteous. Indeed this would be 'a pious indolence which abandons the wicked world to its fate and seeks only to rescue its own virtue'.[12]

Moreover while commitment to Christ is without question a matter for the individual, the question of the consequences of that commitment cannot be avoided. The preaching of the gospel is a public event and response to it carries responsibilities. There is no need to theorize about these; it is possible to be specific and to state what they may be in terms of a particular situation. This indeed is what certain North American Mission Boards felt compelled to do when they engaged in a self-examination about their work in Angola. Prior to the recent revolution and at the time of this self-critical exercise, Portugal was an imperialist power seeking to preserve its dominance and control over a colonial people contrary to the wishes of most of the native inhabitants. On 11 May 1968 the Mission Boards produced a joint statement which they presented to the then Governor-General of Angola and in the course of this they declared:

> The expatriate missionary enters a sovereign state not by right, but by sufferance of the duly constituted authority of that country. It is expected of the missionary that he will render appropriate respect and obedience to the laws of the land. However, prophetic utterance by the missionary and his sending Church, even though they may have political connotations and be regarded by the government as subversives, are always required by the Christian conscience. This is particularly true if the missionary is confronted by a situation in which basic human rights are violated, social injustices perpetrated or tolerated, and the majority of the citizens are ruled by an alien minority by the sole right

of conquest and settlement without the consent of the majority freely ascertained and expressed without fear or reprisals. The compulsion to proclaim the Word of God under such conditions, even though it may incur the displeasure of the government, is inherent in the Christian's duty to God and his responsibility to his fellow men.[13]

Those who produced this statement had no hesitation in asserting that Christianity is not to be isolated in a compartment labelled 'private' – and their logic would appear to be impeccable.

It must also be acknowledged that the association of the privatization of religion with the idea that a state can be absolutely neutral is very dubious. Certainly the Angola Mission Boards held that the then government was in fact reprehensible. Moreover the actions of any state are based upon certain implicit values and concepts of human nature, of society, and of what is good and what is bad. Politics, after all, is related to ethics, and for the Christian ethics is a necessary part of religious commitment.

Again, the view that by changing people you will ultimately improve society is much too facile. A good person is hard to find in an unjust society which itself hinders people from loving others and seduces them into attitudes of dominance and violence. Moreover those whose good will has been cultivated exclusively within personal relationships are frequently blind to social injustice and to the suffering of those they do not meet. Many politicians, whose policies have been humanly destructive, have been known as good family men, kind to children and so on.

To privatize Christianity is to forget that the death of Jesus had political causes and also had political consequences. His cross 'was not planted in the private sphere of individual existence, nor in the sacred space of the religious life, but at the opposite end of the domain reserved to private religiosity. He suffered "outside the gates of the town", as the Epistle to the Hebrews says (13.12), and at the moment of his death the veil of the temple was torn in twain. The salvation which he brought was not just the salvation of the individual soul but *the salvation of the world*: peace, reconciliation, justice in the world, i.e. in the full daylight of social and political life.'[14]

Of course, fundamental to this whole matter is the extent to which Christian ethics should or should not be concerned with worldly institutions and whether or not these are to be regarded as ethically neutral. Is the church's sole task to practise love within the given institutions or has it a vocation towards those institutions to correct, inprove and change them? Bonhoeffer has provided a comprehensive and convincing reply to this. He points out that the ethical question is contingent upon the question of Christ, and that it is only on the basis of the New Testament answer to the question of Christ that one can speak of the relation of the gospel to secular institutions. Approaching the subject from this aspect we have to affirm, first, that according to the New Testament all created things are through and for Christ and exist only in him (Col. 1.16). 'This means,' comments Bonhoeffer, 'that there is nothing, neither persons nor things, which stand outside the relation to Christ.'[15] Further, in Christ all things are reconciled and summed up (Col. 1.17; II Cor. 5.19; Eph. 1.10). Consequently those who believe in Christ have a responsibility for the world which God loves in him. Moreover, as the world's salvation, Christ has dominion over all people and things and it is only through that dominion that everything attains its proper essence. So 'because all created things exist for the sake and purpose of Christ, they are all subject to Christ's commandment and claim'.[16] This means that his disciples cannot escape responsibility for secular institutions. Christianity is not then a private concern, isolated or insulated from the sphere of political action.

(iii) Christianity is concerned with the Kingdom of God and is therefore essentially other-worldly

Even though many Christians may come to agree that their religion is not a private affair, some would still maintain that their beliefs are centred upon the Kingdom of God – the ultimate – and so the things of this world – the penultimate – are of little importance. Over two hundred years ago Jean-Jacques Rousseau made this very point in a telling manner in a passage in his *Contrat Social*, first published in 1762.

> Christianity is a wholly spiritual religion, exclusively concerned with heavenly things; the home country of the Christian is not of this world. It is true that he does his duty; but he does so with profound indifference as to the good or ill success of his efforts. As long as he has no occasion for self reproach, it matters little to him whether things on earth go well or ill. If the state is prosperous, he hardly dares to enjoy the public felicity; he is afraid that his country's glory will make him proud. If the state is declining, he blesses the hand of God which weighs down upon his people.[17]

As an accurate description of what many people have believed and still do believe Rousseau's statement cannot be disputed. Moreover such an interpretation of the Christian position appears to find support in the New Testament. Christians are to seek first the Kingdom of God (Matt. 6.33), that Kingdom which is not of this world (John 18.36, AV). They are not to lay up treasures for themselves on earth but in heaven (Matt. 6.19ff.). Jesus certainly regarded earthly life as the domain of the provisional: 'What does it profit a man to gain the whole world and forfeit his life?' (Mark 8.36). His followers may be in the world but they are not of it (John 17.14); they are strangers and pilgrims (I Peter 2.11). The form of this world is passing away (I Cor. 7.31). All this can be taken to mean that Christians should be concerned with their absolute future to the detriment of their earthly future. Christian hope should be directed towards the final consummation and not pinned to the affairs of everyday life, politics included.

The case is not unimpressive and it has led scholars such as Jacques Ellul to contend that 'there is no continuity between our earthly life and the Kingdom ... The "No" that God has pronounced over man, his works and his history, is a complete "No"; it is a radical and always present negative ... The bringing to nothing of the works of history is a real and complete overthrowing of them.'[18] Perhaps we should admit that Rousseau has won the day and that Christians have to be indifferent to the things of this life. But before reaching such a hasty conclusion, it is necessary to recognize that this position rests upon some faulty exegesis, that it has been affected by Hellenism to the detriment of biblical categories and that it involves a selective use of texts which must be counterbalanced – if you like to do theology in this way – by considerations based upon other passages.

This is not the place to engage in a full scale exegetical exercise, but the questionableness of the interpretation placed on two of the New Testament passages can be demonstrated by way of example. In quoting from John 18.36 use was made of the familiar AV rendering which does declare that the Kingdom is not of this world, but the RSV is more accurate when it translates 'My kingship is not from the world', i.e. the words do not mean that the Kingdom has nothing to do with this world but that Christ's kingship does not have its origin in this world order.[19] Again Paul's statement in I Corinthians 7.31 means that the present order or pattern imposed upon creation is passing away; the existing corrupt system is in the process of dissolution so that creation itself may be 'set free from its bondage to decay' (Rom. 8.21). Here is neither opting out of history nor other-worldliness. These and similar passages can be given such an interpretation only if they are read through the spectacles of Hellenism.

According to the Greek understanding, time is cyclical; it goes round and round like a great wheel, meaningless in its revolutions, and human beings must seek to escape from it into eternity. According to the biblical understanding, time is linear; it progresses and has meaning because it is the field of the divine action leading towards the final consummation. Although the early church accepted this latter concept, it modified it under the influence of Hellenism and taught that, while there is a distinction between past and future, the fundamental distinction is between time and eternity. Consequently emphasis was placed upon the great divide between the present life and eternity in heaven. If to this be added the further, fatalistic, idea that history unfolds strictly in accordance with a divine not human plan, then passivity and resignation, rather than initiative and responsibility, became the norm; the 'other world' is the chief objective of the Christians' endeavours,[20] and salvation is a future possession. But in opposition to this it has to be affirmed that human salvation is not just a matter of the world beyond – the world beyond (if one chooses to use this terminology) represents the transformation and fulfilment of this present life. To speak of salvation here and now is to refer to the religious significance of human action in history. 'To struggle against misery and exploitation and to build a just society,' says Gustavo Gutiérrez, 'is already to be part of the saving action, which is moving towards its complete fulfillment.'[21]

The gospel does not speak of a future which we must await confident in the promises given, but of a future for which we must prepare the way. This preparation involves above all the practice of effective love in all its concrete details (Matt. 25.31–46). So the bishops of the Haute-Volta could declare in a pastoral letter:

The *Our Father* compels us to recognize that we have a role in the world. To ask God that his Kingdom may come while doing nothing to further the rule of love in the world is to mock God. Would it not make a mockery of ourselves, our brothers and of God himself if we were to ask for our daily bread without attempting – in our situation – to resolve the economic problems which we face in our country? Would it not make a mockery of ourselves, our brothers and of God himself if we were to ask to be delivered from evil and at the same time did not strive to develop our political and social institutions which provide the conditions for internal and external peace in the future?[22]

This preparation of the way has two aspects: one positive and one negative. The positive side is that it enables us to understand something of what the Kingdom is all about. So, according to E. Schillebeeckx, 'the hermeneutics of the Kingdom of God consist especially in making the world a better place. Only in this way will I be able to discover what the Kingdom of God means.'[23] The negative side refers to the removal of those obstacles that impede the merciful coming of Christ. Human bondage, poverty and ignorance are all barriers; all that is proud and haughty has to be brought low. But this preparation is not only a programme of social and political action; such a programme is to be understood as a necessary part of the spiritual preparation. This implies, according to Bonhoeffer, 'that the visible actions which must be performed in order to prepare men for the reception of Jesus Christ must be acts of humiliation before the coming of the Lord, that is to say they must be acts of repentance. Preparation of the way means repentance (Matt. 3. 1ff.). But repentance means a concrete turning back; repentance demands action. Thus the preparation of the way does indeed also envisage certain definite conditions which are to be established.'[24]

Christians indeed have an obligation to prepare the way for the absolute future and this means, *pace* Ellul, that there is no necessary disjunction between the ultimate and the penultimate. Concern for the consummation does not of itself involve lack of concern for our future on earth. There is no contradiction between the two precisely because the way towards the ultimate is by means of that which is penultimate, i.e. through the common or garden stuff of our daily lives set within the context of the world of politics. To seek the Kingdom of God is to accept the duty of being involved in human existence now and this allows no basis for a spirituality of evasion which is uninterested in the problems of those among whom we live. Indeed, to use Karl Barth's phrase, it is a 'pious illusion'[25] to suppose that finite beings can stand aside from penultimate developments and concentrate all their attention on a final consummation. After all, eschatology in the New Testament is not just a doctrine of the last things – the present is eschatologically understood because of the inbreaking of the Kingdom through Jesus here and now. So Barth emphasized that the Christian has a hope for the temporal and the provisional and that this hope must assume the form of an action corresponding to its object. 'The Christian hopes as he serves, and he expects provisional and temporal encouragement, equipment and direction for his service.'[26]

However, human hope in the provisional in view of the ultimate is not a private matter but a public one. The Christian hopes 'in and with the community, and in and for the world . . . For each new day and year the Christian hopes. He hopes that throughout the Christian world and the world at large there will always be relative restraints and restorations and reconstructions as indications of the ultimate new creation to which the whole creation moves. And as he hopes for these indications, he knows that he has some responsibility for them.'[27] This excludes any idea of quietism – the position formulated by the Spanish theologian M. de Molinos in the seventeenth century and condemned by the church, that all human effort is in vain and that we must adopt an attitude of complete passivity through annihilation of the will and utter abandonment to God. It also provides an answer to those who reject all political involvement on the grounds that total redemption depends upon a power outside ourselves and that we must therefore resign ourselves to waiting. For Christians believe that God works through human agents and that, in any case, some political action may be imperative now on the grounds of sheer justice and humanity.[28]

Nevertheless, it may be objected that if the parousia of Christ is to come like a thief in the night how can there be any leading up to it, any preparation for it? Have Christians any political role after all? These questions, which expect a negative reply, are misplaced, as Herbert McCabe has pointed out. They miss the mark because they incorrectly presuppose an interpretation of eschatology as entirely futuristic and they fail to see that it is not only to be understood as inaugurated but that this interpretation provides a perspective, i.e. a direction within history. In the second place they treat preparation in terms of an evolutionary model, whereas what is required is a revolutionary advance. The parousia, says McCabe, does indeed 'come as the culmination of our efforts to transform the world, but it comes as the last of a series of revolutions, not as the final term of evolution'.[29] Consequently, while earthly progress, according to *Gaudium et Spes*, 'must be carefully distinguished from the growth of Christ's Kingdom; nevertheless to the extent that the former can contribute to the better ordering of human society, it is of vital concern to the Kingdom of God.'[30] As Christians strive to transform the world – by engaging in the provisional and penultimate field of politics – they are included in a process that leads up to the final parousia.

(iv) Jesus was apolitical and his followers, as imitators of him, must therefore have nothing to do with politics

That Jesus was apolitical, in the sense that he did not identify himself with any of the parties active in the Palestine of his day, would appear to be irrefutable. Although an attempt has been made to represent him as a Zealot sympathizer, i.e. as one who was favourably disposed towards the national liberation movement against the Romans, the case, in my view, is so unsubstantial as not to merit extended examination – it rests upon unprovable hypotheses and tendentious interpretations of isolated passages. The evidence is simply not there and the divergence of opinion is so great that this in itself indicates that we are in the realm of speculation and no more. S. G. F. Brandon could contend that Jesus was deeply influenced by the Zealots;[31] Oscar Cullmann that he was not, although several of his disciples belonged to the party,[32] while Alan Richardson can go so far as to assert that there is 'no evidence for the existence of a political party called Zealots before the outbreak of the Jewish War'.[33]

Instead of belonging to or favouring any of the contemporary parties, Jesus is rather to be seen as confronting them all. He severely criticized the Pharisees who were opposed to the power of Rome and practised separation and not fraternization. He was eventually silenced by the joint plotting of the Sadducees and the Herodians who were afraid of anything that smacked of subversion lest it resulted in greater suppression and loss of religious liberty. His universalist outlook conflicted with the narrow nationalism of the Zealots, assuming *pace* Richardson, that they were active in his day. He would not perform the role of an arbiter in the affairs of everyday life (Luke 12.14); his teaching includes no single statement of a directly political nature. He burst open every category within which men sought to confine him: in the final analysis he was not a rabbi, nor a Zealot, neither a Pharisee nor a Sadducee.

In effect Jesus *was* apolitical and it is vain, on the evidence available, to seek to argue otherwise. It is true that he died at the hands of the political authorities who appreciated that his message and ministry were subversive of the established order; it is also true that he was executed on the, false, political charge of seeking to be a new king of the Jews. But this did not make him a political figure in the normal sense; it merely demonstrates that no one living in that world could operate outside the all embracing framework of politics.

What were the reasons for this apolitical stance on the part of Jesus? It would appear to stem from his realism and from a consciousness of his unique mission. Jesus was perfectly aware that the Jews would not succeed in a trial of strength with the Roman army. He saw the destruction of Jerusalem as a distinct possibility (Mark 13. 14), but would do nothing directly to advance it. In this respect he shared the perspicacity of the Jewish authorities who were not wicked men but realized that Jesus could upset the existing delicate balance of power and produce a Roman backlash. Caiaphas could say: 'it is expedient for you that one man should die for the people, and that the whole nation should not perish' (John 11. 50). It was lack of this political acumen later that led to the disastrous revolt of AD 70. Jesus, as a realist himself, would not endorse a confrontation with the occupying power.

The context of Jesus' ministry was one characterized by widespread support for political messianism or cultural nationalism. To this Jesus appears to have been entirely opposed. Not for him political dominion nor the leadership of an uprising against the Romans, because of his consciousness of a special mission entrusted to him by the Father.[34] He came to preach the Word of God, to reveal the divine will, to execute the plan of salvation. Political power was not his concern. To the end of his life he refused to give countenance to any idea that favoured the current politico-messianic myth. Even when brought before the political authorities, he expressed the view that it was by the Father's will that he was in their power (John 19. 11, which does not mean that political power comes from God). Jesus believed that he had been sent to save sinners (Mark 2. 17), to seek the lost (Luke 19. 10), and to give his life a ransom for many (Mark 10. 45). His concern was with the relationship of humankind to God and of people to one another with respect to God. Of course, it can be argued, and will be argued below, that his teaching is to be applied to the political sphere, but at this point it has to be acknowledged that because of his unique mission he stood aside from direct involvement in contemporary politics.

If Jesus was apolitical in this sense, does this mean that his followers today must also be such? This was the presupposition of the journalist at Geneva whose question was cited in the introductory chapter. Its falseness has already been demonstrated by the preceding considerations: Jesus fulfilled a unique role and no Christian can presume to do the same. In the words of N. Micklem, 'no man can share in his vocation to be Saviour of the world; here he stands alone'.[35] So Christians cannot argue directly from what became Christ to what is required of them. They believe that Jesus was unique – the redeemer of all men and all women at all times and in all places. Because this was his special role, from which he would not be deflected by contemporary political choices, his apolitical attitude cannot be regarded as normative for others. Let us suppose that he had headed a liberation movement, that it was triumphant and that Israel had become once again a self-governing people, freed from the yoke of imperial Rome – would this have made him the Saviour of the world?

It is a false argument to press the imitation of Christ in this connexion and to contend that because Jesus was not directly politically involved Christians should avoid politics. Such an outlook implies that the vocation of Christians is identical with that of Christ – a somewhat presumptuous claim. Once recognize the reason for Jesus' apoliticism – i.e. it was a necessary corollary of his mission – then it follows that this has no bearing upon Christian responsibility at the present day. Indeed the theme of imitation is not to be interpreted literally, otherwise it would result in absurdities. Jesus was a carpenter, but this does not require all Christians to be workers in wood. Jesus was not an industrial worker, but this does not mean that we may not earn our living as such. Jesus was not an active politician, but it does not follow that none of his disciples may be a politician nor that our discipleship is only faithful if it rejects political involvement. The imitation of Christ is not to be interpreted as demanding reproduction of the details of Jesus' life. 'Jesus,' says F. Herzog, 'did not want "Jesus copies". He expected each man to become free in his own freedom . . . Jesus alone had to take upon himself the cross to become the liberator. Discipleship is thus not doing over again what Jesus did. It is freely living *by what he did*.'[36]

To sum up: the unquestionable apoliticism of Jesus provides no grounds for Christians to deny their political responsibility. Yet there is more to be said. Although Jesus was apolitical in the sense that he was neither a politician nor a member of a political party, it is also to be recognized that at that period there was no rigid separation of religion and politics. The idea that religion is a private apolitical matter is a peculiarity of the nineteenth and present centuries. Jesus' public ministry, in the tense political situation between the Roman occupying forces and popular uprisings, was bound to have political effects. 'The ministry of Jesus,' observes Moltmann, 'could have been non-political only if it had been concerned with ineffective inner dispositions.'[37] Moreover when the first Christians came to worship this 'crucified God', this very action had a political significance which is not to be sublimated into the religious sphere. The rejection of emperor worship brought martyrdom in a sense that was both religious and political. Overtly political Jesus was not but that his activities and teaching had profound political significance is not to be denied, as we shall see in the next section.

(v) The teaching of Jesus is not applicable to politics

As long as Christians were a persecuted minority, the question of the political relevance of Jesus' teaching was not prominent. However, with the conversion of Constantine a new situation obtained and the heart searching that this produced found expression in a letter from Flavius Marcellinus to Augustine. The former was an Imperial Commissioner in North Africa; he was a conscientious Christian who had been disturbed by a discussion with a sceptical pagan named Volusianus. To remove his own doubts about his duties as a Christian politician, Marcellinus, in AD 412, reported the arguments propounded by Volusianus to Augustine, and this was one of the factors that induced the Bishop of Hippo to write his *City of God*, which was to lay the basis of political theory for the next thousand years. Volusianus objected that

> the Christian doctrine and preaching were in no way connected with the duties and rights of citizens; because, to quote an instance frequently alleged, among its precepts we find, 'Recompense no man evil for evil', and 'whosoever shall smite you on one cheek, turn to him the other also; and whosoever shall compel you to go a mile, go with him two'; all of which he affirms to be contrary to the duties and rights of citizens. For who would submit to having anything taken from him by an enemy, or forbear from retaliating to evils of war upon an invader who ravaged a Roman province?[38]

The scriptural passages quoted by Volusianus obviously have a direct bearing upon the question of war and violent revolution – and detailed consideration of these may be left until later. But the

main thrust of his stricture, that the teaching of Jesus is inapplicable, and even inimical, to political involvement, requires serious
examination.

There is no denying that the gospels do not contain any explicit
directions about economic and social organization and the New
Testament as a whole may be said to be politically indifferent. Yet,
it may be asked whether it is reasonable to expect Jesus to have
proposed permanent solutions for problems that would constantly
change? Further it has to be noted that Christians in the first century possessed no political power and within the existing structure
of the Roman empire were denied any responsibility. To J. C.
Bennett there is something almost providential in the fact that the
New Testament writings contain no political programme for
Palestine or elsewhere around the Mediterranean basin, otherwise
Christians today could be bound to a political legalism that would
be irrelevant to our changing world.[39] This argument about the
inapplicability of Jesus' teaching is a heads-I-win-tails-you-lose
argument. If there had been detailed political directives, they would
be dismissed, and rightly so, as having no bearing on the twentieth
century; since there are none, the teaching of Jesus is declared
irrelevant.

However the main answer to Volusianus, and his modern copiers,
lies in the fact that Christians are required to live according to the
commandment of love, that this love has to be effective love – not
generalized sentimentality or goodwill – and that love in action
today has to work through political involvement. It may perhaps be
objected to this that love of neighbour is secondary to love of God
and that political activity is therefore to be discounted and, further,
that love of neighbour itself is to be expressed in personal encounter
and not through secular structures. The first part of this objection
cannot stand up to serious analysis. The two commandments –
love of God and love of neighbour – are in fact one and are set
together over against all other requirements of the law: 'there is no
other commandment greater than these' (Mark 12.31). The
'second' commandment is not of secondary importance; it is simply
the second of two which together comprise the 'chief commandment'.[40] Indeed, according to Jesus there is no short cut to God
which bypasses the love of neighbour. As John Baillie has put it:
'it is impossible for me to obey either of the two great commandments without at the same time obeying the other.'[41]

As regards the emphasis upon direct encounter – this is not to be gainsaid. A Christian is required to enter into I-Thou relations with others, but this must not be permitted to restrict Christian love to first-aid. Faced with a starving man, one's duty is to give him something to eat. But Christian love does not stop here. Why is he starving? In certain cases it may be due to the existing social structures; hence the Christian has to change those structures and this will almost certainly involve political action. Suppose one had an uneven path up to one's front door, so uneven that every time one's three-year old walked along it she fell over and cut her knees. Love requires one to treat the cuts, relieve the pain and ensure that there is no risk of infection, but love that stops at this is not effective love in the full sense – love requires the remaking of the path so that first-aid is no longer necessary. Love of the first-aid kind may deal only with symptoms and not with the causes that produce the lamentable effects.

Consequently, while it would be wrong to undervalue in any way the purely personal expression of love, it must be asserted that the gospel of love cannot be distilled into some universal proposition but can only be grasped in its concreteness as it impinges upon specific relationships – direct and indirect – and situations in history. This means that if it is to be effective it must be embodied in political action which today is essential for the service of humankind. How, for example, can we cope with starvation in the so-called underdeveloped countries without political action? To do this is the modern way of giving food to the hungry, just as providing a cup of cold water requires installing an artesian well or an irrigation system in a jungle town in Brazil, neither of which can be accomplished without the use of modern technology and therefore without financial and political decisions to bring them into operation.[42]

Alternatively, the negative approach is equally true, i.e. to refuse to be implicated in public affairs can be a breach of the commandment to love one's neighbour. If we pray 'your will be done on earth', what is God's will but the wellbeing, physical as well as spiritual, of his creatures? And how is that will to be done except through human agents? According to the Genesis myth, God has assigned dominion to human beings over all the earth (1.26). Politics, economics, etc., are the means to exercise that dominion. Nor did Jesus remove from us our responsibility by providing a fixed programme. Yet the exercise of this responsibility is impossible without the devising and implementation of programmes.

Love of neighbour itself implies an ethic of responsibility, and if we do behave as responsible beings we are committed to the creation of a responsible society, i.e. one that assumes responsibility for its members, one of which the structures allow to all the possibility of accepting responsibility for others – without this, love of neighbour is vague sentimentality and the conditions of life at which Christians should aim will not be achieved.[43] 'Brotherly love is realized by the mediation of political structures. It becomes a political task and is made actual by imperatives of a political nature.'[44]

(vi) Politics is party politics and is to be avoided because of the danger to Christian unity and also of the possible emergence of a new integralism

Although in certain countries, in particular those of a totalitarian character, politics is not party politics, in most of the Western democracies this is the form it takes, and so it may be argued that for the church to enter the political arena is to risk its unity. Instead therefore of endangering the oneness of Christians, the church should limit itself to the enunciation of general ethical maxims and/or be entirely neutral in relation to political questions. The short answer to these two points is to say that the first is useless and the second impossible.

No one need doubt that the church continues to exercise some influence on Western society and especially in terms of its moral teaching – but is this sufficient? 'In effect,' says de Clerq, 'it appears that a moral judgment on political questions – which are becoming more and more complex – can only be effective if it is expressed in terms of political action itself and is based upon real technical competence.'[45] Simply to declare that people must be just, peaceful, etc., achieves little. Moral pronouncements only become meaningful if they are directly related to specific situations: one has to decide if a particular strike is really justified, if a certain policy is or is not harmful to the cause of peace. Abstract moralizing is sterile – an appeal to subjective feelings and to the individual conscience is vain. 'If it is true,' continues de Clerq, 'that Christian faith is not indifferent in the face of the major objectives of mankind and of the real course of history, the church must show the proof of it in practice and achievement. It must be able to make itself heard at the crisis points in the human panorama, there where vital decisions are made, where good and evil are forged, the happiness and misery of men, where the future of the world is being built. It is scarcely necessary to add that all this takes place not in the church or the vestry, but above all in the field of politics.'[46]

But should not the church be neutral? Such a supposed neutrality is a myth. There is no neutral area into which one can withdraw from any society. The attitude of Christians, indeed of anyone, to politics is 'shaped by an already accepted political position'. Whoever thinks that his or her beliefs have nothing to do with politics is in fact reflecting a 'reluctance to change the structures of society'.[47] Indeed such a person is understanding his or her faith in terms of an antecedent political choice, whereas Christians should make their political choice as an expression of their faith. If, in an oppressive society, the church is silent, it is condoning the existing régime and is thereby concealing the necessity for an effective defence of the exploited. Such conduct obscures reality. But if the church seeks to illuminate the human situation then it 'has no alternative but to put politics and the struggle for liberation at the centre of its life'.[48] Those who speak of neutrality and apoliticism are those who, often without realizing it, serve the *status quo*. 'No one,' observes A. Miller, 'who is involved, as all human beings are, in the texture of economic and social life can in the nature of the case avoid responsibility for it. In this area of life inaction is a kind of action.'[49] Political neutrality, as the Marxists know well, really favours one side rather than another and far from being neutral is unavoidably partisan.

Moreover the church is a social institution and as such cannot but interact with the society within which it is set. Any claim to stand apart is then simply absurd. The refusal to act means that its influence and power support the existing power structure. The church's decision to do something or to abstain has consequences for the society as a whole, whether its members all enjoy its ministrations or not. Further, it should be obvious that a Christian cannot occupy any political position whatsoever. Can any believer, unless he largely ignores the New Testament and reads much into the Old which is simply not there, be neutral as regards apartheid? Can Christians reconcile their allegiance to God and their love of neighbour with support of a neo-fascist party? Differences between Christians on these issues should be regarded as abnormal, as beyond the pale of what is legitimate for those who would be disciples of Christ.

The number of issues about which there should be no divergence among Christians is by no means negligible. All Christians should be at one in holding that politics are to be used as media for effective love. Such an agreed view would have several consequences, e.g. it would involve doing all that one can to subordinate technology to the service of human beings; it would involve acknowledging inter-dependence between all nations and the duty of the rich to assist those in process of development; it would involve an earnest attempt to establish peace and, to this end, to create and support effective international agencies. Christians should be concerned to give their allegiance to those parties that aim to build up the national community rather than to foster the interests of a particular group, to assist underdeveloped countries, to work for freedom for all and for the recognition of the equality of everyone before God.

Nevertheless, granted this common basis, Christians are bound to differ as to the most suitable means of achieving their agreed ends. All efforts to act in the political field in accordance with the gospel are certain to be partial – such pluralism is inevitable, since the New Testament does not contain prescriptions which can be applied automatically to different situations. There are often several roads leading to the same destination. There will be diver-sity, but this is not necessarily to be regretted if it results in dia-logue. Yet there are limits to this pluralism. It is difficult to see how a Christian could endorse either complete anarchy, which is the negation of politics, or totalitarianism which itself rejects pluralism. Further, in certain situations of oppression, Christians have little choice in that they are called to identify with the oppressed. In such circumstances the Christian may rightly be required to be partisan. This would be a realistic policy to pursue. It would of course call in question the pretension made by some that Christianity should be a mass movement, but as Dean Inge once remarked: 'No religious teacher, even Buddha, has ever been so open as Jesus Christ in predicting that his doctrines would never be accepted by a majority.'[50] If the church, following in the steps of its master, is to be a pioneer group, an *avant garde*, it must expect conflict. To avoid this on the grounds of preserving some supposed unity is to pretend that there can be a unity which accepts injustice, and that this is a harmony, while it is no more than a not entirely overt combat between exploiter and exploited – it is to say peace, peace, when there is no peace (Jer. 6. 14).

However another criticism can be and has been made of this orientation of the church towards the problems of society. It is suggested that it may lead to a new kind of integralism. Integralism, which is more often associated with Roman Catholicism than with Protestantism, left all decisions about the political behaviour of Christians to the hierarchy, and it was obviously a victory for the laity when they eventually obtained autonomy in the political field. If the church enters this arena, will this not constitute a new form of integralism which robs the individual Christian of his personal responsibility for matters political? Again, the socially conscious believer who radically criticizes society tends to become critical also of those Christians who do not share his views or join him in action. This could produce intolerance and so result in another form of integralism, i.e. the legitimate autonomy of the individual Christian to form his own political views would be jeopardized.[51]

Powerful though this case is, it is doubtful if it can stand against numerous counter arguments.[52] In the first place, the concept of an individual Christian must be seen for what it is, viz. an abstraction, if it means one who is not accountable to the Christian community. Further, this is to be set against the fact that Christianity does involve a moral concern for the problems of society and that in relation to certain issues Christians do have to take sides – whether they like it or not. To think otherwise is to suppose that a Christian conscience could still be in favour of slavery. In the third place, whereas integralism locates the authority to decide within the hierarchical structure, the present era demands dialogue and it is the world that determines what the problems are. Hence the Christian community has to be open to the world and this is the antithesis of integralism. It is also obvious that there are different problems demanding different solutions in different areas of the world. Consequently no central authority can decide what is the responsibility of Christians in particular political situations. 'This is not to deny,' comments Theodore Steeman, 'that there should be something recognizably Christian in all these different concrete social positions. It should be possible for one Christian community to explain to another why it takes the position it is actually taking and to account for it in terms of the gospel. This is what constitutes the unity of the Christian Church beyond the local churches: this possibility of testifying to each other of the faith that is at work in their particular involvement in society.'[53]

Since decisions have to be made in the actual situation, it is the laity that must play the major role in working out viable programmes. This may result in some pluralism, but even this, which must have some limits, is not in itself to be deplored. Unity does not mean uniformity, and political involvement of itself does not mean integralism.

(vii) Politics involves the use of power which Christians must reject

At this juncture I do not intend to enter into an analysis of power – this will be undertaken in the final chapter when we come to consider violence. Nevertheless brief note must be taken of the subject here because one argument against political involvement is to the effect that politics is necessarily related to power – both with seeking it and wielding it – and this is to be avoided by Christians because 'God chose what is weak in the world to shame the strong' (I Cor. 1.27).

According to one point of view, the essence of politics lies in a struggle for power. Hobbes believed that the natural condition of human beings is one in which everyone is against everyone else. Politics is then the sphere of violence and the essential role of the former is to control the latter – politics is the mastery of power over violence. Such a view can lead to political pessimism – thus supporting Christian reluctance to be politically involved – and indeed it has done so in Marxism which looks forward to the eventual disappearance of the state. But this, in effect, is to deny politics and to enter the realm of the unreal. The truly realistic view acknowledges the relationship of politics, violence and power and then takes steps to ensure that violence is circumscribed by effective political action.

However, even if it be granted that politics is the use of power to acquire and maintain more power, it should not then also be understood as aimed simply to increase the advantages of a ruling élite. This would be to define what should be proper political action by its misuse. In other words, it is not force or power that ultimately establishes what is right, rather it is the purpose of politics to preserve justice. Christians who seek to evade this responsibility, by repudiating power, are lacking in realism and are not taking steps to ensure that power is exercised in the service of love. So the Roman Catholic bishops of the Netherlands rightly raise these questions:

Is there not an illusion behind this rejection of the factor of power? Is there not the danger of running away from responsibility at the very moment of history when the need to control power has become a question of first magnitude? How can the enormous influence exercised by power be handled and controlled in such a way as to become of service to true responsibility and freedom, and so that we do not fall victim to nameless and destructive forces?[54]

How indeed? The answers are to be found not by opting out of the political sphere but by seeking to direct it in accordance with the divine will for humankind.

Some Consequences for Christianity of Apoliticism

Having considered seven of the principal arguments advanced against Christian political involvement and having shown reason to regard them as unacceptable, we now turn to look briefly at some of the consequences for Christian faith and practice of still persevering in an apolitical stance.

To those who hold that there should be a dichotomy between Christianity and politics there is no need to respond in theoretical terms. One can appeal to historical facts and one can say: Look what disastrous events have happened over the past decades when such a position has been adopted. The tragedy of the Catholics in Germany under Hitler and of their failure to withstand him, with all the terrible results in terms of suffering and death that followed, undoubtedly stems from this very division. As Brian Wicker says: 'The Church actually inculcated an attitude of positive acquiescence towards the Nazi régime.'[55]

An even more vivid example, because it shows the indefensible lengths to which the logic of a Christianity without politics inevitably leads, is provided by the Archbishop of Belem in Brazil. He is an outspoken critic of those priests who engage in political activity to change society with the intention of reducing the appallingly high rate of infant mortality. If the rate were diminished, this unbelievable prelate declares, 'then thousands and millions of baptized children would lose the chance of going to heaven in all their innocence, in order to remain amid the struggles of this earthly life, to offend God, and make their eternal salvation uncertain'.[56] One is tempted to ask, displaying perhaps a certain sick humour: Would it not then be right to kill each baby as soon as born and baptized? To retort that this would be wrong because it involves the taking of life is no reply, for to refrain from political action and so to acquiesce in a system which allows so great an infant mortality *is* to be guilty of taking life.

The Archbishop's words point to another adverse consequence

resulting from a Christian apoliticism – if accepted as a valid
Christian outlook, this would go a long way towards justifying the
Marxist critique of religion. Indeed this has been recognized by
other more perspicacious members of the Brazilian episcopate. In
1967 their Central Commission issued a statement in which they
declared: 'to affirm that the religious mission of the bishops ought
not to go beyond the limits of what is called "the spiritual life", is
practically to accept the Marxist concept of religion.'[57] This concept may be most conveniently represented by reproducing the
words of Lenin himself:

> Religion teaches those who toil in poverty all their lives to be resigned
> and patient in this world, and consoles them with the hope of reward
> in heaven. As for those who live upon the labour of others, religion
> teaches them to be 'charitable' – thus providing a justification for
> exploitation and, as it were, also a cheap ticket to heaven likewise.
> Religion is the opium of the people. Religion is a kind of spritiual
> intoxicant, in which the slaves of capital drown their humanity, and
> blunt their desire for a decent human existence.[58]

It is evident from this that Lenin understood the social function
of religion to be the provision of a justification for the exploiter and
a sedative for the exploited. He held that it obscured the reality of
a situation of virtual slavery in which the proletariat exists and that
the task of socialism was to disperse this fog 'by liberating the
workers from their faith in a life after death, by rallying them to
the present-day struggle for a better life here on earth'.[59] It is
scarcely necessary to insist that if Christianity is separated from
politics and in particular from a politics of liberation, then the
Marxist critique cannot be denied. But if it persists in its apoliticism then human beings are faced with two false alternatives: an
unreal God or a godless reality.

God becomes unreal because, as de Clerq has expressed it, 'why
still believe in God and in the redemption of the world if that
involves no difference in relation to the important things of this
world, if it has no repercussions on the structures, decisions and
actions of which history is made and which affect the destiny of
mankind?'[60] If the only hope is in heaven, what sort of God is
this? Is he not an idol whom the Marxists do well to unmask? Is
he not one who is apparently all powerful on the other side of
death in another realm but has little influence in this present world?
If hope is directed towards a life to come, then in effect this is to

deny the divine concern for his own creation. A God who is in-active here and now does not become credible in terms of action elsewhere in some other time. If one's obedience to God has nothing to do with politics, then the community of believers will become an in-group, cut off from real life; faith will then be an unessential extra and its disappearance will produce no effects.

Again, what does such an attitude make of the Lordship of Christ? If that means anything, it means that he is sovereign over all of life, and we show forth our acceptance of that Lordship by our behaviour in every area of life in the world, in and through which alone God is to be encountered. It is not a matter of indiffer-ence to believers what happens in the world, for the world has been created by God with, through and for Christ, and it is not a mere unsubstantial backdrop against which the drama of salvation is acted out. Apoliticism suggests that Christian ethics has nothing to do with politics, but this is to abandon any serious moral con-cern for the problems of everyday life – which then becomes a godless reality.

Imperatives for Christian Political Involvement

Hitherto in this chapter my approach has been somewhat negative, in that I have considered the arguments against Christian involve-ment in politics and some of the adverse consequences that follow from this apolitical stance. It is now time to review the positive arguments for Christian participation. Some of these have been already mentioned in repudiating the counter position, and by way of introduction to this concluding section they can be summarized before expanding them and adding to them.

Political involvement is an imperative for Christians because God is a political God and politics is our required response. To know God is to be concerned for the establishment of justice and this demands love in action, which is only possible through political activity. Christians have therefore a role in the world which is to prepare the way for the Kingdom, to further the rule of love and so to be concerned with the penultimate in the light of the ultimate. This is the modern way of feeding the hungry and giving a cup of cold water to the thirsty. The fundamental distinction to be noted here is that between micro-charity and macro-charity.[61] The former was the characteristic expression of Christian love in the pre-technological era when virtually the only possibilities open to it

were in terms of one's immediate neighbours. Christian love however has to assume the form of macro-charity in the age of technology when all parts of society, and indeed of the world, are
linked together by impersonal structures which have to be changed
if love is to be effective. This change is only possible through
political action. Politics is also the medium through which we
exercise dominion over the world: 'for all things are yours, whether
. . . the world or life or death or the present or the future, all are
yours; and you are Christ's; and Christ is God's' (I Cor. 3.21ff.).
It is this same Christ who identified himself with the needs of
human beings, physical as well as spiritual, and demands of his
followers an identical service which itself is only possible today by
the exercise of responsibility in and through the political sphere.

Politics, it is time to recognize, is one of the essential dimensions
of all human activity. It is a superstructure that embraces the economic, the social and the cultural fields, as well as that of the family
and of the individual. Each one of us is a member of a political
community and politics has either a negative or a positive influence
upon all the other structures which interlock in modern societies.
Politics is therefore never a side issue, but an essential and constitutive part of life in society. Simply as men and women therefore
Christians have a political obligation. Moreover as human beings,
they participate in relationships in the everyday world, and this
includes political interaction. To adopt an isolationist stance, remarked the late Dorothy L. Sayers, is to believe that 'the Christian
becomes more Christian at the cost of becoming less human'.[62]
Further, the lives of believers should be integrated lives, but if their
faith is to find expression in their day-to-day existence then political involvement is unavoidable. Indeed if Christians are to perceive
any link between their faith and their lives, they cannot ignore the
political superstructure within which their lives are set.

But the imperative for Christian involvement arises directly
from Christian belief, in particular belief in God and in the incarnation, and from the Christian understanding of human nature and
of the scope of ethics.

Christians believe in God as Creator; they are therefore required
by this belief to have a proper reverence for that which God has
created. In a modern technological society this means that Christians have to be concerned about ecology and they have to take
sides with the anti-pollution lobby. To save nature from destruction, it is necessary to engage in political and economic activity –

both at the national and the international level – there is no other way. The maltreatment of God's handiwork reveals base ingratitude and disloyalty towards the Creator, but improvement in the dire state which has resulted from this disregard can only be effected by political means – participation therefore, on this issue at least, is the necessary corollary of belief in God as Creator.

Further the Lord of creation has revealed himself as an incarnate God, and this belief cannot be reconciled with indifference to or contempt for the material body. Christians have to be concerned with the physical since Christ himself was the Word made flesh. But to be concerned with the physical in this day and age is to be engaged in the political and economic spheres which directly affect people as psycho-somatic beings. It is here that the Christian understanding of human nature has its political implications. Human wellbeing is in part a question of food and clothing, of supporting programmes of famine relief, of campaigning on a political platform which aims to tackle worldwide undernourishment by changing the structures that permit it to continue. But human wellbeing is also in part determined by other physical factors that surround our daily lives. Refusing to concentrate, in gnostic and Hellenistic fashion, on the spiritual dimension alone, Christians have to take seriously the material dimension. In South Africa, for example, the black man's response to God is daily tampered with by his poverty, by his separation from wife and children because of the migratory labour laws, by constant insults to his human dignity and daily exposure to corruption and disease – all of this being the outworking of the system in which he is enclosed. But how can any man reach his full human potential if he lives in subhuman conditions such as poverty, virtual slavery and other humiliations? So Sabelo Ntwasa declares that 'any religion, to be meaningful to him, has to take cognizance of his socio-political situation and the need for him to respond in unity with his kind to this political situation in a self-protective manner. For it is only when the physical obstacles in the way between God and man are removed that man can fully realise his spiritual dimension'.[63]

Not only does belief in God as incarnate result necessarily in political involvement in order to promote the proper and just regulation of the material aspects of human life, it is also a summons to change the world. This is what is meant by the statement that Christ came not to judge but to save – restore to wholeness – the world (John 3.17). 'If any one is in Christ,' says Paul, 'there is a new creation; the old has passed away' (II Cor. 5.17). The reference here is not to a return to a previously existing *status quo*; the theme is that of dynamic and continuous creativity. The call of Christ is to transform the world, and his faithful disciples are described as those who 'have turned the world upside down' (Acts 17.6). This is not a programme of preparation for another world but of changing the one in which we live. Accordingly the official report of the World Conference on Church and Society declared

> Christians have been called by God to fulfill a mission in the world, and obedience to this call means full participation in the life of the world. They live responsibly as citizens, and no concentration upon man's eternal destiny can be used as a means to evade responsibility for his welfare now.[64]

A denial of this is a repudiation of the dynamic of the incarnation, since Christ's redemptive work, if it is to be all embracing, must include every aspect of human existence. It is at this point that belief in God as Creator and belief in him as Redeemer meet. According to the Epistle to the Ephesians, creation is not a stage prior to the work of salvation but is the first act of salvation (1.4). According to the prologue of the Fourth Gospel the work of Christ is presented within the context of creation as recreation. So creation and salvation have a christological sense – in him everything has been created, everything has been saved (Col. 1.15, 20). Human beings extend the divine work of creation by what they do and so place themselves within the history of salvation. 'To rule the earth, as is commanded in the book of Genesis, is a work of salvation, with the hope of obtaining fulfilment. To work to transform this world is in itself salvation . . . The struggle for a just society registers fully and correctly in the history of salvation.'[65] In complete accord with these words from a Sodepax Report on Development was the statement of Section III of the Bangkok Assembly which affirmed that salvation has four social dimensions:

(*a*) Salvation works in the struggle for economic justice against the exploitation of people by people.

(*b*) Salvation works in the struggle for human dignity against political oppression of human beings by their fellow men.

(*c*) Salvation works in the struggle for solidarity against the alienation of person from person.

(*d*) Salvation works in the struggle of hope against despair in personal life.[66]

To speak in this way is to recognize a shift in the understanding of salvation as compared with that in the period since the emergence of Pietism. There has been a movement, which appears to be consonant with biblical insights, from a quantitative understanding of salvation – i.e. from the number of persons saved, the possibility of being saved and the role of the church in the process – to its qualitative aspect – i.e. the nature of salvation itself. This qualitative aspect leads to the view that human beings are saved if they open themselves to God and to others – even if they are not consciously aware of their service – and this openness is directed towards the world as the place of encounter with God.

This may be illustrated by reference to the Old Calvinist test for candidates for the ministry: Are you willing to be damned for the glory of God? Although this question is scarcely acceptable for what it implies about the divine nature, yet, as Paul Ramsey has pointed out, one could hardly find a more succinct statement of the bearing of salvation upon Christian behaviour. 'Whoever is willing to be damned for the glory of God is truly saved – for his neighbour. Whoever willingly lets go his supreme interest in eternity presumably among lesser interests in this life seeks not his own but acts always for the glory of God, for Christ's sake and for the gospel, and obediently in love for his neighbour . . . Christianity is the negation of the general religious desire for salvation as the supreme personal value to be gained.'[67] Salvation is then to be understood in terms of love for the neighbour and so is inextricably bound up with politics.

This same conclusion emerges from a consideration of another aspect of salvation and also of human solidarity. In the Old Testament God as saviour is also the liberator. Those in need of salvation are the oppressed and their salvation consists in deliverance from danger or from tyranny (I Sam. 4. 3). Yahweh is the redeemer precisely because he sets free his people from earthly bondage in Egypt – here the political context is quite clear. Similarly in the New Testament, salvation is neither an eschatological longing for escape to a transcendent realm nor an inner serenity which alleviates unbearable suffering – 'rather it is God in Christ encountering man in the depths of his existence in oppression, and setting him free from all human evils, like racism. which hold him captive'.[68] Upon the oppressor falls the righteous judgment of God and his righteousness is at work when he is striving for the salvation of humankind. But this righteous God is the saviour, and justice and righteousness and mercy belong together, being worked out in history and in the sphere of politics. So the psalmist's prayer is

> In thy righteousness deliver me and rescue me;
>   incline thy ear to me, and save me!
>
> Rescue me, O my God, from the hand of the wicked,
>   from the grasp of the unjust and cruel man (Ps. 71.2, 4).

This social and political reference of salvation is also to be related to human solidarity in sin. Any person's sin is not just his or her private affair; each of us is implicated and when what each one does is in part determined by the social conditions under which we live, our duty is to be politically involved in order to change those circumstances that encourage the sins in which we are implicated. So Karl Jaspers says:

> There exists among men, because they are men, a solidarity through which each shares responsibility for every injustice and every wrong committed in the world . . . If I do not do whatever I can to prevent them, I am an accomplice in them. If I have not risked my life in order to prevent the murder of other men, if I have stood silent, I feel guilty.[69]

Political action then becomes imperative for Christians who believe in Christ as their saviour.

All this does not imply a repudiation of the view that the church's task is to confess Jesus Christ and bear witness to him. On the contrary the very acceptance of these functions carries with it the requirement of political involvement. The act of witness, as Karl Barth expresses it,

> can only occur in *unity* with that which I would like to call the *actualisation* of the confession. The actualisation of the confession is its concrete form as an act of *confessing*, as *definite* confession made *here* and *now*. In its actualisation the confession necessarily touches those contemporary problems which are agitating the Church and the world.[70]

Further, the stress upon political action does not imply a repudiation of the view that it is one of the church's functions to worship and pray. On the contrary, the act of praying carries with it political involvement to foster that for which we pray. Prayer is not some magical formula or incantation; it is not just a matter of uttering a petition and then leaving the outcome to God. To pray for something

– peace, the ending of injustice, the overthrow of racism – is to commit oneself to its realization. So Barth goes on to say that 'a prayer in which one would avoid or wished to avoid such a summons would be a worthless, useless one'.[71] After all, he asks, 'what is a choice of faith if it never becomes a political choice?'[72] To similar effect, and equally valid, is the remark made by Paul VI in his address to the Diplomatic Corps on 17 July 1967: 'The Church cannot remove herself from temporal affairs, because the temporal is the activity of men, and all that concerns men concerns the Church.'[73]

There is much more that could be included in this section on imperatives for Christian political involvement, but since this whole book is in effect an attempt to elucidate these I will confine myself here to one final point about the relationship of politics and morals. In the last analysis all major political problems are moral problems. If one selects at random any item before a state legislature, it can be readily perceived that the decisions about what should be done are also ethical decisions. Should blacks have the same civil rights as whites? Should homosexuals have greater freedom under the law? Is abortion to be allowed and is capital punishment to be abolished? Should divorce or contraception be permitted? Even items which at first glance appear to be remote from ethics are soon discovered to rest upon some form of moral evaluation. Thus the questions of increasing the level of old-age pensions or of devoting more money to primary schools raise ethical issues precisely because, with limited resources, priorities have to be determined and they can only be fixed in accordance with some scale of values.[74] But if political problems are ethical problems, they are very much within the area of Christian concern, for although Christianity be more than morality, it is certainly not less.

No one can doubt that racial discrimination is a moral issue. It may be practised within the field of so-called private behaviour, i.e. in terms of one's relations to the person living next door, but when it is embodied in legislation, as it is in South Africa, then it becomes not only a moral issue but a political one, to which Christians cannot be indifferent. After all, to be ethically concerned is to take account of the effect of actions upon other people. What could be regarded as an ethical issue if acting so as to effect others is not ethically significant? No one can be said to behave responsibly if he or she acts in a way that will affect others and does not consider the moral propriety of the behaviour. But this means that political decisions, which have profound effects upon human beings, cannot be divorced from ethical analysis by fully mature persons.[75] The latter alone are moral agents, i.e. ones who perform duties. But to perform duties it is necessary to be able to judge between alternative courses and to do so in full knowledge of what one is doing. Christians are committed to politics because it is within the sphere of morality and therefore within that of moral agents.[76] This is not to say that moral choice is simple. The remainder of this book will illustrate how complex it is in fact, but let the final words of this chapter re-emphasize the imperatives of Christian involvement. In an article on 'Priests and Socialism in Chile', written in October 1971, Maruja Echegoyen had this to say:

> Faith? Our Faith is not something in the air; it has always been an incarnate faith, an historical one. For this reason it implies political involvement. It cannot be separated from human progress, and the priestly function is indissolubly linked to the awakening of human awareness. Hope? Our hope may refer to the Kingdom, to the second coming of Christ, but it begins here and now, in this society in which I happen to live and for whose transformation – humanization – I am inescapably responsible. Charity? Loving one's neighbour, which is the first commandment by definition, today means working to change the structures that can destroy my neighbour, the people, the poor.[77]

3

RESISTANCE TO THE STATE

Granted that Christians should be politically involved – which was the theme of the last chapter – are there circumstances in which it may be right for that involvement to take the form of active resistance to the state? This is a necessary question to raise at this juncture because if the answer were to be in the negative there would be little point in proceeding further to the subject of revolution. Moreover, if one accepts a Weberian definition of the state, which includes the concept of force, this too directs attention to this same question as logically prior to an examination of force as a means to revolution. According to Max Weber, 'a state is a human community that (successfully) claims monopoly of the legitimate use of physical force within a given territory'.[1] The very phraseology of this definition, with its reference to legitimacy, suggests that active resistance is questionable. Indeed many people would hold that Christians at least should play an essentially passive role *vis-à-vis* the state, and they would agree with Rousseau, whom I have already had occasion to cite in connexion with the supposed other-worldly character of Christianity. According to him:

> Christianity preaches only servitude and dependence. Its spirit is too favourable to tyranny for tyranny not to profit always by it. True Christians were made to be slaves; they know it, and do not really mind; this brief life has too little value in their eyes.[2]

This is an amazing statement from a well-read and well-educated man. Had he never heard of John Knox, of Oliver Cromwell or of John Milton? If he were ignorant of the Scottish Rebellion, could he not have known how Charles Stuart was beheaded by those who believed they were numbered among the saints? All of these men were Christians of devout faith who were prepared to justify rebellion in certain circumstances and some of them did promote and engage in armed resistance, confident that this was in accordance with the will of God. They did not do so lightly and they were much exercised about the whole matter. Their arguments, to which we shall come in due course, are well worth consideration and they indicate that the problem to which this chapter is devoted has not suddenly emerged for the first time at the present day.

Nevertheless it is undeniable that throughout the centuries many Christians have been supporters of the *status quo* and they have been so because of their understanding of certain New Testament texts to which we must immediately turn.

New Testament Perspectives

The first passage for consideration is the saying of Jesus about rendering to Caesar what is Caesar's and to God what is God's (Mark 12.17). The context of this saying is quite clear. The question of paying tribute to the emperor was hotly debated at that time – the tax itself had been instituted in AD 6. Hence the query addressed to Jesus was of direct contemporary relevance, but it was put to him in an attempt either to embroil him with the Roman authorities – if he said no – or to discredit him in the eyes of the crowd – if he said yes. Jesus' reply is given three main interpretations at the present day: the ironical, the political and the eschatological. According to the ironical exegesis, Jesus indicates that the problem of the tax does not interest him in the least. Everyone agrees that the emperor should be given what is his own, but that is of no importance whatsoever in comparison with the inbreaking Kingdom. According to the political interpretation, Jesus is adopting an anti-Zealot position and condemns the conduct of those who refuse payment. Either of these two ways of understanding the pronouncement emphasizes that Jesus neither justified the Roman occupation of Palestine – thus siding to a certain extent with the Sadducees and Herodians – nor did he attack it – thus agreeing with the Zealots and, to a lesser extent, with the Pharisees. The third way of reading these words, and this appears to be the best founded, is to acknowledge that Jesus does recommend payment of the tax, but in so doing strives to bring his hearers to a positive attitude to political power which was being exercised *de facto* among them. In effect, he says: discharge your tax duties and hand over the Roman coin to Caesar, because it belongs to him, as they themselves accepted, and indeed they used them in daily transactions. But this does not mean give absolute obedience to the state, because above else there is the divine will to be obeyed. The rule of God is now operative, while the rulers of this world continue concurrently to exercise a legitimate authority, albeit a provisional one.[3] This means that Jesus was not formulating a principle bearing upon the problem of church and state; he was simply saying that people's duty to Caesar need not contradict their duty to God, and at the same time, it is implied, that if there is a clash of obedience the divine will must have priority.

The second New Testament passage is Romans 13. 1–7, where Paul also recommends the payment of taxes and advises subjection to the governing authorities because they exist by divine appointment. Here again the context is all important. Paul's observations follow from his previous remarks in chapter 12. There he had declared that the Christian must not return evil for evil; the state, on the other hand, does the opposite; it does take vengeance on those who do wrong. What then are we to think of those civil institutions whose function is to control and repress evil actions? In so far as they execute vengeance, says Paul, they do so as the 'servant of God'; their function is not therefore outside God's providential will. So Christians should adopt an attitude of obedience as long as the authorities observe the claim implicit in their role. The logical corollary of this, although it is not explicit but implied, is that if they cease to serve the good, Christians would no longer have the same reason to accept their authority. Christian obedience is then to be exercised with a critical approach, and there is nothing in this passage that necessarily supports servility.[4] Indeed the converse is true; if a state does not further the good and instead fosters evil, then it ceases to act as a servant of God. In such a situation there is nothing in Paul's words to rule out disobedience. This was certainly the understanding of John Milton and his comments are a sound exegesis of this passage. Milton regarded Paul's words as applicable only to 'lawful and just power'. The magistrates to whom the apostle refers are such as are

> not a terror to the good but to evil; such as bear not the sword in vain, but to punish offenders, and to encourage the good. If such only be mentioned here as powers to be obeyed, and our submission only to them required, then doubtless those powers that do the contrary are

no powers ordained of God, and by consequence no obligation is laid upon us to obey or not to resist them.[5]

Romans 13. 1–7 then provides no charter for passive submission. But before leaving these verses there are three other factors related to them that need to be taken into account. First, it should be recognized that Paul was giving practical advice to fellow Christians living in Rome half way through the first century AD. Now the Roman government from 54 to 62 was in the hands of the capable Seneca and as such it satisfied the basic requirements of authority in Paul's eyes – this is also evident from his readiness later to appeal to Caesar (Acts 25.11). However the very fact that Paul was addressing a particular group in a particular situation means that his words are not to be regarded as enunciations of eternal truths. Indeed, and this is the second factor to be noted, in modern democracies, where the people are regarded as the source of political authority and no one is set over them without their consent, the concept of complete obedience, understandable in the light of a realistic appraisal of the situation when Paul was writing, is neither adequate nor readily applicable.[6] The present era does provide opportunities for political action by Christians which were simply not there in the days of the early church. Moreover there is no real parallel between contemporary totalitarian states and the Roman empire, since the latter was in intention based upon law and to that extent differed considerably from modern tyrannies.[7]

The third factor refers to the recognition that neither this passage nor any other in the New Testament provides the basis for a metaphysical understanding of the state. It is true that according to Paul the state possesses a legislative power, of which the essential aim is the good, and it also has an executive power, the sword. Such statements merely record the givenness of the state by listing its actual functions. However Paul also remarks that the state exists through an 'ordinance of God' (13.2, RV). This does not mean that God instituted or ordained political authority in the sense that at one time it did not exist and then he caused it to come into being at a particular time and place. Political institutions evolve – this is the historical fact – but they can be recognized by a man of faith as being in accordance with the divine will and, as such, accepted as an ordinance of God. But Paul was not concerned to provide a theological interpretation of the state's essence and meaning. Accepting it as given, his purpose was to direct Christian conduct in that context, i.e. this passage in Romans has a bearing upon Christians' relations to the state but it does not provide the basis for a theory of the state. Indeed it is a mistake to isolate statements such as Paul's and then seek to establish obedience to earthly powers on some peculiar power believed to be inherent in them. On the contrary, in this, as in all aspects of discipleship, the Christian begins from the confession of Jesus as Lord – Jesus who is sovereign over the individual's relation to the state.[8] 'Instead of enquiring into the nature of the state, to derive therefrom the necessary ethical injunctions . . . we must understand the state in the context of the command to love one's neighbour.'[9] Since Christian action is a response to the divine love, obedience to the state is to be judged by the extent to which its laws serve the neighbour. In certain circumstances disobedience and resistance could obviously be justified.

That the state is not a divine entity is made clear in I Peter 2.13, where the emperor is equated with a human institution. However, that particular passage adds little or nothing to the Pauline statement, but Revelation 13 carries us a stage further. Here the author declares that if governmental power exceeds its proper bounds, it becomes the embodiment of Satanic power. So Oscar Cullmann sums up his survey of the state in the New Testament with the words: 'according as the State remains within its limits or transgresses them, the Christian will describe it as the servant of God or the instrument of the Devil.'[10] Therefore the relationship of Christians to the state cannot be a fixed one – neither necessarily obedient nor necessarily resistant.

Patristic and Medieval Teaching

Although, as we have just seen, the New Testament does not really provide the basis for a metaphysical understanding of the state and confines itself to pointers for working out the relationship of Christians to it, the fundamental institutional questions could not be ignored. Christians are confronted with the particularities and peculiarities of the political order and they have to consider in what ways the divine purpose for humankind can cast light upon it as a human institution. The ends of the state have to be examined in the light of general theological convictions. It was to this task that Christian thinkers turned from as early as the second century, and indeed the development of political theory in Western Europe was very much a Christian enterprise.

In general, the view taken was that the state is a necessity because of human sin and is a divinely appointed remedy for it. Irenaeus was the first to express this clearly:

> Earthly rule has been appointed by God for the benefit of the nations . . . so that under the fear of human rule men may not eat each other up like fishes, but that, by means of the establishment of laws, they may keep down an excess of wickedness among the nations.[11]

The implication of this position is that the institutions of the state are to be regarded as an ethical second-best, in the sense that in the perfect society they would not be necessary.[12] This rather negative approach is to be contrasted with the Greek view as represented by Aristotle. He held that the state is a means for the moral improvement of its members; it should be an association of people working together to achieve the best possible life, and that good life he deemed to involve participation in the life of the state, i.e. for Aristotle the good life is not and cannot be just something private.[13] So to him the state is a necessary condition for civilized living; it is a positive agency of human perfection. In similar vein Cicero maintained that the state is a corporate body and membership of it is the common possession of all citizens; it exists to supply them with the advantages of mutual aid and just government.[14] To the patristic writers however the state is a coercive power to make earthly life tolerable, while at the same time it is of divine institution and rulers are representatives of God. This, of course, is not the same as saying that rulers are accountable to God alone, be they never so absolute or irresponsible.

In the medieval thought world, the different approaches of the Romano-Greek theorists and the theologians merged. In particular Thomas Aquinas, under the direct influence of Aristotle, argued that civil government is necessary in itself to the good life and is therefore justified by its ethical benefits, even apart from its sanction as a divinely appointed means of coping with sin.[15] Hence it became a commonplace of medieval political theory that the state is of divine origin and that its end or purpose is a moral one, viz. the maintenance of justice. But while the authority of the state is good, since it derives from God, its exercise may be evil; while its function is to promote justice, the abuse of this function has no divine sanction.[16] Thus the possibility of resistance was recognized.

In order to appreciate this position more fully, it has to be noted that it was developed within the context of the feudal system which was one of mutual and fixed obligations. Within this system, the ruler had his own binding duties to perform; in no sense was he absolute; he was not above the law but its servant.[17] Consequently, if the monarch failed to fulfill his obligations, disobedience was perfectly justified,[18] and Aquinas advocated the removal of a tyrant[19] while John of Salisbury had no hesitation in saying that such a one could be legitimately killed.[20] Thus, while accepting that the state has a divine authority, these medieval writers did not draw from this the conclusion that the king so represents God that he cannot be resisted when his actions are evil and unjust. This understanding of the state and of the right of citizens to resist in certain circumstances is all part of a coherent whole. Just as in medieval thought there cannot be an absolute monarch, so there cannot be an absolute community, for all are under God. This means that the whole system of law (*jus*) was to be derived from righteousness (*justitia*), which was interpreted to refer to the constant will to render to all their dues, as that which gives expression to the principle of fairness or equity (*aequitas*). This principle of equity resides in God himself.[21] Any ruler then who acts contrary to righteousness and to equity and therefore to God himself is to be resisted, not only as a right but as a duty. Here, briefly summarized, is a coherent case for resistance to the state in accordance with a particular political theory accepted by Christians in the past – this is in itself an answer to those who hold that Christians must always be servile citizens. But political theory has not remained static and numerous changes were introduced as the feudal system began to crumble and as the Reformation made an ever increasing impact.

The Reformation and Its Aftermath

The teaching of Luther and Calvin as to the nature of the state does not in itself stray far outside the medieval understanding. Luther tended to stess that the political order was the result of human sin, while Calvin was inclined to see it a little more in terms of the providence of God. However, while the medieval theory allowed resistance in certain circumstances, these two reformers were

opposed to the idea. While considering that disobedience may on
occasion be obligatory, they were more or less at one in deeming
active opposition to be wrong.[22]

In reaching this position, they were clearly influenced by the
contemporary situation which pushed them towards the acceptance
of the divine right of kings – an idea foreign to the medieval outlook. Many reformers discovered that they needed the royal support to achieve their ends in the teeth of opposition from papacy
and hierarchy. Hence both Lutherans and Anglicans were compelled to ascribe authority to the monarch in order to put their
programme of reform into effect. So Luther could insist that 'even
if the government does injustice ... yet God would have it
obeyed'.[23] This theory of the divine right of kings was then in part
a reaction to papal pretensions and, to that extent, was a development of the position of the medieval imperialist writers who
endeavoured to refute the claims of the popes to universal sovereignty.[24]

At the same time another factor was influential in promoting
complete obedience to the state, as embodied in the prince or king,
and that was the widespread desire for peace and order. In England,
for example, the Wars of the Roses had dragged on for thirty long
years and the people were only too eager to accept a strong central
authority who would prevent a recurrence of these violent disrup-
tions. It is against this background that we can understand William
Tyndale's sycophantic advocacy of royal power in *The Obedience of
a Christian Man* which he published in 1528.

> God hath made the king in every realm judge over all, and over him
> there is no judge. He that judgeth the king judgeth God; and he that
> layeth hands on the king layeth hands on God; and he that resisteth
> the king resisteth God ... Though he be the greatest tyrant in the
> world, yet is he unto thee a great benefit of God.[25]

As for those who oppose rulers,

> whoever resisteth them, resisteth God, for they are in the room of
> God; and they that resist shall receive the damnation ... neither may
> the inferior person avenge himself upon the superior, or violently
> resist him, for whatsoever wrong it be.[26]

Time and again this note was sounded, whenever there was
danger of civil strife. So under Elizabeth I, after the Northern
Rebellion of 1569, a sermon on rebellion, running to six parts and

many pages, was added to the second Book of Homilies and this is full of condemnations of resistance.

> Such subjects as are disobedient or rebellious against their princes disobey God, and procure their own damnation . . . What an abominable sin against God and man rebellion is, and how dreadfully the wrath of God is kindled and inflamed against all rebels, and what horrible plagues, punishments and deaths, and finally eternal damnation doth hang over their heads.[27]

For a final example we may cite the canon issued by convocation on the eve of the civil war in England.

> The most high and sacred order of kings is of divine right, being the ordinance of God himself, founded in the prime laws of nature, and clearly established by express texts both of the Old and New Testaments.[28]

Consequently those who suffer from an evil monarch have to regard this as a punishment for their sins, and faithful Christians will make no attempt to have him removed. They will certainly not resort to arms because, as James Ussher, Archbishop of Armagh, declared: there is 'no other refuge but fervent prayers unto Almighty God'.[29]

It is not my intention to give an historical account of the development of ideas about Christians' relations to the state. The views formulated in the sixteenth and seventeenth centuries are summarized here to illustrate one attitude adopted by the faithful at one period of time. This attitude, as I have already remarked, is contrary to the medieval outlook. It is understandable in the light of the contemporary situation but, if my previous exegesis of the relevant New Testament passages be correct, it cannot be regarded as having a sure foundation in scripture, despite the Anglican bishops' categorical assertion to the contrary. Indeed it would appear actually to be denied by Jesus' dictum about the poll tax. Whether or not, in the circumstances of the sixteenth century, it was right to stress order is one question; whether or not absolute obedience is required by Christian ethical teaching in all situations is another. Jesus in fact said that the tax was to be paid but that obedience to God is on a higher plane. Hence he did not provide the Roman emperor with the halo of divine right, otherwise he would not have contrasted Caesar with God. Although the state has its importance, Christian citizens are bound to have reservations about the exercise of its powers. One cannot therefore appeal to the passivity of these people as providing the standard and norm of Christian conduct at all times. This does not mean that there is no difference between right and wrong; but it does mean that ethics has to be accepted as relative, in the sense that it has always to be related to existing situations. Change that situation and then Christians have the responsibility to discover new creative responses. This too can be illustrated from the same period and there are arguments to be examined rejecting submission and recognizing the duty to resist.

Luther himself in one particular found he had to modify his outlook. The Germany of his day was divided into a number of separate principalities, but over these the emperor of the Holy Roman Empire exercised sovereignty. Hence the question of resistance had two aspects: resistance within each state to the ruling prince and possible resistance of each state under its prince to the emperor. At first Luther pursued a conservative line, advocating nonviolent disobedience and allowing the possibility of refusing to execute unjust orders from above. In general he accepted the prince as supreme and counselled submission. He was also emphatic that a prince should not wage war against his overlord. However in 1531 Luther became convinced of the right of a prince to take up arms against imperial authority if that were ranged unjustly against him. He adopted this position, not primarily on moral grounds but, because he believed that this was allowed by the law. He argued that the emperor was not free to act as he pleased and that under the law he could be opposed by force if he were guilty of notorious injustice. He did not incidentally acknowledge such a right for the peasants, whom he regarded as having no legitimate authority. In permitting princes to take up arms, he was however granting the right to declare war to a group within the empire below the supreme ruler.[30]

Calvin took the next step and contended that in any nation officials in an established position could initiate armed resistance,[31] i.e. when they act by virtue of their office as magistrates and oppose tyranny, their conduct may be justified. Followers of both Luther and Calvin were to go even further.

In 1550 ministers at Magdeburg, where Lutheranism was in danger of forcible repression, published a tract in which they made three main points. They argued, first, that any ruler who seeks to abolish true religion forfeits his authority. Next, they declared that such a one reveals himself to be of the devil and not of God and that passive resistance towards him will achieve nothing. Finally, they asserted that to believe that God always commands non-resistance is to suppose that he wills the maintenance of evil and requires disobedience to himself. While mainly concerned with opposing the suppression of what they held to be the true faith, the authors of this document also affirmed that for a ruler to attempt to take by force the lives, liberties and property of his subjects is to act unjustly and to overstep the bounds of his authority. Since God gives authority for the sake of justice, there can be no authority when a ruler acts contrary to it – the right to resistance is therefore plain.[32]

The Arguments of John Knox

Amongst the followers of Calvin, it was John Knox in Scotland who went the furthest in developing this line of argument, and indeed what he had to say represents an impressive case for the rightness of resistance. Knox was no impetuous hothead. He was fully aware that to engage in resistance was to behave contrary to the prevailing view as represented by Tyndale. He was careful to seek advice wherever he thought it might be helpful, and so he addressed a series of questions to leading reformers. One of his queries reads as follows:

> Whether obedience is to be rendered to a Magistrate who enforces idolatry and condemns true religion; and whether those authorities, who are still in military occupation of towns and fortresses, are permitted to repel this ungodly violence from themselves and their friends?[33]

In 1554, the Swiss reformer J. H. Bullinger replied to the effect that the examples of Daniel, of the apostles and of many Christian martyrs show that we do not have to obey rulers when their commands are opposed to God. He further cited the action of the Armenian Christians who, according to Eusebius, fought against 'their lawful sovereigns, the Roman emperors' when the attempt was made to force them into idolatry, and also, on another occasion reported by Evagrius, withstood their Persian rulers, 'slew their ungodly commanders' and transferred their allegiance to the emperor Justin. Resistance is therefore legitimate on the grounds of past Christian practice and moreover, added Bullinger, 'the Holy Scripture not only permits but even enjoins upon the

magistrate a just and necessary defence'. At the same time he acknowledged that 'it is very difficult to pronounce upon every particular
case. For an accurate knowledge of the circumstances is here of
great importance.'[34]

Knox himself admitted that obedience should be the norm and
that rebellion should not be undertaken simply for 'worldly promotion' but only as a last resort. The populace must do all in its
power to assist those in authority to perform the right, but if rulers
persist in unjust actions, you 'lawfully may attempt the extreme
. . . you are bound to defend your brethren from persecution and
tyranny'.[35] In reaching this conclusion Knox moved to a position
beyond that of Bullinger and Calvin who reserved the right to
rebel to duly constituted officials. In Knox's view the duty to resist
evil rulers is laid upon all.

> The punishment of such crimes, as are idolatry, blasphemy, and
> others, that touch on the Majesty of God, does not appertain to kings
> and chief rulers only, but also to the whole body of that people, and
> to every member of the same, according to the vocation of every man,
> and according to that possibility and occasion which God does
> minister to revenge the injury done against his glory, what time that
> impiety is manifestly known.[36]

This passage comes from *The Appellation to the Nobility and
Estates of Scotland*, published in 1558, but Knox also pursued this
theme in *A Letter to the Commonality of Scotland* of the same year.
In this he pointed out that every one has been created in the divine
image and that Christ died for every one. Hence, while there is a
distinction of status between ruler and ruled, no one can surrender
to another the primary responsibility for what takes place in one's
own country. In relation to moral duty and religious calling all are
equal. 'It will not excuse you, dear Brethren, in the presence of
God . . . to say, We were but simple subjects, we could not redress
the faults and crimes of our rulers.'[37]

In advocating rebellion, Knox was not solely concerned with
matters religious. He contended that the task of taking up 'the
sword of just defence' was not only for 'Christ Jesus his glorious
Evangel' but also for 'the liberty of this our native country to
remain free from the bondage and tyranny of strangers' – the
reference is to the danger of foreign domination by the French.[38]

Turning now to Knox's positive arguments,[39] it is important to
recognize them for what they are. His main concern was the legitimacy of rebellion against the charges of disobedience and lawlessness.

He did not have to consider whether the violence that might result was a moral bar to rebellion. Neither he nor his contemporaries doubted that war, self-defence, capital punishment, etc., were permissible in certain circumstances. The question of violence will occupy us in a later chapter, but in this present one it is the question of resistance – without direct attention to its methods – that is under examination and to this Knox's position is very relevant.

Knox rested his case upon a compound of realism, biblical, especially Old Testament, precedents, and upon an appeal to reason. He did not keep these various factors separate but, as far as possible, in presenting his views I shall, for the sake of clarity, attempt to distinguish between them.

Knox's realism and his appreciation that ethical decisions must be related to existing circumstances is apparent both in his conversation with Mary, Queen of Scots, and in his debate with Sir Richard Maitland of Lethington. Knox defended disobedience before the former by appealing to the actions of Daniel and the Three Children. The queen pointed out that these were examples of nonviolent resistance, to which Knox rejoined that 'God had not given unto them the power and the means'.[40] That is to say, the situation under Nebuchadnezzar was such that there was no possibility of armed resistance, which therefore was neither a viable nor a sensible option. In similar vein Lethington contended that we have to leave judgment and punishment to God and that subjects cannot assert the right to condemn and remove a ruler. Here again Knox was ready to admit that in some situations there might be no other alternative. He instances a minority of Christians in an 'infidel' state, and says that they might have 'no other force only to sob to God for deliverance'.[41] Change the situation however and right action may require resistance, so when Abraham was in Egypt he was required to keep himself from idolatry, although he was not charged to destroy the local idols; when his descendants took possession of the promised land and had subdued the inhabitants, then they were commanded to root out all idolatry.[42] In these two examples we see Knox's realism supported by an appeal to the Bible, which is a perfectly reasonable position for a Christian to adopt.

Biblical precedent did indeed bulk large in his long debate with Lethington and in his *History* Knox summarized his main points as follows:

1. That subjects had delivered an innocent from the hands of their king, and therein offended not God.

2. That subjects have refused to strike innocents when a king commanded, and in so doing denied no just obedience.

3. That such as struck at the commandment of the king, before God were reputed murderers.

4. That God has not only of a subject made a king, but also has armed subjects against their natural kings, and commanded them to take vengeance upon them according to his law.

And, last, That God's people have executed God's law against their king, having no further regard to him in that behalf than if he had been the most simple subject within this realm.[43]

From his account of the debate in the Assembly in June 1564, to which this summary is the climax, the particular biblical precedents to which Knox was appealing become evident. In support of the contention that the people were acting in accordance with the divine will when they refused to acquiesce in the execution of an innocent man, despite the king's decree, Knox cited the case of Jonathan condemned by Saul for taking food in ignorance that it had been forbidden: 'Then the people said to Saul, "Shall Jonathan die, who has wrought this great victory in Israel? Far from it! As the Lord lives, there shall not one hair of his head fall to the ground; for he has wrought with God this day." So the people ransomed Jonathan, that he did not die' (I Sam. 14.45).[44] Saul similarly figured in another incident, when he condemned Ahimelech and others to be killed, but 'the servants of the king would not put forth their hand to fall upon the priests of the Lord'. Indeed only Doeg obeyed and his compliance with an unjust sentence made him a murderer (I Sam. 22.17–23). As for God's commanding opposition to a ruler, the supreme example was that of the prophet Elisha who entrusted Jehu with the mission of destroying king Ahab and all his house (II Kings 9.1–10), while Amaziah was slain as if he had been a private citizen (II Kings 14.19). Knox was not short of example to pile upon example: he instances the attack of Elijah upon Ahab and Jezebel (I Kings 21)[45] and the opposition of Jeremiah to Zedekiah (Jer. 21.3–7), as well as the slaying of Queen Athaliah (II Kings 11.1–16) – indeed he saw the last as providing grounds to justify the similar execution of Mary Tudor.[46] Oppressive rulers should be removed because they play the same iniquitous role as Pharaoh and are destined to perish in the same manner.[47] If the people do not do this they suffer, and their suffering, as is evident in the Old Testament, is to be regarded as a punishment from God for their failure to overthrow wicked régimes by revolution.[48]

When it is recalled that according to the Old Testament the king is the divine representative, the Lord's Anointed or Messiah, one cannot fail to be impressed by the number of occasions when this sacred personage was resisted on the grounds of a higher justice than that which he manifested by his own actions. It is of course true that these examples are all culled from the Old Testament, and at the time of the English Civil War John Corbet could accuse the Covenanters, who reproduced Knox's arguments, 'All your testimonies are out of the Old Testament, but not one out of the New Testament'.[49] Yet Christians do accept the Old Testament as part of their Bible, and in any case Knox could find nothing in the New that contradicted his position. In particular he did not regard Romans 13 as a charter for absolute obedience. He contended that there is a necessary distinction to be drawn between an ordinance of God and those persons in authority, so that one may resist the persons but not offend the ordinance. He held that the passage gave no countenance to the view that one must obey rulers if they order unlawful things; instead, the passage implies that they have to be resisted. Those in authority are intended by God to preserve peace and to punish the wicked. If these functions are not performed, the ordinance stands, despite men's unfaithfulness, but the rulers are to be resisted. There is nothing in this exegesis that runs counter to that which I have outlined earlier, and Knox, in putting forward his exposition, can be held to be nearer to the meaning of the text than was Lethington, who denied the validity of this interpretation.[50] 'To resist a tyrant,' said Knox, 'is not to resist God nor yet his ordinance.'[51]

Knox further defended himself by a series of reasoned statements. Expanding the subject of obedience, he differentiated between that obedience which is right and that which is wrong, saying that God may command resistance and has rewarded obedience to such a command.

Now the common song of all men is, We must obey our Kings, be they good or be they bad; for God has so commanded. But horrible shall the vengeance be, that shall be poured forth upon such blasphemers of God, his holy name and ordinance. For it is no less blasphemy to say, that God has commanded Kings to be obeyed, when they command impiety, than to say, that God by his precept is author and maintainer of all iniquity. True it is, God has commanded Kings to be obeyed, but like true it is, that in all things which they commit against his glory, or when cruelly without cause they rage against their brethren, the members of Christ's body, he has commanded no obedience, but rather he has approved, yes, and greatly rewarded such as have opposed themselves to their ungodly commandments and blind rage, as in the example of the Three Children, of Daniel, and Ebedmelech.[52]

Moreover, in conversation with Mary, Queen of Scots, he justi-fied resistance on the analogy of children whose father has become insane: should he attempt to kill them, they have every right to withstand him.[53] Nor is there really any neutrality in this matter. To be silent before tyranny is to confirm the unjust actions of vicious rulers. They who do this

> give no true obedience; but as they are apostates from God, so are they traitors to their prince, whom by flattery they confirm in rebelling against God. Only they which to the death resist such wicked laws and decrees are acceptable to God.[54]

One cannot stand aside, for this does not preserve one's inno-cence nor ensure freedom from guilt:

> God craves not only that a man do no iniquity in his own person, but also that he oppose himself to all iniquity as far forth as in him lies.[55]

Finally, Knox would have none of the argument that oaths or promises bind a people to obey or maintain tyrants against God. He intended to take this up in a work he never completed to be entitled *The Second Blast of the Trumpet*, but he did indicate its contents; in particular he was going to discuss that

> if either rashly they have promoted any manifest wicked person, or yet ignorantly have chosen such a one as after declareth himself unworthy of regiment [i.e. government] above the people of God (and such be idolators and cruel persecutors) most justly may the same men depose and punish him that unadvisedly before they did nominate, appoint and elect.[56]

The Revolution of the Saints

Within seventy years of Knox's death – he died in 1572 – England itself was plunged into the turmoil of the Great Rebellion, as king and parliament struggled against each other. The question of resis-tance was once again a burning issue; arguments for and against its justification were plentiful, often echoing those advanced in the previous century. Thus, from the royalist side, we find Edmund Verney writing to his brother Sir Ralph: 'I beseech you consider that majesty is sacred; God saith, "Touch not mine anointed".'[57] This is a statement faithful to the outlook of William Tyndale. In opposition to this are these words of John Milton, which could well have come from the pen of John Knox: 'Absolute lordship and Christianity are inconsistent.'[58]

Milton was representative of the Puritan attitude, which itself was the product of changing historical circumstances and the working out of Reformation emphases. Medieval society had been largely composed of nonparticipants, of inactive men. The feudal system had seemed closed to planned reconstruction because it was conceived as a chain of being and not as a hierarchy of office. Each citizen had an allotted place in the God-given structure which was not to be tampered with. The Reformation introduced a radical alteration in attitudes in that it regarded the state as subservient to the Word of God and to be changed if necessary.[59] Since the state was bound to subserve the divine will, if it did not do so the seventeenth-century Puritan was prepared to revolt against lawful authority, not just in the sense of resisting it but of seeking to overthrow it. His allegiance was to God's Word and to the community of the future. Evil was not just to be combatted within the individual but wherever it was found, including the political sphere. So the word 'reformation' acquired a new meaning. Originally it had suggested renewal, restoration to some initial form – a view based upon a cyclic interpretation of history. Now it came to mean transformation of the kind associated today with the concept of revolution. Reformation was to be radical change for the better.[60] So resistance was not just defensive struggle against a tyrant, but a violent effort to transform society. In a sense this radical stance is to be understood as the politics of exile,[61] i.e. the Puritan believed that Christians are strangers and pilgrims, but this led not to indifference and apoliticism: instead he faced the world with the intention of changing it. Not being at home, having here no abiding city, he could not settle down in comfort or conformity and he was driven to take steps to transform the society in which, in one sense, he was an alien. Moreover the divine demand for obedience was held to set people free from all kinds of alternative jurisdictions and authorities – 'we must obey God rather than men' (Acts 5.29). In such a struggle the Christian was by no means comfortable; indeed he was one of those 'sensitive men who embodies and articulates the stress of a changing society'.[62]

This sensitivity may be illustrated and some of the arguments for resistance outlined from a letter by Oliver Cromwell to Colonel Robert Hammond – both the writer and his correspondent reveal an extremely conscientious approach to the whole question.

Hammond was worried, in the first place, about the principle that 'it is lawful for a lesser part, if in the right, to force a "numerical majority" '.[63] Cromwell's reply, to what is a new point, was in effect to say: Look at what has happened. Can you not see the hand of God at work on our behalf against tyranny? If you can, so he implies, then the principle should not cause you concern. Cromwell was not answering the query in theoretical terms, but pointed to the historical events and, like an Old Testament prophet, declared that this is the sphere of the divine action which may be discerned by faith.

Hammond's second difficulty related to the exegesis of those New Testament passages which some held to require subservience to the state. 'God', he wrote, 'has appointed authorities among the nations, to which active or passive obedience is to be yielded.'[64] Hence to fight against them is to question the divine authority. Cromwell rejoined:

> Authorities and powers are the ordinance of God. This or that species is of human institution, and limited, some with larger, other with stricter bands, each according to its constitution. But I do not think the Authorities may do *anything*, and yet such obedience be due. All agree that there are cases in which it is lawful to resist . . . The query is, Whether ours be such a case?[65]

One cannot but be impressed by Cromwell's diffidence and his refusal to lay down the law. In approaching an answer to this last question that he himself raised he did not make a series of categorical statements, but posed further questions. His own replies are implicit, but he left Hammond free to adopt his own position once he had been helped to face the issues involved. The first query raised by Cromwell was: Is *salus populi* a sound argument? By this Cromwell indicated that the justness of a rebellion in part rests upon a decision about what best will serve the safety and wellbeing of the populace at large. Obviously he thought that the contemporary situation was such that defence of his fellow countrymen against the dictatorship of Charles was essential – but he left it to

Hammond to weigh the pros and cons for himself. The second question was: whether our actions have defended the people's welfare? Again it is obvious that Cromwell would return an affirmative to this, but again Hammond is presented with the issue to determine in his own way. Finally, Cromwell asked: whether the army is a lawful power called of God to oppose the king? Clearly he thought that it was.

In a further demonstration of his charity and nonjudgmental attitude, Cromwell went on to declare that he himself would not 'slight' those who opt for 'the principle of suffering', i.e. for passive obedience. But one should take care not to be led astray by this principle; we have 'to beware lest fleshly reasoning see more safety in making use of this principle than in acting'.[66]

> Have not some of our friends, by their passive principle (which I judge not, only I think it liable to temptation as well as the active, and neither of them good but as we led unto them of God . . .) – been occasioned to overlook what is just and honest, and to think the people of God may have as much or more good the one way than the other? Good by this Man, – against whom the Lord has witnessed; and whom thou knowest?[67]

Moreover the principle of active suffering is applicable to the Roundheads who, by engaging in rebellion, have experienced anguish and many have died. This engagement is 'all contrary to our natural tendency, and to those comforts our hearts could wish to enjoy as well as others'.[68]

Hammond's final doubt was that 'by acting against such opposition as is like to be, there will be a tempting of God'.[69] Cromwell went immediately to the heart of the issue by considering what is meant by tempting God. To him it is behaving presumptuously in carnal confidence or in unbelief through diffidence. What makes people tempt God is 'acting before and without faith'.[70]

> If the Lord have on any measure persuaded his people, as generally he hath, of the lawfulness, nay of the *duty*, – this persuasion prevailing upon the heart is faith; and acting thereupon is acting in faith; and the more the difficulties are, the more the faith. And it is most sweet that he who is not persuaded have patience towards them that are, and judge not.[71]

The final sentence of this statement shows Cromwell's earnest approach to the whole debate. He will not condemn those who in deep anguish of moral decision do not share his views, but equally

he will not accept any suggestion that his own views are not conscientious nor worked out in relation to his ardent faith in God. He
threw in his lot with the army, preferring 'to take my share with
them, expecting a good issue, than be led away with the others'.[72]

Cromwell's was by no means a lone voice in arguing for the propriety of resistance, and two other writers may be taken as express-
ing, in typical manner, the reasons advanced in its favour, viz.
Samuel Rutherford, a Scottish Presbyterian in the line of Knox,
and John Milton who, while his *Paradise Lost* was 'to justify the
ways of God to men', produced a number of treatises to justify the
ways of his fellow revolutionaries before God.

Both Rutherford and Milton commented on the passage in I
Peter 2 which some held to demand passivity. Rutherford considered that it had nothing to do with the question of political
resistance *per se*,[73] and Milton that submission was only to be
accorded as long as the authority of the state was exercised 'for the
punishment of evil doers, and the encouragement of them that do
well'.[74]

The pith of Rutherford's argument is contained in this quotation
from his *Lex, Rex*, which was published in 1644.

> For the lawfulness of resistance in the matter of the King's unjust
> invasion of life and religion, we offer these arguments. That power
> which is obliged to command and rule justly and religiously for the
> good of the subjects, and is only set over the people on these con-
> ditions, and not absolutely, cannot tie the people to subjection without
> resistance, when the power is abused to the destruction of laws,
> religion, and the subjects . . . There is not a stricter obligation moral
> betwixt king and people than betwixt parent and children, master
> and servants, patrons and clients . . . but the law granteth, if these
> betray their trust committed to them, they may be resisted.[75]

Milton repeated this argument in his *Tenure of Kings and
Magistrates* (1649) in which he defended the execution of King
Charles. He reasoned that just as an individual has the right to
defend himself against another, so a body of people may defend
themselves against a tyrant.[76] But what particularly offended him
was the idea that Christians should manifest a slave mentality.
Those who eschew true liberty on the grounds of loyalty and
obedience do so 'to colour over their base compliances'.[77] To Milton the sword of justice is to be wielded against every tyrant by
anyone 'in whose hand soever is found sufficient power to avenge

the effusion, and so great a deluge of innocent blood. For if all human power to execute, not accidentally but intendedly, the wrath of God upon evil doers without exception, be of God; then that power, whether ordinary, or if that fail, extraordinary so executing that intent of God, is lawful, and not to be resisted.'[78] Neither Christ, nor his gospel, is to be made 'a Sanctuary for Tyrants from justice'.[79]

Two years later Milton wrote his *Pro Populo Anglicano Defensio*, which was an answer to those who charged the English people with regicide. In this he returned to his attack upon the idea that Christianity demands the outlook of slaves. To those who advanced the example of Christ as grounds for humble obedience, he replied that Christ accepted the condition of a servant in order that we might be free, and he quoted from the *Magnificat* about bringing down the mighty from their seat, declaring: 'How ill suited to that occasion would these expressions be, if the coming of Christ rather established and strengthened a tyrannical government, and made blind subjection the duty of all Christians!'[80] Christ, according to Milton, died under a tyrannical government in order to secure freedom for us. He was ready to grant that God may afford us grace to endure slavery if there is no way of avoiding it, but he also contended that God does encourage us to seek liberty whenever possible. 'Were you a slave when called? Never mind. But if you can gain your freedom, avail yourself of the opportunity' (I Cor. 7.21).

> You are very impertinent in endeavouring to argue us into slavery by the example of our Saviour, who, by submitting to such a condition himself, has confirmed even our civil liberties. He took upon him indeed in our stead the form of a servant, but he always retained his purpose of being a deliverer . . . Our liberty is not Caesar's. It is a blessing we have received from God himself. It is what we are born to. To lay this down at Caesar's feet which we derive not from him, which we are not beholden to him for, were an unworthy action, and a degrading of our very nature.[81]

It is difficult to see what there is in either the Old or New Testaments to set against this advocacy of resistance in certain circumstances. While Rousseau, as previously cited, may say that 'true Christians were made to be slaves', he would have received scant sympathy from these seventeenth-century revolutionaries. Indeed in opposition to this characterization is to be set the words of the Leveller John Lilburn who could refer to 'the most faithful servants of Christ in every country where they lived' being 'ever the greatest enemies to tyranny and oppression'.[82] The historical accuracy of both Rousseau's and Lilburn's assessment is questionable, but the freedom of the Christian requires us to face the question ever afresh in the changing circumstances of our day to day existence.

Some Assessment of the Arguments for Resistance

The argument of this chapter would not be greatly advanced by tracing further the development of political theory or by reproducing later arguments in favour of resistance.[83] The function of the preceding sections has simply been to demonstrate that some Christians in the past have believed that they were not required to adopt an unvarying role of passive submission and that, on the contrary, resistance was their positive duty in their situations. In the course of this demonstration an account has been given of the grounds upon which they decided that their action was justified. It now remains to attempt some assessment of these grounds, i.e. I wish to examine them as possibly useful pointers to assist Christians at the present day in their several countries to determine their relationship to the state.

As we have seen, much was made of the appeal to biblical – especially Old Testament – precedents. It must be acknowledged that this is a doubtful proceeding. It involves a highly selective use of certain incidents to the ignoring of others. After all, there are a number of events recorded that no Christian is likely to regard as sanctioning the like conduct at the present day. Although Samuel 'hewed Agag in pieces before the Lord in Gilgal' in response to what he believed to be a divine command (I Sam. 15.33), this would scarcely be taken as an example to imitate. The most that one can say therefore of this line of argument is that the Bible does provides accounts of resistance which were understood to be divinely inspired, but whether or not resistance at a different time and place is justified has to be determined on other grounds.

In relation to the few New Testament passages that do speak of Christians and the state, we have to notice a clear division of opinion as to how to interpret and apply them. Indeed it must be admitted that here is evidence of the twisted nature of Christian thinking on this subject. Believers have, without question, manipulated the sources in order to arrive at the answer they wanted in particular situations. Twentieth-century Christians should take this as a serious object lesson pointing to the need for a critical questioning of the honesty of their own thinking and conclusions. However I think it is fair to affirm that Knox and the Puritans appear to have been closer in their exegesis of the New Testament passages to their original meaning and intent than were their opponents. In no sense was Paul in Romans nor the author of I Peter laying down prescriptions that were to be regarded as binding on all future generations. They were dealing with specific conditions in which obedience was the most realistic course to adopt. Paul, in particular, indicated the functions that he expected a state to perform. He did not assert that if these functions are not discharged or are directed towards evil then disobedience is a duty. The question did not arise at that point in time. Yet one cannot brush aside the implication, drawn by Milton and others, that if the state is unjust and acts, in the terms of Revelation 13, as an instrument of the devil and not of God, then disobedience may be required. At least the question is an open one and the Christian's freedom to make moral choices is not foreclosed.

However there is one passage that I have not touched upon previously and which surprisingly played little part in the debates, and that is the saying in the Sermon on the Mount: 'Do not resist one who is evil' or, even more general in the AV: 'resist not evil' (Matt. 5.39). If this be regarded as a categorical imperative, as the promulgation of an absolute law of conduct, then all resistance is condemned. The question of violent or nonviolent means does not even arise, for nonviolent resistance is still resistance (or, conversely, nonresistance is *not* nonviolent resistance), and this would appear to be excluded by this verse. Consequently, if we persist in a theological method that bases itself upon passages of scripture which are taken to be directives, we are touching upon the nub of the argument about resistance. If political obligation is a species of moral obligation or somehow partakes of it, then 'it is difficult to understand how there can be *any* obligation to a morally unjustifiable state, unless there was a substantive moral rule that proscribed all resistance'.[84] Does then Matthew 5.39 constitute such a rule? I shall argue later that Jesus' sayings are not to be accepted as either absolutes or laws, but here it is sufficient to notice that, if this verse were taken as a rule, then something is drastically amiss as regards Christian moral thinking, for it seems immoral to assert that there is any such moral rule that has the effect of requiring one to co-operate in the perpetuation of immorality.

Moreover, to hold that this saying does preclude all forms of resistance is to do violence to it, by wrenching it from its context and elevating it, in an entirely ahistorical fashion, into an absolute. Whereas, as Roger Mehl has put it, 'concrete precepts relating to a definite, given situation are not transformable into universally valid rules, especially in the field of social ethics'.[85]

There are two principal ways of interpreting the Matthean saying, although they are not necessarily contradictory, and each pays attention to the context and historical circumstances. The first method lays stress on the Old Testament background and on the elaboration of this teaching by Paul. The other pays particular attention to the setting in the gospel itself.

The Old Testament background clearly includes such statements as these:

> Do not say, 'I will do to him as he has done to me;
> I will pay the man back for what he has done' (Prov. 24.29).

> What you hate do not do to any one (Tobit 4.15).

The Pauline elaboration is to be found in Romans 12 where he seems to be echoing these ideas and where he asserts that Christians must 'repay no one evil for evil'; they must 'never avenge' themselves, and they should 'not be overcome by evil but overcome evil with good' (Rom. 12.17, 19, 21). Taking these pronouncements as providing the general thought context, then Matthew 5.39 does not refer to craven acquiescence in evil but rather to a yielding at one level, while at the same time engaging in another kind of action which is to overcome evil.[86] Hence Jesus was not teaching nonresistance but that evil cannot be resisted by a further evil.[87] So the antithesis between resistance and resignation is a false one.

Turning now to the actual context in Matthew 5, we find that this is an attack upon the *lex talionis*. This law of retaliation was to the effect that the reparation required of a criminal should be in proportion to the harm caused. This was generally accepted in the ancient world and indeed appeared in the Code of Hammurabi two thousand years before Christ. In the Old Testament it is to be found in Exodus 21.23-5:

> If any harm follows, then you shall give life for life, eye for eye, tooth for tooth, hand for hand, foot for foot, burn for burn, wound for wound, stripe for stripe (cf. Lev. 24.20; Deut. 19.21).

Despite the rigour of the punishment, this represented an advance upon the archaic system of personal vengeance. If someone suffered an injury, he was not allowed to retaliate by taking the aggressor's life – he could only demand the inflicting of an equivalent injury. This principle has two aspects: on the one hand, it protects the criminal, but, on the other, it lays down the penalty that he merits for his wrongdoing. In Matthew the charge not to resist would appear to be related to this second aspect and to be a demand to replace the law of retaliation with that of love. Though the *lex talionis* was an advance, Christians must go even further: any response in a spirit of vengeance is contrary to the way of the Kingdom. Simple retaliation is insufficient to enable people to live in peace and harmony. So the saying is aimed to encourage behaviour based upon love and not upon hatred. 'Do not treat vindictively someone who harms you' – this would be a fair rendering. In this form, it is evident that there is here no general law against resistance *per se*.

However there are two other matters to be noted. First, the verb translated 'resist' means 'retort' and the reference is almost certainly to opposing someone in front of a judge. This someone is neither the devil nor evil in general but one who wishes you harm. Hence this saying could also be rendered: 'If someone wishes you harm, do not rush off to the law court and arraign him before a magistrate.' Further, in this very specific sense – which illustrates the law of love that is to replace the *lex talionis* – there is no universal rule forbidding resistance to evil – possible disobedience to a state is therefore not precluded by this saying.[88]

Turning next to the more general arguments, it seems reasonable to agree in one particular with Knox against both Luther and Calvin. The two continental reformers, as we have seen, maintained that only those who hold public office can initiate resistance, whereas Knox was of the opinion that every citizen had this right and that this right may on occasion become a duty. The view of Luther and Calvin arose directly out of their contemporary situation which is no longer ours. The masses were both ignorant of politics and had little means of effective participation. Because of their lack of knowledge and of their possibly poor judgment, it was understandable that some Christian thinkers should limit resistance to a certain group or class; but at the present day with mass media, democratic institutions, etc., conditions are entirely different. It would be a mistake therefore to be too much influenced by this aspect of reformed thought. Other aspects of that thought are more relevant as possible guide lines for conduct, and indeed they have a direct bearing upon the concept of a just revolution which will be considered in the final chapter.

First, it would appear to be a sound argument that God cannot be supposed to command nonresistance at all times and in all places no matter how oppressive a situation may be; to think otherwise is to suppose that he wills the maintenance of evil. Further, while obedience is the proper course when a state is relatively just, to continue obedient under tyranny is to condone it, and a conflict will arise between obedience to human authority and obedience to God who condemns all evil. In such circumstances, heed must be paid to the apostles' declaration that 'we must obey God rather than men'.

Much was made of the argument that an unjust state forfeits any claim to authority. If this be so, then the question of obedience does not arise, for there no longer exists any authority to which obedience may be due. If the just exercise of authority is a condition of its acceptability and legitimacy, injustice nullifies that authority. This same argument is considered to carry weight at the present day. So Karl Barth affirmed that Christians should condemn National Socialism which, because of its totalitarian form, was no longer subserving the will of God and indeed had resulted in the fundamental dissolution of the just state. It had destroyed all order, justice, freedom and authority.[89] In similar vein, the authors of a report of the Board of Social Responsibility of the Church of England state:

> If government utterly fails to fulfil its God-given function, authority lapses back to God who may then call new rulers.[90]

Authority is of course to be distinguished from tyranny to the extent that its correlate is the free partner, whereas the correlate of tyranny is the slave. Christians believe that they are called to be free and therefore they cannot but acknowledge that 'even the earthly external ordering of human affairs is best carried on if it appeals to the free man instead of taking freedom away from man'.[91] To pray for a just state or for lawful authority is to assume responsibility for its preservation, if it exists, or for its creation if it does not exist. This creation may well involve, in the first instance, a clearing of the ground by resisting the powers that be. When an attack upon an existing order is part of a struggle for freedom, it is difficult to see how Christians, who believe in redemption or liberation, can stand aside. Milton was not speaking against a balanced understanding of the Christian faith when he stressed that freedom is a blessing from God which we must establish and preserve in all areas of life.

The Christian then is free to be disobedient, but at what point he or she will resort to resistance is a matter that can only be decided in relation to specific circumstances. We have to determine when a state has ceased to discourage social evil and encourage social good and has become an instrument of the devil. We have to determine too if the situation is propitious for active resistance, since it would be blind not to take account of the resources available and of the prospects of success. Cromwell in fact was entirely right in contending that an estimation of the *salus populi* is an essential element in moral decision. Cromwell was equally correct in stressing that all forms of government are man-made, so that no one form is sacrosanct. To a certain extent his thought was moving towards the utilitarian consideration that government is a means to an end, viz. the good of the people it serves, and that if it does not further that end it should be changed, by active resistance if no other way can be found.

In the last analysis, it is one's understanding of ethics that will determine the individual's choice. This will concern us in the final chapter, but here it is relevant to note the distinction that Max Weber drew between an ethic of intention or ultimate values and an ethic of responsibility.[92] According to the former, a person is committed to a particular value, e.g. obedience, which is to be actualized always regardless of cost; according to the latter, a person recognizes that there may be a number of values that can conflict and that in making a moral choice it is responsibility to others that must be the determining factor. The first tends to be private and individualistic – and fits in well with the idea that religion is a private concern – the second is more public and corresponds with the Christian emphasis upon love of neighbour. There can be situations in which disobedience and resistance are the only ways of embodying that love in effective action. Those within the church who follow this course are opting for the party of charity and seeking to make justice inspired by love the mainspring of their social action. They differ therefore from the party of order which seeks to preserve the *status quo*, with or without some modifications. Cromwell, as will be recalled, refused to sit in judgment on those who differed from him about this issue. This is wise Christian proceeding, but it does mean freedom to choose, in the knowledge that the justice of resistance is in proportion to the injustice of an existing state.

4

LAW AND ORDER

Over the past decade or so the question of law and order has come very much to the fore. The occurrence of protest marches, demonstrations, sit-ins, aggressive picketing and the taking over of factories by workers, together with the atrocities of urban guerillas and the increase in crime, both against property and against the person, all have combined to disturb those concerned for the stability of society. Indeed one major political party in England has sought to gain votes by projecting its public image as the party of law and order. Obviously this subject bears directly upon Christian participation in revolution, for revolution by its very nature involves illegal activity and the creation, if only for a short period, of disorder. There is indeed no reason to question Lord Devlin's statement that 'the law knows nothing of the right, and it may be the duty, to rebel and cannot recognize it'.[1] Consequently the Christian understanding of and attitude towards the law has to be investigated.

The New Testament sheds little light on this subject. The word 'law' appears frequently, but what is usually in view is the Jewish Torah, i.e. that which was believed to be the revealed will of God set down in the Pentateuch and elaborated in oral tradition. It is of this that Paul was speaking when he said that 'Christ is the end of the law' (Rom. 10.4). This is what the author of Ecclesiasticus could term 'the law of the Most High' and 'the law of life' (9.15; 17.11).

However, few today would think that the laws embodied in civil and criminal codes, in law reports or on the statute book have any claim to being regarded as direct expressions of the divine will. They are man-made rules to regulate social interaction – they do not constitute that 'law' from which Christ set us free. It could therefore be said that Christianity has desacralized law. Yet precisely because a country's laws are of human devising, there has always been a certain degree of antinomianism in Christian thought, in the sense that members of the church have regarded obedience to the legal system as secondary to what they believe is the will of God for them on those occasions when their understanding of the latter conflicted with what the law required. An obvious example of this is the law, which operated up to the Peace of the church, requiring the worship of the Roman emperor as lord. Christians, who claimed in other respects to be loyal and law abiding citizens, would not act in accordance with that particular law and paid the penalty for their disobedience with trials and executions. So, according to Lactantius: 'when men command us to act in opposition to the law of God, and in opposition to justice, we should be deterred by no threats or punishments from preferring the command of God to the command of man'.[2]

A further instance was when the emperor Diocletian declared all gatherings for Christian worship to be illegal. The proconsul Anulinus, cross-examining a member of the congregation arrested at Abitina in North Africa in 304, could demand: 'Why did you celebrate the eucharist (*dominicium*) contrary to the imperial edict?' The answer of the accused was: 'It is a foolish question, as if anyone could be a Christian without the eucharist.'[3] Consequently we find C. J. Cadoux summing up the position adopted in these early centuries in the following words: 'Christians reserved to themselves the right of deliberately and avowedly disobeying the laws and orders of the state, whenever those laws and orders came to conflict with what they felt to be the law of God.'[4] Steadfast in their illegal conduct, these martyrs were but following in the footsteps of Peter and the apostles when they told the Sanhedrin: 'We must obey God rather than men.' The validity of this position has of course been generally accepted, as indicated by the dictum of Chief Justice Hughes that 'in the forum of conscience, duty to a moral power higher than the state has always been maintained'.[5]

Nevertheless, it would not be incorrect to say that over centuries Christians have sought to be law abiding citizens and they would agree in a general sense with the author of Proverbs:

> Those who forsake the law praise the wicked,
>   but those who keep the law strive against them (28.4).

Nor is this attitude without a reasonable foundation.

The function of law within any community may be said to have a number of interrelated aspects. It exists to ensure justice, to restrict conflict and to create channels of co-operation. It acts to promote the common welfare. It aims to safeguard individual freedom by protecting people from arbitrariness and from oppressive actions. Under the rule of law no one is wholly unrestrained, but there is a valid distinction to be made between subjection to another's capricious will and to a law which has a right to be respected. Law too provides the context for order and security and it serves to enforce community standards. Of course most would agree that no state and no body of laws ever achieve absolute justice. Every state exists between two poles: that of righteousness, on the one hand, and that of order, on the other. States constantly violate true justice, but in so far as they preserve order they have some claim to a citizen's allegiance. Consequently law as an expression of relative justice is necessary to maintain some sort of order. Hence 'although law is in the unenviable position of never being able to reflect pure justice and is, indeed, often highly coloured by the reverse, yet because it aspires to justice and generally speaking is to be preferred to a life without law, it is entitled to a certain reverence'.[6]

But Christians would want to go further than this. They acknowledge that law need not degenerate into legalism. Having a concern for social order and social justice, they recognize that the legal system is one of the means for embodying effectively that concern. Just as Christian involvement in politics, as I have argued in the second chapter, is the necessary working out of love in action in today's world, so too Christian support of and persistent efforts to improve the law are motivated by love of neighbour. Indeed law plays an essential part in social relations and it can subserve the purpose of creating the conditions in which love can flourish.[7]

But it is possible to go even further than this and acknowledge that there are certain moral reasons which favour obedience to the law. Thus to accept the benefits of a society is in part to be committed to accepting its laws. Moreover, since the law is an instrument for advancing the purposes of a state, if one agrees with those purposes then observance is called for. So, to give one example, if the legal system does safeguard personal security and if I, as an individual, value personal security, I have moral grounds for obedience. Again, all human beings have certain moral obligations towards their fellows; we should respect their rights and interests, and whenever these are protected by law, we ourselves should uphold it.[8] Because law can have these positive, and indeed beneficial, aspects, it is not lightly to be disregarded, and I must emphasize – lest the point be lost amidst much else I have to say – that no Christian will lightly act in an illegal manner or irresponsibly encourage any easy lack of respect for the rule of law.

Order

In speaking in this way of the valuable functions of law I have not infrequently referred to order and this concept needs further explication. It is almost impossible to separate law from order since the definition of the latter is partly given in terms of the former. According to the *Oxford English Dictionary* order is 'a natural, moral or spiritual system in which things proceed according to definite laws'. To act against order in this sense means to act contrary to these definite laws and, conversely, to behave illegally is to conduct oneself against order. The two are so interrelated, as far as their application to a social context is concerned, that order is more or less synonymous with the rule of law. Consequently, to insist upon the need to observe the law in order to uphold order is to commit a tautology which adds little to the discussion.

Because law and order reinforce one another and indeed reflect one another, it is possible to conceive of an unjust system of law upholding an unjust order. In such a case, however, the argument against resistance to injustice is not reinforced by adding the folly of disorder to the moral problem of illegality.

If law and order – in their social setting – are more or less identical, then the only way to increase order in a society is by the strictest enforcement of the law, but this completely overlooks the possibility that some of the laws may be unjust. Conversely, what may be regarded as order may itself be anything but just, and so we find Helder Camara objecting to those who wish to support the social order in all circumstances. 'What social order?' he asks, 'I cannot speak for the developed countries, but the so-called "social order" in the underdeveloped countries is nothing but a cumulus of stratified injustices.'[9]

Even where there are relatively just laws, the prevailing order may be unjust because of the malfunctioning of the law, i.e. the law may be misused by its administrators. So on occasion the police may harass and suppress protest groups in ways that really have no legal backing. An example of this is provided by the case of the blacks in the USA who opposed the illegal but traditional practice of segregation. When some of them sat in at a department store they were quite wrongly charged with disturbing the peace. Hence the existence of law, even when just, guarantees no sure preservation of proper order, in the sense of the rule of law, if the law malfunctions.[10]

Too readily traditional Christians equate law and order with Christianity. In so doing, they are seeking to attain a false security and so to avoid the anxiety and complexity of moral choice. They then contend that the existing system is less evil than others, that the issues lack clarity, or that they do not possess a sufficient knowledge of the facts and so assure themselves of the righteousness of doing nothing. This is to behave in unfreedom. It is to fail to recognize that law and order often find freedom threatening, for they wish to keep the old, while freedom strains after the new. Jesus himself was killed because he represented a danger to the order of his society.

It is here that we have to take issue with the view exemplified by Cicero when he declared that 'we are servants of the law in order that we may be free'.[11] It is a mistake to identify the law with freedom. From one aspect the law is a piece of machinery which can be used either for or against liberty.[12] In any case, order should not be regarded as the presupposition and condition of freedom; rather freedom is the presupposition and condition of order,[13] for true order is the practice of freedom. To hold that order is prior and freedom is consequential is to reverse the proper sequence. This reversal is constantly being made and provides a self-justifying legitimation of the *status quo*. Once it is acknowledged that freedom is necessary for good order and that justice is the proper foundation and criterion of law, then it is possible to perceive that law and order may have to be opposed in the interests of freedom and justice. Freedom then comes before order and justice before law. It is, after all, the function of a state to structure order as the practice of freedom. Yet the order upheld by a state may lead to exploitation and slavery; when this is so, an existing order, because it does not allow the practice of freedom, is to be condemned. Order *qua* order is nothing in itself – the question is whether it is or is not just, whether it does or does not allow freedom and whether, if it favours both injustice and oppression, it can be changed without an increase of either. Order, indeed, may be a barrier to freedom; it may be institutionalized disorder which has to be resisted to bring liberation and to establish a new order corresponding to freedom.

All this is not to say that law and order are not valuable; it is to point out that they cannot be regarded as the supreme value before which all other moral considerations have to give way. As F. Herzog affirms:

> Man benefits from institutions that maintain his society. But he also abuses them as means of manipulating his neighbour. Law and order should help man attain a fuller life. But, in the dimension of freedom, man is accountable ultimately to his origin in God and not man-made institutions.[14]

Law

Even granted the positive functions of law, which I have briefly described previously, it is necessary to recognize that there is, in the phrase of M. Q. Sibley, a certain 'dubiety about the law'. At the present day, it is the Marxists who have most questioned its impartiality and therefore its justice. Their view, which is by no means superficial, is that law is often an instrument to promote the economic and status interests of the ruling class. They were, of course, anticipated in this long ago by Plato, who made Thrasymachus, a Sophist philosopher, define law as 'the interest of the strongest party'.[15] In this sense law may function as a means of social oppression. Indeed Helder Camara, himself no Marxist, can say: 'As for "law", it is all too often an instrument of violence against the weak.'[16] So Sibley reveals that the American legal system enshrines a property scheme which has permitted a distribution of income in 1955 not greatly different from what it was in 1910.[17] Laurence Veysey points out that 'without laws to establish it and maintain it, the institution of slavery would have been impossible'.[18] Similarly in South Africa the apartheid laws are a scarcely veiled expression of racial oppression. A government can pervert justice while hiding behind the protective cover of legality; judicial processes are then used to achieve political ends.[19] Or again, from December 1973 to January 1974, there was a confrontation in Great Britain between the Conservative Government and the Trade Unions and this was regarded by the former as a question of authority and obedience to the law. To many in the Trade Union movement, however, the so-called laws were so many examples of social discrimination, favouring the haves against the have-nots. To oppose or to refuse to obey such laws is not necessarily to opt for lawlessness, but to declare that there are laws that fall short of that degree of justice that alone will command respect for and observance of the law. As M. Q. Sibley says: 'To the degree that the positive laws of the state represent primarily the special interests of particular groups within the state, it would seem that my obligation to obey them is correspondingly lessened, other things being equal.'[20]

Augustine, although writing many centuries ago, was not lacking in a similar discernment. He posed the question: 'Remove justice, and what are kingdoms but gangs of criminals on a large scale?' He then argued that no human institution can ever achieve complete justice – it may go some way towards it but always falls short. Hence an obligation to obey the laws of a country in such a condition corresponds to the duty to obey the rules of a robber band.[21] It is perhaps also to be noted that although Marxists share this insight and apply it to bourgeois capitalist societies, when they themselves achieve power they have to date used the law in precisely the same way, i.e. as an instrument of oppression; it is only the identity of the victims that has changed. Illustrations of this abound in the history of the USSR since the October Revolution – millions of White Russians, kulaks, returning prisoners of war, 'dissident' intellectuals, etc., have been imprisoned or executed and many of them quite legally.[22] But then the Russian Communists are quite consistent, in that they define law as that which safeguards 'arrangements agreeable and advantageous to the dominant proletarian class'.[23] Even in a constitutional democracy, some of the legislature may be ill-educated and motivated by self-interest. It is quite conceivable that some of the laws they may promulgate will embody their own prejudices.

It begins to look as if the rule of law is not always and in every place so sacrosanct as may at first appear. Historically speaking human beings have vacillated between understanding law as a cumbersome device for regulating social intercourse and as the epitome of human achievement. The truth probably lies somewhere between. One's obligation to obey the law – and I repeat that I do not hold that the rule of law is lightly to be disregarded – will obviously be affected by the precise role it is seen to play in specific situations. Whenever law functions as a means of social, racial or sex oppression, one can scarcely congratulate the upholders of law and order; they have to be sensitive enough to detect when the so-called order is no more than a generalized disorder.

Of course there is an apparently simple way of resolving the moral problem of Christian disobedience to the law and that is by adopting a non-positivist understanding of it. This turns on the question: what is law? There are, broadly speaking, two main positions with respect to this. The positivist position is to the effect that that is law which is promulgated by the person, group or association which has authority to make it. Such a view separates the definition of law sharply from morality. The alternative position is that that is law which meets certain moral standards, is reasonable and is proclaimed by a legitimate government. So John Locke, who condemned resistance to the law, argued that laws which transgress certain fundamental principles are not laws 'properly so-called'.[24] Nazi Germany will serve as an illustration of these two approaches. From the positivist side, the decrees of Hitler were law; to the non-positivist they were not law at all.[25] However in terms of practical moral decision the two approaches are not very far apart. The positivist accepts that a law is a law, but then as a moral agent he may condemn it and refuse to obey it. The non-positivist may reject what purports to be a law on the grounds of its immoral demands and refuse to acknowledge its authority *qua* law. In each case the person concerned exercises moral discrimination which may result in identical conduct. But strictly speaking the question of illegal behaviour only arises in the case of the positivist. To the non-positivist, an immoral decree is simply not a law and to refuse to obey it cannot therefore be contrary to law. In this case it is a matter of disobedience towards a duly constituted or *de facto* government and the moral problem turns on one's relation to the state, which was examined in the previous chapter. For the purposes of the present discussion therefore I propose to adopt the positivist definition,* as this does pose acutely the problem of the morality of acknowledged illegal behaviour.

---

* To adopt the positivist definition in this instance and for this specific purpose does not mean that I accept the positivist position *in toto* nor that I am unaware of the many serious objections that may be brought against it.

Justice

The morality of illegal behaviour depends in part upon the distinction between just and unjust laws. This distinction does not rest upon the standing of those who promulgate them. A dictator can issue just laws and a majority, in a democracy, may create unjust ones. Rather the distinction turns upon one's understanding of justice. Consideration of this subject is sometimes bedevilled by looking at it in the context of the law courts and this leads to a superficial view that justice is that which is administered by them. But justice is not primarily a legal term at all. Of course, a legislator, when formulating a law, should, as a moral being, take into account whether or not the proposal is in accordance with justice, but his or her appreciation of justice will not derive from the law itself but from ethical considerations.

The present day view of justice is dominated by Aristotelian categories. He distinguished between arithmetical or contractual justice on the one hand and geometrical, proportional or distributive justice on the other.[26] Contractual justice is based on the idea of equality and involves giving like for like. Distributive justice recognizes the existence of inequality. So in war-time Germany ration cards were issued and their circulation was initially based upon contractual justice, i.e. everyone received the same quantity of certain commodities. It was then recognized that the diversity of persons and of their circumstances should be taken into account and so heavy labourers and expectant mothers were allowed more. This was an example of distributive justice.[27]

By accepting this Aristotelian position as his starting point, Emil Brunner, in *Justice and the Social Order*, was led to the conclusion that love goes beyond justice; it is a superadditive. He was also moved towards this conclusion by another factor, viz. that the Christian norm of love has never been fully embodied in any historical system of law. This too results in a distinction between justice and love. But when a Christian speaks of justice, he or she should do so on a biblical basis and not in terms of Hellenistic philosophy nor of a knowledge of law courts past and present.

In the Bible justice is an attribute of God or, rather, it is descriptive of his essential nature. There is however no single word that corresponds to the English one; in the Old Testament at least six Hebrew terms bear on its meaning.[28] God's justice or righteousness – the two are synonyms – is revealed in action when he defends, vindicates and saves the poor. It is not then fair treatment according to the law that is justice, but loving treatment that is justice. The divine justice is therefore to be equated with love and mercy.[29] Although, as supreme judge, God condemns the hard hearted, he also, according to the New Testament, justifies the ungodly, i.e. he acquits sinners and this acquittal is at the same time his saving activity, which is also his merciful love in action. Justice, from this perspective, is much more than is contained in the Aristotelian categories. It is not a question of fair shares all round[30] – contractual justice. Nor is it a question of distributive justice – to each according to his or her condition or status in the community. Rather biblical justice is rooted in the idea of to each according to his or her needs. Love then is not something added to justice, but is of its very essence.

In the New Testament, Jesus not only reveals the divine love in effective operation, he is himself the righteousness of God (I Cor. 1.30). Love then does not do more than justice demands; it is the ultimate principle of justice.[31] When justice and love are not married, then Christians are misled. According to Paul Tillich, 'it is regrettable that Christianity has often concealed its unwillingness to do justice, or to fight for it, by setting off love against justice, and performing works of love, in the sense of "charity", instead of battling for the removal of social injustice.'[32] True justice, however, cannot be separated from love; love is not something extra, over and above justice; rather love is justice in effective operation. 'Justice,' says Tillich again, 'is just because of the love which is implicit in it.'[33] Consequently that is unjust which is a denial of love. It is not difficult to find numerous examples to illustrate this, but one alone will suffice. The property laws relating to women in many Western countries are anything but just; they are the embodiment of a male chauvinism that denies to women what love would freely bestow.

Legality and Morality

This understanding of law – and of its justice or lack of it – was basic to Thomas Aquinas' view that law should promote the common welfare, i.e. it should be motivated by and embody love. A law that is not directed to this end is then unjust, and so Aquinas was prepared to affirm that it does not bind anyone in conscience and no one is under an obligation to obey it.[34] It is evident from this that neither Aquinas nor indeed any other Christian thinker about this subject would equate *simpliciter* legality and morality. So Lord Devlin has no hesitation in recognizing a gap between what he calls the moral law and the law of the land and in rejecting the equation of crime and sin.[35] It follows that one cannot identify legality with morality and so an illegal act is not necessarily immoral *per se*. Indeed if the two were identical we should be faced by the absurd position that to propose a change in the law would be to advocate an immoral action. This would be so because whatever were to be required or permitted by the new law would necessarily deviate from the morally acceptable behaviour required by the law as it is.[36] Hence Lord Devlin can affirm that

> I am not under the delusion that the law has the ultimate answer to every moral problem and I am not asserting that there is in all circumstances a moral obligation to obey the law. There may be times in the future, as there have been in the past, when a man has to set himself up against society. But if he does so, he must expect to find the law on the side of society.[37]

There are too occasions when to act in obedience to the law is to behave in an immoral fashion. For example, in Holland during the last war it was illegal to harbour Jews. Many Christians and non-Christians sheltered these unfortunate victims of Nazi hatred, seeking to shield them from torture and death. By doing this they risked and in many cases sacrificed their lives. Can any one doubt that their illegal conduct was entirely moral? Conversely, of course, to act in accordance with the law is not necessarily to behave in a moral fashion. Many Roman Catholics hold that abortion is wrong. British law does allow it in certain circumstances, but to take advantage of this legal permission would be, according to the Catholic understanding of the matter, to be guilty of an immoral act; he or she would be acting legally but immorally. What may be deemed immoral then can be legally right.

Socrates provides a paradigm case of this distinction between immorality and illegality. As depicted by Plato in his *Apologia* and in *Crito*, Socrates argued that, in his view, he had not disobeyed the law, but that if the court should hold that his conduct was indeed illegal, then in that case he would have acted deliberately in an illegal manner because it was his moral duty to do what he had done. When sentenced, he acknowledged the right of the state to find him guilty of unlawful conduct, but maintained that the line he had adopted was unavoidable in the light of his understanding of his moral duty. In effect therefore, both by his conduct and his remarks, Socrates was demonstrating that moral principles may compel us to disobey a particular law.

Of course there are occasions when to act illegally is to act immorally, but this is so only when law and morality exactly coincide. Thus to batter a baby to death is to make oneself liable to a charge of murder or, at the least, of manslaughter. The act is illegal, but battering a baby to death is also in most circumstances held to be immoral. Conversely, that to act illegally is not to act immorally has already been demonstrated by the example cited above from Holland. As E. van den Haag says: 'Individual conscience can be morally right and legitimate authority wrong; and in some cases the individual should act illegally to make his conscience prevail over legitimate authority.'[38]

Especial emphasis upon individual conscience in connexion with this subject was laid by Henry David Thoreau. Thoreau refused to pay his Massachusetts poll tax as a protest against slavery. The consequence of this illegal act was that he was imprisoned for one night in July 1846: he was released when a well meaning – but, according to Thoreau, wrong-headed – friend paid the tax on his behalf. Two years later Thoreau defended his action in a lecture before the Concord Lyceum and this was first published under the title 'Resistance to Civil Government' but is now more usually known as 'Civil Disobedience'.

Thoreau's approach was very much that of the individualist who asserts the autonomy of the conscience. His arguments are not therefore directly related to social ethics, but they are powerful ones nevertheless. For Thoreau, to be a human being involves the free exercise of 'the judgment or moral sense'. So he asserted that 'the only obligation which I have a right to assume, is to do at any time what I think right'.[39] Hence he posed the question, to which he obviously expected there to be a negative reply: 'Must the citizen, even for a moment, or in the least degree, resign his conscience to the legislator?'[40] He was prepared to allow that one should submit to an injustice which arose simply from the inevitable clumsiness of government; he was also willing to accept injustice towards himself, but he would not acquiesce in injustice towards others. In his view, to pay taxes and so to support a government that was condoning slavery was to be an agent of injustice towards the neighbour. In such a situation, 'then, I say, break the law . . . What I have to do is to see, at any rate, that I do not lend myself to the wrong which I condemn.'[41] Thoreau then poured scorn on those who 'in opinion' are opposed to slavery but do nothing in actuality to bring it to an end and just wait for others to remedy the evil. 'There are nine hundred and ninety-nine patrons of virtue to one virtuous man'[42] – the former being those who do no more than express regret at the existence of unjust laws, while the latter actively opposes them by disobedience. It was in this way that Thoreau mounted an attack upon the acceptability of automatic obedience to external authority and in so doing he focussed attention upon the nature of moral responsibility itself, which is such that it rules out the identification of legality with morality.

Moral Choice and Law

If an individual is to remain a moral agent, i.e. one who acts according to ethical principles, he must ultimately be responsible for deciding whether or not to obey a law; otherwise he surrenders his own freedom and wills his own slavery. Even if he or she decides to do what could be regarded as objectively wrong, it cannot not be done without surrendering moral responsibility and admitting that a majority or a special group can tell the individual what he or she thinks it is not right to do.[43] In making this statement I have to admit that such an approach could lead to anarchy, where every person does what seems right in his or her eyes. But this is a necessary, and indeed inevitable, risk if we commit ourselves to human freedom and responsibility. Moreover the risk can be exaggerated; only in the most extreme circumstances is a large number of people likely to disobey more than a particular law at any one time, and such extreme circumstances, involving widespread and massive injustice, could of themselves be held to justify wide disobedience.

One may be disobedient either to preserve personal integrity or to change the structure and practices of society. Many of the early Christians acted illegally in accordance with the first type, when they refused to worship the emperor. Martin Luther King belongs rather to the second category; he headed a movement which relied on disobedience to achieve its ends, but those ends comprised more than the alteration of a single law; they related to the position of blacks within their total social, economic and political setting. No one however is likely to take seriously the view that King was either an immoral person or behaved in an immoral fashion.

Not only does one's understanding of moral responsibility involve the freedom to act illegally on occasion in accordance with
conscience, but the nature of moral choice too is such that subservience to the law can never be absolute. Tillich is certainly right
when he declares that 'The moral imperative is the demand to
become actually what one is essentially and therefore potentially
. . . Therefore, a moral act is not an act in obedience to an external
law, human or divine.'[44] Further, since Christ has set us free from
all legalism, the basis of Christian ethics does not lie in any code,
such as the ten commandments; it is founded upon faith working
through love. But from the point of view of Christian love, any
and every law is to be transcended or breached which stands in the
way of serving the needs of others. It does not matter whether we
define the law as a divinely revealed set of imperatives nor as a
man-made code nor as so-called natural law* – Christian ethics
transcends them all.

This freedom carries an obligation, viz. to do absolutely everything that love requires.[45] For the Christian therefore the question
of absolutism and relativism in ethics is resolved. Since the principle of Christian ethics is love, it is love that remains an unchang-
ing element; but love can transform itself according to the concrete
demands of every specific individual and social situation without
losing its unconditional validity. The principle is: 'Love and do
as you please.' This does *not* imply: 'Do as you please', for by
definition Christian love will be pleased only by doing what the
neighbour needs. Hence I agree with Paul Ramsey: 'What should
be done or not in a particular instance, what is good or bad, right
or wrong, what is better or worse than something else, what are
"degrees of value" – these things in Christian ethics are not known
in advance or derived from some preconceived code. They are
derived *backwards* by Christian love from what is apprehended to
be the needs of others.'[46] If illegal action is the only way to serve
the neighbour, then it cannot be deemed bad or wrong or worse
than anything else; it can only be held to be morally right. 'We are
to live by the law of love,' says J. Fletcher, 'and not by the love of
law.'[47]

This living according to the law of love is necessary for

* One way to approach the question discussed in this chapter would
have been from the point of view of natural law. I have deliberately
refrained from examining this, since I hold that the concept is highly
ambiguous.

Christians because, although I have suggested earlier that law can create the conditions in which love may flourish, we have to take account of the fact that, in the words of Lord Devlin, 'the criminal law is not a statement of how people ought to behave; it is a statement of what will happen to them if they do not behave'.[48] This sets limits to the extent to which law can be an embodiment of love. Here Lord Atkin's famous dictum is very relevant.

> The rule that you are to love your neighbour becomes in law, you must not injure your neighbour; and the lawyer's question, Who is my neighbour? receives a restricted reply.[49]

To express this in a different way: if one is always law abiding, one is not thereby being a fully moral person, because morality must go beyond existing laws which tend to be negative (what will happen to people if they do not behave) and not positive (how people ought to behave). So, if I go into my neighbour's house and take his goods, I am liable to prosecution; but if I do not go into his house to take him some food when he is starving I am not guilty of any breach of the law but I am guilty of a sin of omission.

The case may perhaps be said to have been made that Christians may have to disobey the law in certain circumstances. As I stressed at the outset, they should never do this lightly, for illegal behaviour undermines that order which is necessary for harmonious living. Not that order has a higher value than justice, since the only real justice is an ordered justice. Equally justice is for the sake of order, since the only order in which human beings may really live together in peace is one that is just enough to command their allegiance.[50] Moreover, granted that all existing political orders are only relatively just and may in part be extremely unjust, they are to be preserved as long as they cannot be superceded by another order which is equally effective and more just. But if a government or social system is unworthy of support, as was the Fascist régime in Italy, loyalty to such a system and its laws is not a moral obligation, and if the attempt is made to coerce citizens, this too would have no moral justification for there is no ethical foundation for seeking to compel people to act in immoral ways.

Resort to illegal action must depend upon two factors. Although on the basis of moral principle one may decide that a law is unjust, there is still the decision to be taken as to whether or not to act upon one's moral judgment. That action could be justified if the moral objections to the injustice of the law outweigh the moral reasons in favour of obedience. Further such action, to be justified, would have to be taken after all possible legal means of obtaining the objectives had been exhausted. The temptation to act illegally will obviously be greater when there exists no means of changing unjust laws. In a democracy, illegal action is less likely, or, perhaps it should be said, less necessary than in a totalitarian state. There are devices in a democracy for calling attention to abuses and for the alteration of laws. While these processes may take time, one should not hastily seek to circumvent them. But it is not just the existence of means but their effectiveness that is important. At a certain point a person may reasonably consider that, while the means exist, it is obvious that no change is going to take place. If his efforts are continually frustrated, it is unrealistic to go on and on.[51]

All this does not mean that it is possible to frame a universally valid statement which would indicate exactly when a person may legitimately disobey the laws of a state. Nor is there any easy appeal to the example of Jesus. It is true that he was regarded as a law breaker – he certainly did not observe, for example, the sabbath regulations. It is also true that by casting out the money changers from the temple court he violated their civil rights. But Jesus provides no model to copy literally and everyone has to wrestle with the problem in the situation that confronts him or her. We simply have to recognize that there are occasions when the Christian may have to act illegally if God is to be obeyed rather than men. So Bonhoeffer, speaking not on the basis simply of theory but out of his agonizing decision to participate in the plot to assassinate Hitler – certainly an illegal action – was led to say:

> In the course of historical life there comes a point where the exact observance of the formal law of a state, of a commercial undertaking, of a family, or for that matter of a scientific discovery, suddenly finds itself in violent conflict with the ineluctable necessities of the lives of men; at this point responsible and pertinent action leaves behind it the domain of principle and convention, the domain of the normal and regular, and is confronted by the extraordinary situation of ultimate necessities, a situation which no law can control.[52]

5

REVOLUTION

It is not unusual for historians to employ a certain kind of short-hand when they give names to particular periods, indicating by this means some overall characteristic. So church historians often refer to the fourth century as the Age of Conciliar Creeds, while the eighteenth century is commonly styled the Enlightenment. There seems little reason to question the view of Hannah Arendt that the twentieth century can properly be designated the century of revolutions.[1]

Since revolution is indeed a widespread contemporary pheno-menon, Christians cannot simply ignore it. They may not like it; they may wish to repudiate it, but they cannot pursue their dis-cipleship in the world and pretend it does not exist. They have no real alternative but to seek to understand it and its relationship to the gospel and to define their own position *vis-à-vis* revolution in the light of this critical appraisal. Christians indeed have a respon-sibility to and for the world – a responsibility they share with all human beings – but this demands a theological understanding of revolution so that believers can orientate themselves. The con-temporary world raises the questions we cannot evade: why, or why not, revolution?

To face these questions is, in the first instance, a theological enterprise rather than an ethical one. The ethical question relates to the means whereby a revolution is initiated and carried through. Since there is empirical justification for saying that most revolu-tions have involved and therefore probably will involve bloodshed, the moral problem focusses upon the subject of violence. But it cannot be denied that a revolution could be achieved by peaceful means; insurrection and violence may accompany a revolutionary movement but they are not essential to it. To speak of a nonviolent revolution is therefore not to perpetrate a contradiction in terms. In other words, violence is not logically necessary to revolution, although it may be highly likely that it will accompany one. For clarity of exposition therefore I propose to deal in this chapter with revolution *per se*, leaving the subject of strategy or tactics – and so of power, force and violence – to be considered later. If the disjunction seems a little artificial, it is nevertheless, as I have just pointed out, logically defensible and will make the disentanglement of the various elements that much more easy.

The Concept of Revolution

Marx's concept of revolution, which is the one I propose to use, was that it should not refer simply to the political sphere; this would render it superficial. Instead he sought a social revolution, i.e. he wished to alter not just the political superstructure but the underlying economic causes of social inequality. In strict accord with this is Marcuse's definition that it is 'the overthrow of a legally established government and constitution by a social class or movement with the aim of altering the social as well as the political structure'.[2]

This means that certain types of so-called revolution will not be considered here. The palace revolution or *coup d'état*, which simply substitutes one group of power-hungry people for another, is not the kind of movement with which I am concerned. Indeed it is difficult to see why Christians should regard such an action with any sympathy at all. If, for example, one clique of right-wing army officers ousts another, partly out of ambition to be in power and partly out of a desire to make the existing system work more efficiently, the general condition of the people will be but little changed. This qualification of the group in the example as right-wing is not tendentious but accurate, because, as Debray has stressed, a government brought to power by this means always tends to the right. It does so because it is compelled to rely for its continuance upon the same support as its predecessor and therefore has to base itself upon the existing institutions.[3] *Plus ça change, plus c'est la même chose*. This type of political shuffling does not call for a theological appraisal here, precisely because it is no more than a change of personnel and is not revolution in the sense I have in mind. Rather, I accept, also from Debray, that true revolution 'is the installation for the first time of popular power, based upon the awakened majority of the nation'.[4] Thus conceived it has nothing to do with the putsch or coup. It differs too from evolution through the speed and purposiveness of its process. It implies an element of rupture with the current social order and the building of a new one.[5]

Not only are *coups d'état* outside the scope of this chapter, but so are protest movements. The latter serve to call attention to a particular injustice and those who engage in them believe that by adopting a certain course – demonstrations, sit-ins – a change will be forthcoming. From the perspective of revolution however a particular injustice is understood to be one aspect of a total pattern that has to be transformed, i.e. the aim is not corrective adjustments within a continuing system but the substitution of a new system for what is deemed corrupt.[6] Merely to seek to redress grievances or ease suffering – both admirable activities – without engaging fully in the revolutionary struggle is, from this point of view, to relieve symptoms and to ignore the deep-seated causes of the disease. First-aid is not the same as major surgery.

Of course there are those who would say that this chapter is attempting the impossible. There are those – Christians and non-Christians alike – who would agree with Malcolm X that Christianity is a 'slave religion' and would therefore suppose that it and revolution are absolute antitheses. No relationship between them exists and cannot therefore be explored. This is but to reproduce Rousseau's opinion that Christianity preaches servitude and dependence – an opinion I have already criticized in chapter 3. There is some truth in this: the churches in the past have often supported the *status quo*, but it is equally true that the Christian faith has inspired many liberation movements. The slave risings in the USA were prompted by a belief in God as the God of justice and in Jesus as the Liberator;[7] the Civil Rights Movement of Martin Luther King was similarly motivated and much of the demand for freedom in Africa has the same root. However let us not pre-empt the exploration but undertake it and see what the result is, beginning with a brief description of certain situations which would appear to demand a revolution in order to transform them.

Sinful Situations

In Cuba, before the Castro-led overthrow of the existing social and economic structures, 91 per cent of the workers were under-nourished; 96 per cent lived on only beans and rice and no more than 4 per cent could afford a real meal. As regards health: 36 per cent suffered from parasitic illnesses, 31 per cent from malaria, 14 per cent from tuberculosis and 13 per cent from typhoid, and yet only 8 per cent had official medical care; 44 per cent of the population never went to school and 89 per cent of those who did had no more than three years' teaching.[8] Was not Aristotle right when he said that 'the universal and chief cause of . . . revolutionary feeling is . . . the desire of equality, when men think that they are equal to others who have more than themselves'?[9]

Or take a slightly wider view of Latin America, contained in the 'Second Declaration of Havana', which is not to be questioned because of its source, since the estimates can be checked:

> In this continent of semi-colonies about four persons per minute die of hunger, curable illness or premature old age; five and a half thousand a day, two million a year . . . A holocaust of lives which in fifteen years has caused twice the number of deaths produced by the First World War, and it still continues.[10]

Or again, to refer once more to a particular country, Colombia has witnessed a population explosion from some nine million in 1939 to something over nineteen million thirty years later. Today 61 per cent of the ground belongs to 3·6 per cent of all landowners, and 4·6 per cent of the population receives 40·6 per cent of the national income. Of the fifteen thousand entering the labour market each year, only twelve thousand find jobs. The infant mortality rate is at 10 per cent; there are 2·5 doctors for every ten thousand people, and every year twenty-five thousand children die of malnutrition.[11]

These are cold, hard statistics, and blunted as our sensibilities are through the receipt of incessant information via the mass media about large numbers of casualties due to natural disasters – drought, floods and hurricanes – it is difficult to grasp the sheer sum of human suffering that they represent. We cannot rest content with gradualism to cope with this – what is the use of smooth, even evolution to these people? If the necessary transformation were to take only two days – and even with a revolution it would certainly take longer – eleven thousand more people would have died in Latin America. Nor is there any point in counselling patient sub-mission – what father, dragging out his existence in these conditions, can calmly witness his children starving around him and do no-thing, *when he knows it is not inevitable*? These italicized words draw attention to a great change that has taken and is taking place in the world today. At its simplest level, when someone becomes aware that while he or she is living in poverty there are those in the same country enjoying affluence, when a country as a whole recog-nizes its underdevelopment compared with and dependence upon much richer Western nations, it is natural that there should be a refusal to accept this deprived situation as unalterable.

Prior to the modern era, nature and society were regarded as parts of a divinely given order. All social structures had ascribed to them a sacred character and they were not to be changed. Today this aura of holiness has departed – and rightly so – and we regard all structures as open towards the future and to be shaped accord-ing to human will. This difference of attitude, wedded to a desire for justice and wellbeing for the deprived, produces a movement towards rapid change which may take the form of revolution. This is especially so when the possibility of altering society is hindered by a minority that possesses economic and political power. Suffer-ing is no longer regarded as inevitable; it is not a punishment from God but a man-devised affliction, and so hope is born, and a polarization develops between those who benefit from the *status quo* and those who desire to change it. Revolution seems a viable, and possibly the only, option.

Christians have been slow to come to terms with this possibility for they have tended to think of the world as given, as a kind of heaven-sent order within which they may work but which they cannot themselves create. But this invests the world of human rela-tions, mediated by institutions, with an element of immutability, for what is given is, by definition, largely outside human control. So Christians have been prone to support the *status quo* and have regarded revolution as an act of impiety, especially since in the past it has often involved an attack upon the church itself, mainly because it was a bulwark of privilege. This outlook is typified by a verse in the hymn 'All things bright and beautiful', which is as blasphemous in its understanding of God as it is rigid and unjust in its social determinism.

> The rich man in his castle,
> The poor man at his gate,
> God made them, high and lowly,
> And order'd their estate.[12]

This particular verse in *Hymns Ancient and Modern* was omitted when the hymn was reproduced in the *English Hymnal,* and there is little excuse for the persistence of such an idea within the church. There is little excuse because the model of a closed system is obviously absurd and un-Christian. A system can become closed by the action of either human beings or of God. If human beings are responsible, then they too can change it. To hold God responsible is to deny his otherness and to equate his will with historical determinism, which is another name for fate. Rather God in Christ subverts any and every system, otherwise they become idols, nor does he accomplish this *ab extra* but from within by identifying with the oppressed. So in recent years a number of studies, many prompted by the World Council of Churches, have stressed the necessity for the churches to come to terms with change and have revealed the fallacy of identifying man-made institutions with God-given realities. This is but to recover the insight of Oliver Cromwell who, it will be recalled from chapter 3, acknowledged that authorities are the ordinance of God but declared that 'this or that species is of human institution and limited'. He therefore had little hesitation in seeking to change them.

The redemption that Jesus preached, according to J. H. Cone, 'has nothing to do with stabilizing the *status quo*. It motivates man to be what he is – a free creature.'[13] Nor is this understanding confined to the New Testament. In the Old Testament, the Exodus is presented as a revolutionary uprising in which God is revealed as liberator. The divine action, in the series of events leading up to the sealing of the covenant on Mount Sinai, produces radical change within history and in this transformation human beings had their part to play. According to the New Testament, the mission of Jesus introduces a very specific kind of change. In the person of Jesus the rule of God is present with power (Matt. 12.28). His words and deeds bring unrest into the world (Matt. 13.33; Mark 2.22). They begin a new movement; they introduce a fresh beginning in a dynamic way. This change has two aspects: it has *already* taken place – 'the old order has gone and a new order has already begun' (II Cor. 5.17) – and it is *still* taking place. Thus history is experienced as change, of which Jesus is both the initiator and the final goal. So far then from resisting change – from opting out of the world as history – Christians are required to see in it the hand of God (Isa. 45. 1–7). They are not to be conformed to this world or age (Rom. 12. 2); they are not slavishly to endorse the *status quo* because their faith in God cannot but induce dissatisfaction with it.

This general attitude becomes specific when it is applied to particular circumstances. So, for example, Thomas Merton, speaking of racism in the USA, points out that his fellow believers have to face a choice: 'The choice is between "safety", based on negation of the new and the reaffirmation of the familiar, or the creative risk of love and grace in new and untried solutions, which justice nevertheless demands.'[14] It is quite understandable therefore that Neil Middleton should assert that 'revolution is a condition of mankind; in a very real and important sense it becomes a synonym for life – people change their societies as they are changed by them. We should be able to rephrase the word in the New Testament thus: "I am the way, the truth and the revolution" – and do so with no sense of incongruity. For revolution, not necessarily bloody, is life – it is the indication that life is still there.'[15] It is difficult to see how the most conservative of theologians could deny this or maintain that God is concerned simply to preserve existing situations. If one employs traditional categories and speaks of human beings as sinners living in a fallen world, then obviously sinfulness and fallenness are characteristics of the *status quo* which God must condemn and must will to have transformed.

But what is the sinfulness of present situations? How do we define that which is to be overcome? Or, to put the latter question in different words which mean exactly the same, what are those evil features in human circumstances that demand revolution in order to remove them? Briefly put, those evils include degradation, abject poverty, slavery and inequality, all of which induce suffering. In opposition to these Christians affirm dignity instead of degradation, a reasonable living standard instead of poverty, freedom from slavery and equality for inequality. In antithesis to colonialism they set justice; they fight dehumanization to forward the process of humanization. All these conditions, that characterize a situation in which nothing short of revolution is called for, are closely interconnected. So economic oppression leading to poverty, which may result in degradation, is a form of enslavement. Conversely, humanization and justice embrace equality, freedom and dignity. To further the argument, we need to analyse these conditions and their effects upon human life more precisely.

We may begin with poverty. To be in a state of constant want and acute misery is to become subservient to physical needs, to the dictates of the body above all else and so to live in the domain of necessity. As psycho-physical entities, the starving of the world can only be stunted in their humanity. This is more than a condition of deprivation: it is one of ignominy. Consequently Helder Camara says that 'poverty disfigures the human person'.[16] Poverty is not just a lack of material goods – one can indeed speak of the poverty of the affluent. In its pejorative sense, it refers to the impoverishment of the whole personality. It is therefore to be distinguished from poverty in its positive sense, as embraced, for example, by a St Francis. Poverty to him and to many Christians does not mean limited growth, lassitude, etc.; rather it involves liberation from subservience to material desires. It does recognize the material basis of life, and amongst other things the consequent need of nourishment, but it refuses to regard this as the be-all and end-all of existence. This is totally different from the condition of today's poor, whose material wellbeing is non-existent. Here is one impelling motive for revolution: give us food! Let our children eat so that we may not see them waste away before our eyes! Yet even when this has been said, it has to be added that 'the essence of revolution is not the struggle for bread; it is the struggle for human dignity'.[17]

In order to affirm the basic dignity of persons, one cannot acquiesce in a system which denies it; if one does, one is in fact abdicating one's own humanity. 'Being a man means that you do not permit others . . . to decide what you are or what your place in society should be . . . You must decide these things for yourself.'[18] So far as the underprivileged are concerned, it is not just a matter of improving their physical condition; they themselves have to be enabled to participate in the process of determining their own goals and shaping their own future. So T. W. Ogletree continues: 'Being a man – a mature man – involves the exercise of power, the act of assuming responsibility for your own life and the life of the world.'[19] It was the negation of this truth that led to the emergence of Black Power in the United States. The blacks came to realize that they did not want mere integration and a greater share of the economic cake; they wanted to play a creative role in determining their own future. Not just economic deprivation then, but powerlessness corrodes human dignity. In so far as its aim was to correct this, Black Power is to be understood as a humanizing force as the blacks sought to affirm their being.[20]

George Jackson has documented this rise to consciousness of an individual black in his letter from prison. Writing to his mother, he says:

> You must realize, understand fully, that we have little or no control over our own lives. You must then stop giving yourself pain by feeling that you failed somewhere. You have not failed. You have been failed, by history and by events, and people over whom you had no control. Only after you understand this can you then go on to make the necessary alterations that will bring some purpose and value to your life; you must get some control![21]

Jackson then charges the system and its supporters with responsibility for the blacks' condition of alienation and abandonment and declares: 'If a good god exists then they are the ones who must make an appeal to him for forgiveness: forgiveness for relinquishment and dereliction of duty. I don't need god, religion, belief, etc. I need control, control of determining factors.'[22] In short, Jackson and his fellows have awoken to the fact that they are the victims of colonialism, i.e. of a relationship in which the dominated are not free to be creators of their own history. Colonialism, in fact, may be a feature of national life and is not only applicable to one country's control by another. In this situation, the lives of the colonized are not organized according to their needs but according to that of the master group and the result of this is the creation of conditions of virtual slavery and of what Rubem Alves terms an 'oppressed consciousness'.[23]

An oppressed consciousness is one which is domesticated by the situation in which it is placed. It is a reflexive consciousness. Those who suffer from it accept the values of those who dominate them. As Berdyaev said: 'Master and slave are correlatives. Neither of them can exist without the other.'[24] The slave finds identity in a subservient relationship to the powers that be, so that any questioning of the existing authority is understood to be an attack upon oneself. This can be illustrated from the reaction of some blacks to the efforts of those struggling against segregation in the southern States of America. When four protestors sat-in at a Woolworth's lunch counter in Greensboro, North Carolina, a black assistant called them 'ignorant' and 'a disgrace to their race'.[25] The oppressed consciousness is then paralyzed because 'creative action is possible only in the context of hope and power'.[26] Nor can those who suffer in this way have their own future created for them by others. The masters cannot do it because the slaves then become the objects of the dominators' activity and are not the subjects of their own emerging freedom. Humanization is only possible when the people act freely to create their own future and thereby are liberated from the passivity in which they have been imprisoned.[27]

There is little point in an inhabitant of one of the Western democracies seething with moral indignation at the plight of those just described. Especially is this so if it be assumed that this refers just to blacks in the States or in South Africa or to the poor in Latin America and not to the West itself. We Westerners have to be sufficiently critical of the societies in which we live to perceive that there exists a flagrant disproportion between what is formal and what is real and that an apparent equality in the existing democracies masks economic class inequality. We pay lip service to formal liberty, but within it there are many who fear for the morrow and are hungry, homeless and in want, while others enjoy vast fortunes. 'The existing disproportion between formal liberty and real liberty,' commented Berdyaev, 'is due to the fact that in the economic world liberty is not determined formally but materially, by the means and methods of production.'[28] Further the growth of technology under conditions of *laissez-faire* is producing a new determinism. Technology was originally a tool; then it became a system – the technological society. So there has been a transition from a situation in which technology provided instruments for human beings to exercise their freedom to a structure which now lays down the rules they must obey. There is consequently a current tendency to retreat into a closed universe where technology functions as once nature did. Human subservience to nature and to its rhythms and the consequent need to conform excluded the radically new,[29] but the demands of technology and the future that it permits, being frequently no more than an extrapolation of the present, similarly rule out what is new. So a fresh form of unfreedom has developed which can only be overcome – not by destroying technology or ignoring it in some back-to-nature commune – by a revolution which transforms the social and economic spheres.

Christianity and Revolution

In the face of these conditions in the First, Second and Third Worlds, what are Christians to think and do? Simply to counsel patience is useless. Acceptance, passivity – these are empty words in the face of massive unfreedom. To advocate such behaviour would be the same as if Jesus had said to the leper who approached him: Just put up with it! Instead he restored to wholeness the one who was incapable of healing himself. Of course the parallel is not exact: in today's world, especially among those who suffer because of others, there is a growing awareness that people *can* do something to alter the situation. They do not ask Jesus to do it for them; they are liable to seize the opportunity to do it for themselves. But one cannot suppose that Jesus would condemn them and say: Accept your lot – as if it were divinely sanctioned and unalterable, instead of being humanly created.

It is not surprising that, when it is assumed that this is precisely what Jesus would say, many repudiate him. George Jackson, it will be recalled, declared: 'I don't need god . . . I need control.' He went on to say: 'I've been patient, but where I'm concerned patience has its limits. Take it too far, and it's cowardice.'[30] We are not to be resigned, as if fate determined all – believing in the dynamic God of the future, we have to work to establish what is in accordance with his will. Can anyone really doubt that Christians are called to condemn injustice and to work for change? Various theological considerations combine to lay this twofold duty upon all believers.

First, let us reject once and for all the heretical distortion of the Christian faith that it is concerned only with some other-worldly reality – a view already criticized in chapter 2. These words of René Coste put the position with admirable clarity. 'One can only become a citizen of heaven if one strives to the utmost to be a citizen of earth, because it is only in this way that the command to love one's neighbour can be put into effect during his earthly existence.'[31] To actualize neighbour love is to create a new world in which the neighbour will be freer tomorrow than he or she is today. Neighbour love is not some romantic I-Thou island; it must include social awareness and an obligation to create healthy cultural, economic, political and social structures for all.[32] In the West we have to implement the moral imperatives of the love commandment under the conditions of a technological age.[33]

Elsewhere, the God who identifies with the oppressed and condemns injustice demands an active discipleship directed towards the transformation of dehumanizing structures. Throughout the Bible there is a constant emphasis upon the divine concern for the outcasts, for the needy and the poor. Conversely service to these is interpreted as the service of God. To despise the neighbour is to offend God (Exod. 22.21ff.; Deut. 24.14f.; Prov. 14.21; 17.5), while to love God is to do justice to the poor and the oppressed (Jer. 22.13–16). Where there is justice and righteousness, there is knowledge of God (Isa. 1; Hos. 4.1f.). To know God is also to love him, and this is equivalent to seeking to establish just relationships among human beings. Where there is no justice, even worship is vain (Isa. 1.10–17; 58,1f.). But justice is inseparable from the abolition of slavery and the creation of the conditions for freedom. Slavery in any form contradicts God and denies his will, for 'to be enslaved is to be declared *nobody* and that form of existence contradicts God's creation of people to be his children'.[34]

There should be little doubt in any Christian's mind that the church has to fight slavery in the name of God; to acquiesce in it is to fail in witness. Indeed if we are to show forth God to the world, we must seek to deliver the oppressed from bondage, for it is in and by social deliverance that God's righteousness is revealed. This struggle for freedom is essential because of its interrelationship with justice. Where there is no justice, you cannot have freedom, while the absence of freedom is itself a result of injustice. But the concept of divine justice or righteousness is meaningless if it is not related to the daily experience of humankind. It is here and now that God's justice, i.e. his vindication of the poor and helpless, is to take effect. Christians as chosen agents of the divine will are also agents to bring this about. They have to 'join God in the fight for justice. Therefore, whoever fights for the poor, fights for God. Whoever risks his life for the helpless and unwanted, risks his life for God.'[35]

Consequently one must not separate the God of love from the God of righteousness, in Marcionite fashion. Love and righteousness (justice), as argued in the previous chapter, belong together, but precisely because of this we must realize that God will take sides. It is true that God loves both the just and the unjust, but his love for the oppressor is revealed in his concern for righteousness, which involves his identification with the oppressed, because only when the oppressed are liberated can the oppressor know true liberation. This means that, in terms of righteousness, God is partisan: he does take sides. With complete honesty Gustavo Gutiérrez points out that 'one cannot be *for* the poor and oppressed if one is not *against* all that gives rise to man's exploitation by man'.[36] But the divine love embraces both masters and slaves, and in relation to the former this love demands that they cease to be oppressors in order to be free. Here again love is to the fore – but 'love is an act of courage, not of fear; love is commitment to other men. No matter where the oppressed are found, the act of love is commitment to their cause – the cause of liberation.'[37]

Towards a Theology of Revolution

This reference to liberation serves to direct attention to what is variously called the theology of revolution or the theology of liberation. What we are concerned with here is the nature of the gospel itself, its relationship to freedom and salvation and the connexion of all these with the subject of revolution.

The good news is an eschatological proclamation, i.e. it declares that that which was expected to happen at the *eschaton* or end has here and now began to take effect through Jesus of Nazareth. In other words, the gospel denies what is, in the face of the future which is operative in the present. In this sense gospel and revolution are analogous, for the latter is 'a transforming movement from *what is* to *what ought to be*; it seeks to make an *is* out of an *ought*. A Christian is a maker of revolution, not just a talker about it.'[38] The Christ event is thus declared to be the introduction into history of a subversive power that negates the old to make room for the new. Indeed Christianity originated in a tension between the old and the new – exemplified by the division of its sacred book into Old and New Testament. So Paul can say that 'the old has passed away, behold, the new has come' (II Cor. 5. 17;cf. Gal. 6. 15; Col. 3. 9f.). The new wine bursts the old wineskins (Mark 2. 22). This proclamation of newness arouses hope and Christians look towards a new future which through the resurrection of Christ is already present and effective.[39]

All this means that Christianity is an eschatologically oriented faith; it seeks to change the world rather than explain it; it is concerned to transform existence; it asserts the possibility of revolutionary change. This understanding of the gospel does not rest upon a few isolated texts; the good news is itself revolutionary.

That the time has been fulfilled with the coming of Christ means
that there is no longer any future for a closed order in which all
human beings have a fixed place and destiny; rather all must be
made new. Hence while the message of Christ was not revolutionary
in the superficial sense of seeking to upset certain political institutions, it was revolutionary in the more radical sense of aiming to
reorientate men's and women's understanding of their nature and
to restructure their relationships. So Jesus attacked the Jewish law
in so far as it failed to function as an instrument of human fulfilment. This attack called in question the dominant values of his
society and challenged the pattern of social organization, while
revealing its authority to be bogus.[40] When this truth is accepted,
then it has to be worked out in life,[41] and such a working out
requires a transformation of the conditions of existence – a transformation that can properly be described as a revolution. Indeed
the gospel, as a summons to a new life, only obtains substance as it
is embodied in an attack upon those structures and values that
daily distort and crush human beings.

But the gospel is not only the negation of what is for the sake of
what can be, it is also a powerful instrument of what the Latin
Americans call conscientization. Conscientization means awareness
building; it is an opening of the eyes to the present situation; it is
an awakening of the critical consciousness which produces an
experience of social discontent,[42] as, through the gospel, the disparity between what is and what may be becomes apparent. The
gospel declares that the reality of the present is to be found in its
potentialities for the future, but in the very process of pointing to
this reality the gospel lays bare self deception, rejects fatalism –
even when it is blasphemously called the will of God – and requires
us to become agents of change. 'What really motivates Christians
after all to participate in the process of liberation of the oppressed
people,' comments G. G. Merino, 'is . . . the radical incompatibility
of the demands of the gospel with an unjust and alienated society.'[43]

As the poor and exploited learn, on the one hand, to perceive the
truth of their existing socio-political conditions, and on the other
hand, hear the gospel call to freedom, they are motivated to act
against dehumanization. This does not lead to fanaticism; instead
it makes it possible for those who accept the message to enter into
the historical process as responsible subjects. Moreover the Jesus
who is proclaimed is not an example of patience and submission
to fate. As Moltmann has emphasized, 'Jesus did not suffer

passively from the world in which he lived, but incited it against himself by his message and the life he lived . . . he provoked the hostility of the guardians of the law. By becoming a "friend of sinners and tax-collectors", he made their enemies his enemies.'[44] The gospel then is a message of liberation and freedom.

According to the Johannine Christ 'the truth will make you free' (John 8.32), while according to Paul 'for freedom has Christ set us free . . . you were called to freedom' (Gal. 5.1, 13), and he sets before the Romans the vision of 'the glorious liberty of the children of God' (8.21). That liberation is the purpose of the mission of Jesus is apparent from the Lucan account of his reading from the book of Isaiah in the synagogue at Nazareth and his announcement of the fulfilment of that prophecy.

> The Spirit of the Lord is upon me,
> because he has anointed me to preach good news to the poor.
> He has sent me to proclaim release to the captives
> and recovering of sight to the blind,
> to set at liberty those who are oppressed,
> to proclaim the acceptable year of the Lord (Luke 4.18f.).

While it has to be acknowledged that it is difficult to say exactly what freedom is before it has been fully experienced, Paul in particular has provided some guide lines for a preliminary understanding. According to him Christ's act of deliverance brings freedom from sin, from principalities and powers and from death (e.g. Rom. 6.18; I Cor. 15.24ff.; II Cor. 1.9f.). If these interconnected themes are analysed with the specific intention of discovering their meaning for the present day, then the statement above that the gospel is a message of liberation will be further clarified.

To be set free from sin is not to be understood solely in terms of individual, personal and private sin. Deliverance, from this aspect, if it is to be other than partial, must also involve liberation from the social sins that dehumanize people.[45] It must include too liberation from the consequences of sin, such as 'racial discrimination . . . money concentrated in a few hands, lands possessed by a small number'.[46] In other words, freedom, if it is to be anything other than private self-adulation, has to be embodied in corporate life. Freedom, says F. Herzog, 'must become concrete in the structures which hold us captive. Otherwise it is not freedom at all.'[47] So the freedom that Christ makes possible is to be interpreted not just as subjective inner freedom, for true freedom is never a private affair; it can only be with and for others. Hence repression, which is the outworking of sin, when it assumes political and economic forms, has to be overcome for freedom to be established. From this perspective, the gospel message of deliverance from sin implies revolution as its cutting edge to transform those institutions which incarnate and perpetuate sin itself.

Equally the proclamation of the dethroning of the powers is to be related to revolution. In the Pauline letters there are numerous references to the exposure and defeat of the principalities and powers which hold human beings in servitude. There is no need to provide here a detailed exegesis and application of these passages because this has already been admirably done by Albert van den Heuvel in *These Rebellious Powers*. Suffice it to say that he has convincingly established that these powers are to be understood as constituting the framework of our lives, as the structures within which we exist. Necessary as they are for social interaction, they readily assume an absolute authority, becoming the equivalent of idols, and function as domination not service structures. Supra-personal, and sometimes subhuman, these powers assume political, social and economic forms. According to Paul it is precisely their demonic character that has been exposed by Christ and the process of deliverance from their crushing authority has been set in train. 'Paul's conception of the powers,' says van den Heuvel, 'comes to us not only as an account of our new freedom from the powers, but also as a command to go with Jesus to bring the powers under his feet.'[48] They have to be unmasked publicly; they have to be stripped of semi-divinity and they have to be humbled by Christ's victory. Freedom from these powers therefore demands revolution, when revolution is understood to be a transformation of the existing structures so that human beings are no longer in bondage to them but serve mankind.

When these powers remain in control, we have what may be termed a necrophiliac society. In one sense this description can be taken quite literally: when over 50 per cent of the global community exists below the starvation level, one can accurately speak of the reign of death. But wherever oppression and injustice hold sway, human beings are denied that fullness of life which it is their Creator's will they should enjoy – instead their life is a living death. It is to this condition that the gospel of the resurrection may speak and indeed does speak in different and complementary ways. To the exponents of Black Theology, Easter enables them to find meaning in their suffering. They understand that experience in terms of Good Friday – the suffering of alienation and the risk of annihilation. But the blacks, engulfed in a necrophiliac society, descend into this death in hope because of the promise of resurrection. Latin American theologians see the very possibility of doing theology in their situation as requiring the experience of Easter, i.e.. theologians, who mainly belong to the educated and privileged middle class, have to die as members of an élite to be resurrected on the side of the oppressed. To them such phraseology about Easter is not commemorative rhetoric; it is praxis. It is historical involvement because it is only through historical action that Easter becomes the death that makes life possible. But the link with revolution is not lost. 'Resurrection is verified when rebellion against the demonic thrives.'[49] Thus to engage in revolution is to challenge the reign of death in a society, going forward in hope which is founded upon the resurrection of Christ. Conversely it may be said that to assail the life denying forces within a society is to focus upon the theme of resurrection. Hence Herbert McCabe affirms:

> The resurrection of Christ means that death is not just a matter of destruction, the end of life, but can be a revolution; the beginning of a new and unpredictable life. All revolution means radical change in the structures within which we have our existence, all revolution produces a new kind of man; resurrection is the revolution through death, the radical change of those structures within which we exist at all . . . The new world only comes through the death of this world. Thus every revolution which deals with structures less ultimate than this is an image of, and a preparation for, the resurrection of the dead. The Cuban or Vietnamese revolution is a type of the resurrection in the sense that we speak of Old Testament events as types of Christ.[50]

This reference to Old Testament typology also serves to call attention to another aspect of the resurrection of Christ that has a direct bearing on our subject. One of the ways in which Luke understood the work of Christ was as a new Exodus (9.31). Jesus' death, resurrection and ascension are seen as an act of deliverance that rivals and surpasses that from Egypt under Moses. The meaning of the Easter happening is thus formulated in terms of a secular and political uprising. Indeed in the Exodus revelation became revolution and the 'tyranny of the given was dethroned, for the children of Israel recognized that what can be is worth the risk of what is'.[51] The divine action, mediated through Moses, produced a radical change in all the existing structures of Hebrew society. To the writer of the book of Exodus this deliverance from bondage had been accomplished by God's 'outstretched arm' (6.6). It is no coincidence that this same imagery appears in the *Magnificat* which announces the revolutionary programme to be initiated by Jesus.

> He has shown strength with his arm,
> he has scattered the proud in the imagination of their hearts,
> he has put down the mighty from their thrones,
> and exalted those of low degree;
> he has filled the hungry with good things,
> and the rich he has sent empty away (Luke 1.52ff.).

These verses continue the Old Testament teaching that temporal realities exist to serve the divine purposes for humankind and that they can and must be changed in accordance with that purpose. So God is the one who tears down to build up (Jer. 1.10); he breaks the power of the oppressor to establish justice (I Sam. 2.10; Pss. 9. 72; 146). To Thomas Münzer these words in the *Magnificat* were to be taken with the utmost seriousness; to believe that they are impossible of fulfilment is to doubt God, while to recognize that God judges here and now is to take an active part in the overthrow of the forces of domination.[52]

But what do these militant verses mean in contemporary terms? Victor Hayward has recently applied them to the Chinese revolution, showing a point by point correspondence, which cannot be said to be contrary to their original spirit. Thus the scattering of the proud is to be seen in the overthrow of Chiang Kai-shek and his corrupt entourage. The putting down of the mighty has been fulfilled by the loss of their privileged position by the capitalists allied to foreign imperialism. Those of low degree, previously exploited and oppressed, have been freed. Despite the population explosion, there is still food for the hungry, even if it is not yet plentiful, and the rich have lost their status and personal wealth. 'Has there ever been,' asks Hayward, 'in all human history, anything comparable to the Chinese experience for giving literal historical embodiment to those declarations of radical revolution?'[53] All this is not to say that the People's Republic of China has now become the Kingdom of God! Various caveats against absolutizing revolution will be entered later in this chapter. At this junction however we must distinguish between liberation and freedom, between freedom-from and freedom-for.

Liberation

Liberation is the necessary condition of freedom, but the two are not identical nor need the one lead to the other – one may be delivered from one tyranny only to fall under the domination of another, equally if not more oppressive. To a certain extent this is what has happened with the Russian Revolution: liberation from the absolute rule of the Tsar did not result in freedom but in the new absolutism of a Joseph Stalin. Many so-called liberties too are negative, e.g. freedom from want, freedom from fear, etc., and they do not provide the actual content of freedom. In a sense freedom-for is the other side of the coin to freedom-from. So, for example, to Christians freedom from the power of death means freedom for a new life in the service of òthers. Freedom-for therefore comprises openness and dialogue as well as equality of opportunity and the reign of justice. From one aspect, freedom is the power to take the material conditions of life and give them form according to one's intention. But this involves, as Hannah Arendt rightly stresses, participation in public affairs or admission to the public realm.[54] We may recall George Jackson's demand for 'control'.

Freedom is also the power to transform the world and to create continually a new future. It requires the development of a new consciousness, the acceptance of a new model of human nature, of which Christ is the exemplar. The oppressed consciousness, to which reference has previously been made, must be replaced by what Paul calls 'the mind of Christ' (I Cor. 2.16). This mind is an independent one, in the sense that it is neither superior nor inferior in its attitudes towards or in its relationships with others. Hence the vital importance for liberation to be accompanied by conscientization through the gospel, if the end of revolution is to be the foundation of freedom. 'A free man,' says Berdyaev, 'does not desire to lord it over anyone.'[55] Yet precisely here is the rub – 'there is no native who does not dream at least once a day of setting himself up in the settler's place' – François Fanon.[56] Similarly Hannah Arendt draws attention to the fact that most of the poor do not think in terms of 'to each according to his needs' but of 'to each according to his desires', and that while freedom is only possible when needs are fulfilled, there will be no freedom for those who

are bent on living solely for their desires.[57] To identify freedom
with the assumption of the role of the oppressor is a betrayal of
freedom. So for example in the Congo, in 1960, independence for
many blacks was symbolized by meting out indignities to white
Belgian women, but the perpetrators of these crimes had not fully
understood either the content or the exercise of freedom; they were
acting as mirror images of those they had replaced. Instead of
openness and service, there was continued exploitation and
domination; instead of love there was hatred.

Love itself is to be regarded as the name for the dialectic of
liberation in history. 'Love,' says Rubem Alves, 'is what God does
in order to make men free.'[58] In other words, the historical
practice of liberation is a practical version of the liberating love of
Christ – *diakonia* is the praxis of liberation. But love must also be
the content of freedom and must be embodied in new structures
once liberation has been achieved. Because the encounter between
people is the essential means of coming to personhood, all social
structures have to be subservient to dialogical communication.
Liberation-from requires the overthrow of those institutions which
prevent the free approach of person to person; freedom-for
requires the creation of institutions which facilitate meeting. 'The
Christian reaches out beyond this world towards a future world of
freedom, towards real communication between men and therefore
full human life.'[59] Moreover, since it is within the social structures
of human existence that we receive the life-sustaining gifts of the
Creator, the meeting place with God is precisely within our socio-
political settings. Therefore hope for the poor and oppressed
consists in providing them with a passport to the meeting place
with God, which is what freedom is all about.[60]

However, when all this has been said – and much more could be
said – it has to be admitted that no clear blueprint of freedom
exists, or can exist, for freedom is not a static state but a process.
We derive from Christ the responsibility to seek freedom; he does
not predetermine its shape. As we create our own future, we shall
discover new dimensions of freedom. Indeed it is only as Christians
'participate in a liberating and creative history that they are able to
understand and give an account of the Word of God by coming to
understand their humanity'.[61] Freedom is not to be circumscribed
or frozen within some facile definition.

Salvation

Just as one has to distinguish between freedom-from and freedom-for, so one must differentiate between salvation-from and salvation-for. Indeed in the final analysis liberation/freedom and salvation are synonyms. So the freeing of Israel from the bondage of Egypt was regarded as God's act of salvation (Ex. 14.30), while in the New Testament, as Kümmel has shown, the general concept is that of deliverance, which is usually translated as salvation.[62] We are saved/liberated from our sins, etc. But salvation also has the connotation of wholeness and this helps to fill out a little the content of freedom-for. Since human wholeness is interpersonal and social, it is defective within structures of bondage, and so salvation embraces not only the individual but society too. As evil works in personal life and in exploitative social structures which humiliate humankind, so God's justice manifests itself both in the justification of the sinner and in social and political justice. Consequently struggles for economic justice and for political freedom are elements in the total liberation of the world by God. Hence the statement from the Bangkok Assembly, which I have previously quoted, that

> within the comprehensive notion of salvation, we see the saving work in four social dimensions:
> (a) Salvation works in the struggle for economic justice against the exploitation of people by people.
> (b) Salvation works in the struggle for human dignity against political oppression of human beings by their fellow men.
> (c) Salvation works in the struggle for solidarity against the alienation of person from person.
> (d) Salvation works in the struggle for hope against despair in personal life.[63]

To accept and endorse this formulation is to acknowledge that Christians must repudiate any spiritualization or individualization of salvation, as well as any resigned acceptance of the *status quo*. On the contrary, the historical liberation of humankind has to be understood as an essential component of salvation. Human emancipation is then an indispensable element of the divine saving action. It follows from this that if the construction of a more just society is fully inserted in the history of salvation, then the church has a role to play in establishing a new order. Indeed 'participation in the revolutionary movement of liberation is the social visibility of the life of faith'.[64] So the church cannot be conceived simply as a community of believers who have had a spiritual experience. Rather it is called to be the company of those who reveal the quality of Christ in his struggle against human bondage. The church's election is to be the company of human liberation – in a revolutionary situation it cannot stand on the side lines.

Revolutionary Situations

So far in this chapter I have been contending that the gospel is a summons to revolutionary participation in order to act in accordance with God's will to establish freedom and justice. But this should not be taken as a clarion call to Christians to rush hither and thither in a hot-headed attempt to start revolutions all over the place! I have already suggested that there are caveats to be entered against the absolutizing of revolution and the full import of what has been said previously can only be grasped when it is read in the light of certain necessary reservations. Christians are required to be as innocent as doves but they are also to be as wise as serpents in the sense that when they act they do so with a clear-sighted appreciation of exactly what the situation is with which they are confronted and what is involved in coping with it.

The first and most obvious matter to notice is that not all situations are revolutionary situations, i.e. situations in which revolution is either desirable or possible. This means that we must recognize that there are countries where it is really the established forces that require support. Currently there are a number of African states, newly emerging from colonialism, that are endeavouring to create viable national communities out of tribes scattered over vast territories. In Tanzania, for example, it would be absurd to attempt to hinder the efforts of President Julius Nyerere to build a humane society. The term 'revolution' has to have a different meaning in such a context from what is usual in some Latin American countries.[65] Further, to identify a revolutionary situation, it is necessary to have a typology in order to distinguish between different contexts. There are three main categories to be noted:

1. *Colonialist imperialism* This refers to a situation where a foreign power is in possession of a colony. Examples of revolutions against this kind of domination include that of the Chinese against the

Japanese, of the North Vietnamese and the Algerians against the French and of the Cypriots against the British.

2. *Imperialist colonialism* This refers to a situation where a foreign power, without being in physical control of an area, still exercises political, socio-economic and psychological domination. Examples of revolutions opposing this include Cuba against the USA and the Hungarian and Czechoslovakian attempts to achieve independence of the USSR.

3. *Internal colonialism* This refers to the situation in a particular country where one privileged group oppresses others. Such oppression may take the form of economic and social domination; it can also have the character of racism, with white exploiting black. Also under this heading is to be included male domination of women – women's liberation is therefore one example of a revolutionary movement seeking to transform the situation.[66]

Even in countries, such as those in Latin America mentioned earlier, which fall into the third category and where suffering is rife, such misery does not of itself provide the possibility of revolution. For revolution to take place, there must be widespread acceptance of a goal, constituting an image of freedom which enables the misery to be recognized.[67] This recognition may be achieved in one or more of several ways. I have already spoken of the conscientization role of the gospel and this is something Christians should undertake; in so doing they will foster the growth of revolutionary consciousness. So Helder Camara declares:

> It is imperative, in the name of the gospel, to make the underdeveloped masses aware of their human dignity, of their rights, because it is impossible to elevate them to a human level until they are conscious of living at a sub-human level, until they are aware of their right to a better life, one which is worthy of man. This is our christian duty, quite apart from all local and contingent circumstances ... We must open the eyes of the deprived masses to their misery, and tell them: No, the life you live is not just, something must be done.[68]

One effect of this awareness building will be a change of values – from passivity to action, from meek acceptance of injustice to a vigorous demand for social righteousness. Out of this there develops an alteration in the value structure that unites people within a society. The authority which has been legitimized by the previous values then becomes illegitimate in the eyes of the people and its overthrow and transformation is perceived as a distinct possibility.[69] As long as people's conceptions of themselves are faithfully mirrored in the principles upon which a society is organized, revolutionary feelings do not exist, but when Christians present an image of wholeness and proclaim the Kingdom of God, they disclose a sharp contrast between what may be and what is. They then foster dissatisfaction with the present and act to subvert it and encourage revolutionary aspirations. What is the gospel but a form of conscientization?

A further factor promoting revolutionary consciousness is the phenomenon of relative deprivation. While some Marxists have emphasized increasing poverty as a basic source of worker revolt, de Tocqueville noted that on the eve of the French Revolution the peasants had achieved a far higher standard of living than ever before.[70] An improving social and financial situation induces expectations of more accelerated amelioration. What is then significant is not the absolute level of poverty but what people have come to feel is their proper due as compared with their existing relative deprivation. In other words poverty does not of itself engender revolution. It is when it is combined with some progress that a new amalgam is created. The hope of social change can, for example, be fostered by even a minimal educational programme – then a fresh social phenomenon is to be seen in the form of the rebellious poor who have nothing to lose but see much around them to gain. The more power a ruling élite devolves, the greater the degree of freedom it allows, the higher the expectations of the oppressed, and if these are frustrated then revolution appears that much more feasible. The lesson that Christians must draw from this is that the sheer existence of misery is insufficient to justify a call to immediate revolution.

Here we are touching upon the discussion between theoreticians of revolution as to how far they are the result of certain social conditions which suddenly explode in a general crisis and how far they do not happen but are made. So Trotsky took the view that 'the active minority of the proletariat, however well organized it may be, cannot seize power independently of the general situation in the country'.[71] While R. Blackburn has pointed out that if one looks at the first fifty years of this century, we find that there have been revolutionary situations, e.g. post-war Europe, which have come to nothing, and there have been revolutions, e.g. in China, created by long years of struggle.[72] Perhaps this either/or approach is a mistake. Revolutions can be made – Castro made one in Cuba

– but in the absence of propitious social circumstances they will not succeed – Che Guevara in Bolivia. Debray was right when he said that it is an irresponsible and criminal act to lead a mass of peasants into a social and political struggle which will certainly lead to their repression.[73] In sum: while Christians have a part to play in creating the conditions for revolution, resort to direct action must be determined in the light of a careful examination of the existing situation.

We must next note that Christians cannot support any and every so-called revolution. There can be no doubt that Hitler carried through an immense transformation of German political, social and economic structures. There was then in the 1930s a highly successful Nazi revolution, but one that by its very nature was dehumanizing and far from warranting Christian enthusiasm required vigorous opposition. Moreover, revolution should not be regarded as a normal remedy, as a beneficial panacea, but as a last desperate operation[74] and it carries with it certain serious risks.

The Risks of Revolution

The most serious danger is the possibility that as a revolution progresses it may come under the control of extremists, of men so radical in their outlook that the purpose of the initial rebellion to overthrow oppression is itself subverted. There is a tendency for the moderates to exercise authority first, only to lose it in due course. According to C. Brinton, they lose it for four reasons. First, in seeking to re-establish order, they have to use the machinery of government and so tend to be regarded as the heirs of the old régime. Second, because the revolution is made in the name of freedom, it is difficult to suppress extremists without incurring the charge of betraying the revolution. Third, placed between conservatives on the one hand and extremists on the other, lacking the support of the former and unable to regard the latter as opponents, they become isolated. Fourth, being realists and therefore not possessing the singlemindedness of fanatical idealists, they are vulnerable to attack from all sides.[75]

Once the extremists achieve power, they forget the freedom and toleration for which they appealed and become highly authoritarian. They then rationalize their position by claiming that freedom *will be* established by them, but first its 'enemies' must be rooted out. This analysis is based upon the French and Russian Revolutions which do present a salutary lesson. But if one examines the Mexican Revolution then one finds, according to C. Leider and K. M. Schmidt, that moderate forces remained sufficiently powerful throughout all the stages to prevent the extremists from fully implementing their programmes or ideologies.[76] In other words, while there is an undeniable risk of a movement from moderation to fanaticism, thus compromising the very freedom in whose name the revolution was undertaken, it is not inevitable. Such a conclusion coincides with a Christian view of history. To say that extremism is bound to take the lead is a negation of faith and the endorsement of an historical determinism. The gospel declares the openness of the future; it summons human beings to create their future, not along predetermined lines, fixed by God or by an inescapable process of history, but in freedom. In short, the pattern of certain past revolutions is not ineluctable but is a warning against repeating the same mistake. The Christian in revolution is not that caricature of a liberal who does not know where he stands, but one who, being a realist, is capable of saying: This far and no further.

A further and possibly even more serious risk is that of regarding revolution as an end in itself, as something perfect. In reality no revolution will bring an end to history, whether it be envisaged as taking place in the near future or some thousand years hence.[77] Nor, it should be noted, did Marx fall into this error. According to his scheme the revolution will usher in only the dictatorship of the proletariat; eventually, according to his vision, the state will wither away and the classless society will emerge. Only then will the end be reached – but this end seems very like a secularized version of the Christian expectation of the future Kingdom of God, whereas as humankind moves forward it should not expect complete fulfilment. It is not disillusionment but accurate observation that leads Moltmann to say that 'hopes which we connect with the future always shoot over the mark and are not able to redeem themselves in history'.[78] Revolution as an end in itself is simply a new version of nineteenth-century *laissez-faire*. If it be true that human beings exist in sin, the new revolutionary authorities will be subject to the same temptations as those they have replaced. Indeed Berdyaev, speaking out of his experience in Russia, enunciates nothing but the truth when he says that 'a revolution may be necessary, it may be just, but it cannot be sacrosanct. It is always sinful, just as the order of society against which it was directed was sinful.' He continues:

The truth and right of revolution lies in the fact that it always destroys the excessively false and corrupt past which was poisoning life. Revolution always brings realities to light, it reveals the unreality of that which gave itself out as reality. It puts an end to many fictions, but it creates new fictions. It destroys by force the right that had ceased to be right and had turned into brute force. Revolution is a paradox of might and right. The old right is turned into violence upon consciousness because it has its might. Revolution becomes might and seeks to create new right.[79]

To exalt revolution as the great and perfect way of adjusting society to necessary change is to conceal the fact that some evils are apparently inherent in human government. No revolution ever sweeps away the evil past as completely as is intended and no revolution ever carries out entirely the programme with which its supporters began. It may do more; it may do less; it will certainly do many things that its promoters do not promise and do not want.[80]

These sombre and sobering thoughts will find a sympathetic hearing among Christians. They acknowledge that to declare judgment upon injustice will have its political effects in the day of reckoning when the injustice is overthrown. They are aware that, while concerned to build a new society, their relationship to it is bound to be ambiguous because even a new society will stand under the judgment of God. But this very awareness may tempt them to adopt one or other of two false options: either they become quietists and declare that in view of the risks it is better to do nothing and simply await the final Day of Judgment, or they ignore the risks and equate the revolution with the Kingdom of God. Those who chose the former are entirely futuristic in their eschatology; those who are in favour of the latter tend to accept a fully realized eschatology or one fully realizable before the final end. The whole of this present study is an attack upon the first position. To scorn what might be achieved is to hold that our hopes are beyond reach, whereas those very hopes should lead us to new efforts and experiences which themselves will result in a revision of our aspirations. Further, to accept the future of God as disclosed in the present and thereby to become discontented with the existing structures is to opt for radical change. God's eschatological presence is here and now – not in some remote future. Futuristic eschatology of this kind is simply an excuse for leaving the world as it is – usually advanced by those who benefit from the world as it is – and that is not the Christian's vocation.

Equally wrong-headed is the identification of revolution and Kingdom. This is where Camilo Torres revealed the limitation of his historical perspective and the naiveté of his theological apprai- sal. Torres gave up celebrating mass because he believed it to be meaningless, if not hypocritical, in the Colombian situation. How- ever he declared that 'when my neighbour no longer has anything against me, and when the revolution has been completed, then I will offer mass again'. There is, certainly unconsciously, a quasi- millenarian undertone to such an affirmation. To the millenarian the new age of perfection is soon to be established; to Torres the revolution will bring in 'a system which is grounded in love of neighbour'.[81] He failed to realize the need for Christians to engage constantly in social criticism in terms of the eschatological proviso, i.e. in the knowledge that every social situation – even one created by a revolution – has a provisional character. Those prone to this absolutizing tendency need to read these words of John C. Bennett:

> There is no basis in the New Testament for identifying the Kingdom with a new social order and there is no basis in our experience for doing so either. But the Kingdom is relevant to all social orders and Christians serve the Kingdom whenever they seek 'justice, truth, humanity, and freedom' in any social order.[82]

Yet the expectation of the Kingdom is sentimental and abstract unless it is accompanied by the belief that there are present signs of its activity in the rejection of injustice and in renewal. Without this perspective eschatology loses its ethical significance. Moreover a theology that takes hope seriously becomes vague and insufficient if it does not involve fighting for that hope.

This absolutizing tendency has been present throughout history. It was there in the fourth century when Eusebius of Caesarea, in a flush of enthusiasm, declared the empire of Constantine to be the messianic Kingdom, with Constantine as the new David and the Church of the Holy Sepulchre as the New Jerusalem;[83] it was there in the sixteenth century when John of Leyden proclaimed afresh the setting up of the heavenly city. It was present in the thought of Hitler with his thousand-year reich. It is present today when generous minded people yearn to hear good spoken of the Cuban and Chinese Revolutions and look with expectancy at the current Portuguese Revolution, hoping that the absolute has indeed found a home in history. This is part of the mythology of revolu- tion which the Christian must demythologize. For the Christian there can be no glorifying of a revolution, even though he be committed to it. He must not expect a replica within history of what his eschatology tells him must await the final consummation. While he should not claim to be more revolutionary than the revolutionary, his role must be to hold to the original revolutionary programme, once events are in train. He must oppose the revolution becoming an end in itself, in the name of that freedom which alone makes a revolution a justifiable choice. Recognizing that revolutionary groups tend to ideological rigidity, he must remain critical of all ideologies. Believing that freedom is not a static condition but has to be struggled for constantly, he will reject the view of automatic improvement of the human condition. Indeed he will be sensitive to the fact that revolution has tended to replace the inevitability of progress as a dogma; but it is the same dogma, with speedy, critical action replacing gradualism. In either case the confidence in betterment is central. But while a revolution may bring greater freedom and greater justice, these can neither be developed nor preserved without constant vigilance. It is therefore not just the victory of the forces of revolution that is important, but the implementation of a social and economic policy that allows for liberty and humanization.

This means that revolution must have an orientation towards organization. 'Revolution,' Jacques Ellul rightly observes, 'inevitably channels itself into institutions and constitutions.'[84] The overthrow of existing structures has to be followed by construction. There have to be 'managers' through whom the revolution fulfils its meaning. Unless this takes place, there will be no real revolution, only a revolt. Here again the implicit concept of *laissez-faire* – which denies both freedom and responsibility – has to be exposed and opposed by Christians. The assumption that all that is needed is an uprising is a false one; it has to be followed by a building-up process.[85] It is true that one cannot make an omelette without breaking eggs, but one can break eggs and not make an omelette. In other words, revolution has to be goal-directed and must not be – I repeat – an end in itself. It always belongs to the realm of the penultimate, although in and through it the ultimate may be seen at work.

The hope of Christian faith mobilizes on the one hand the Christian to make visible on earth signs of the Kingdom of God, through active protest against misery, against the sloth and lack of imagination of

reactionary stubbornness, and places him on the side of the revolutionary, unites him with the latter's revolt against the existing order,
and makes it possible from time to time for a whole series of steps to
be taken in common.[86]

Yet while a revolution may represent a step forward in the
search for human freedom, that freedom is not itself an easy style
of life. In a sense freedom is a burden; it too is risky; it produces
anxiety and conflict. Consequently the Christian can never oppose
revolution on the grounds that its outcome is never completely
certain, because if people are to be free in a post-revolutionary
situation, that very freedom will bring its own dangers. Revolution
cannot be the final answer; it cannot release us from the responsibility of freedom.

Nevertheless, if the above arguments are accepted, this means
that some revolutions may be interpreted as signs of the Kingdom
and that a revolution may be a true attempt to express historically
something of the eschatological renewal of all things. In Christ the
future is already present, and his followers are to work towards the
consummation by transforming the world. Within some revolutions may be detected signs of the divine activity, but not to mis-
understand such a statement it is necessary to pay heed to T. W.
Ogletree's carefully phrased caveat.

> To speak of God's action in history does not mean to absolutize or to
> embrace uncritically developments which are identified as peculiarly
> significant bearers of his presence. Nor does it mean that such
> developments are guaranteed certain or immediate success . . . The
> primary significance of identifying particular historical phenomena as
> crucial expressions of God's activity is to underscore their creative
> potential for moving process toward forms of organization more
> adequate to the vital energy operative in human personal and social
> existence.[87]

Possible Criticisms*

Having now sketched some of the main features of a theology of

* I am drawing on the criticisms formulated by three writers, viz.
J. Ellul, G. Giradi and R. Padilla.[88] Of these three Ellul is the least
convincing as he unfortunately adopts a method which he is prone to
employ too often, i.e. he presents an absurd caricature which he has
no difficulty in demolishing. It seems to me that scholarly discussion
demands full justice being rendered to that with which one may finally
disagree.

revolution, it remains to consider some possible criticisms that may be brought against it – criticisms that have been taken into account in the preceding formulation but which merit direct attention on their own. Such an undertaking is to a certain extent anticipatory, for while I have drawn on existing studies I have not confined myself merely to reproducing points that others have previously made and I have added new material of my own. Hence the preceding is a fresh formulation of one more theology of revolution or liberation which has still to undergo critical appraisal by others. However attacks upon existing essays are indicative of the kind of reservations that are likely to be brought forward and to these I now turn.

It would be possible to present these points systematically by contrasting a revolutionary attitude with that which is held to be the traditional Christian outlook. But this latter is based upon a highly selective use of tradition and ignores numerous chapters in church history, for as Jacques Ellul has correctly noted, it is a matter of record that in every revolt and revolution between the fourth and eighteenth centuries the church did take a part and a number of the clergy have always supported rebellions of the poor.[89] But it is only right and proper that the supposed opposition between revolution and Christianity should be presented as cogently as possible.

1. While the revolutionary says 'no' to the actual state of the world and strives to transform it, the religious person regards the world as the divine handiwork to be inhabited and not changed.

For Christians to adopt this standpoint is to accept fate under the name of God, whereas God created human beings to be free. This implies that he does not seek to predetermine our actions by imposing fixed and unalterable conditions nor to manipulate by overriding liberty of choice. On the contrary, the Bible affirms that we are called to be co-creators with God, in relation not only to nature but also to society. We would have strayed far from the apostles' example if today we adopted submissiveness as our watchword. Were not Paul and Silas described as those 'who have turned the world upside down' (Acts 17.6)? What this means in terms of social and financial upheaval can be illustrated from the episode at Ephesus. The silversmiths realized that the gospel of Paul was undermining their whole trade in the silver shrines of Artemis and they sought to have him silenced (Acts 19.23–41). Christians today can remain silent and inactive, but they cannot at the same time claim to be walking in the footsteps of the apostles.

2. The revolutionary stresses human initiative, seeing human beings as the creators of history, whereas the religious person leaves all to God as the transcendent author of history, believing that the temporal order has no value in itself but is simply a period of progress towards eternal destiny.

In effect the charge is that a theology of revolution denies the gospel of grace and puts human beings in the place of God. In contradiction to this, it has to be asserted that trust in God is never to be made an excuse for evading the responsibility of Christian participation in the struggles of this age.[90] It is true that the *Magnificat*, as we have previously seen, ascribes the reversal of privilege, wealth and power to a divine act, but, according to the Bible, God acts in human history through human agents – agents who may be outside the immediate covenant relationship, such as the Assyrians or Cyrus, or within it, like the Messiah. As for Christians, who believe they are living under the new covenant, they must acknowledge that God does not call a people simply to have a people, but that through them, if they are obedient, he may actualize his will in history. Jim Cone is right when he declares that 'Christianity has to do with fighting with God against the evils of human life. One does not sit and wait on God to do all the fighting, but joins him in the fight against slavery.'[91]

If this is not so, then what is a Christian to do in a situation that has become intolerable? It cannot be denied that there has been a tendency to affirm that God will help us to bear it, i.e. the intolerable may be made tolerable through divine grace. This is no doubt true, but why should God expend his power in every situation to support people to endure patiently unjust conditions? What sort of a God is this who leaves a situation unchanged and forbids us to attempt to alter it, while at the same time enabling us to endure it? This whole concept is a mockery of God and turns his fearful presence in judgment and liberation through human agents into an unreality.

Of course, the acceptance of suffering as in some sense the will of God may make it bearable, and this may be the only possibility in certain situations of massive oppression. But what one is accepting as the divine will is the enduring of suffering, in unity with God who is compassionate (i.e. a co-sufferer); one does not thereby endorse the view that the suffering is itself imposed from on high, or that the enslaved experience is the consequence of human neglect and wrongdoing. To suppose that God wills murder and bondage is to turn him into a devil and not the Father of Jesus Christ.* On the contrary, God identifies with the poor and the outcasts and Christians must do so too, but this is not the assumption of a passive role. If we identify, and those in bondage decide to revolt, then that identification, if it is to be wholehearted, has to include revolutionary activity.

3. Evil, says the revolutionary, is to be fought and overcome; evil, according to the religious person, is a punishment for sin and to be endured.

Evil, it may be readily admitted, is often a consequence of sin; but evil, especially in the form of social evil, was consistently condemned by the Old Testament prophets, and few would doubt that the church's role includes the declaration of God's judgment on all that robs human beings of their wholeness. But if such a pronouncement is lacking in precision and if it is not supported by involvement in the affairs of those who suffer, it will be so much hot air. The verbal witness, which may satisfy the conscience of some, will be meaningless unless accompanied by action. Such action requires political involvement and may also, in certain circumstances comprise revolution. God after all is not some vindictive tyrant, brandishing suffering as a punishment, but is himself the liberator calling us to give ourselves to the process of liberation.

4. The revolutionary idealizes human beings, sanctifies the revolution and has a misplaced hope, whereas the religious person knows that we are sinners, refuses to identify revolution and Kingdom and hopes in Christ alone.

Any revolutionary who holds the views here imputed can only do so if he absolutizes revolution – this is a temptation but not an inevitable stance. Consequently the suggested contradiction is apparent rather than real. I have previously argued that Christian faith, while impelling believers towards revolution, should safeguard them against millenarian expectations. One can accept that we are sinners, that the revolution is not the Kingdom and that our hope is in Christ and still be a revolutionary. Revolution,

---

* Did not God then will the crucifixion? Christians believe that he did, but they also hold that this was not the divine will for someone other than himself; he himself was involved in the suffering of his Son.

after all, is neither a vocation nor a predetermined end but a means.*

Perhaps even more serious is the charge that theologians of revolution are no more than conformists. Since revolution is in the air, certain Christian thinkers have become fascinated with, not to say hypnotized by, the subject, and are seeking to exonerate their religion in the eyes of revolutionary movements of its continual conformity to the *status quo*.† If such be the case, then one kind of conformism is simply replacing another. There is the danger of either a conservative conformity or of a revolutionary conformity, but neither is what is required of the Christian and to elaborate a theology of revolution is by no means *ipso facto* to be guilty of the second. Of course, if one absolutizes revolution, then conformism has taken place, but I have sought to show the falsity of regarding revolution as an end in itself nor is it ever free from the eschatological proviso.

Those who write on this subject are, after all, intelligent enough to know what they are doing. They appreciate that atheism has emerged as an obligatory doctrine of many revolutionary movements precisely because religion has so often rejected the possibility of revolution. They see that the Christian faith may commend itself to some revolutionaries if revolution is interpreted in a more favourable light. They are therefore very concerned with the subject of relevance – i.e. with the relevance of theology to revolution – and Jim Cone makes no secret of it: unless theology takes seriously the hope of the suffering for historical liberation, 'it will remain irrelevant for the oppressed who view the gospel as the good news of freedom'.[93] But this does not mean that Christianity *must* endorse revolution in order to commend itself. Christianity can only support it if there are sound theological and ethical grounds for so doing. Christians who speak favourably of revolution on the grounds of relevance alone are simply adopting an ideology which

* Other counter arguments are that a theology of revolution denies that violence is evil and so contributes to its increase, that it minimizes the role of reason in political evolution and that it questions the absoluteness of the values laid down in God's law. These criticisms will be examined in the next chapter.

† So Jacques Ellul.[92] While he rightly takes to task certain named writers for their exaggerations, his critique is, as I have already suggested, superficial and is regrettably lacking in understanding and charity. Are those he castigates such fools as he suggests? They are never given the benefit of the doubt.

projects and protects their own interests. Conversely, those who stand aloof from the subject, possibly from fear of the risks and possibly from an unimaginative conservatism, become advocates of despair over against atheists who profess a great hope for humanity. But Christian faith itself is based upon a new hope for this earthly world, yet it differs from Marxism in being more realistic, i.e. it recognizes what may be altered and seeks to change it, while acknowledging the persistence of greed, selfishness and death.

Any person in any society, short of emigrating, has only three possible options: indifference, acceptance, rejection. Which one the Christian chooses will depend upon the responsible exercise of freedom in specific circumstances. Indifference has characterized some believers in the past. They have taken the view that 'the world to come' is their real concern and the present life is merely a testing ground. But the argument in chapter 2 in favour of political involvement, together with the discussion of revolution in this chapter, may be taken to show that God cares for the poor and underprivileged and that therefore indifference should not characterize those who seek to obey his will. To actualize at-one-ment is to be involved in the cause of brotherhood on earth. This is what should motivate Christians in their social and political commitment.

Acceptance may be right and proper in certain situations – I have previously instanced Tanzania – but, in general, Christians, who are not to be conformed or moulded to the pattern of this age (Rom. 12.2), should never be uncritical supporters of the *status quo*. As strangers and pilgrims, they cannot give steadfast adherence to the tyranny of what is.

Rejection – again to be adopted only according to circumstance – can lead either to a movement for reform or to revolution. If the argument of this chapter is sound, then the latter, at certain times and in certain places, is a viable and proper choice.

6

VIOLENCE

Even if it be granted, on the basis of the previous chapter, that Christians may, on occasion, be required to engage in revolutionary activities, in so far as these may lead to greater freedom and justice, there remains the question of the extent to which they should be directly involved in the process of liberation if that process is a violent one. Two matters indeed require to be investigated: the first is the Christian understanding of power and the second is the Christian attitude to force and violence. When attention has been paid to these, it will then be possible to consider the concept of a just revolution and to conclude with some observations relating to reconciliation and peace.

Power

To participate in a revolution is undeniably to be involved in a struggle for power. The attempt to seize it therefore raises the question of the nature of power and of the morality of its exercise. It is of course possible to contend that there is no need to pursue these issues further because the logical corollary of accepting the arguments for political involvement, presented in chapter 2, is the acceptance also of responsibility for the use of power by Christians. Since there are no politics without power, since every human community has to have a centre of power in order to exist,[1] to be engaged politically is to act within the area of power. Moreover it is to be noted that from the reign of Constantine up to and including the present day, Christians have occupied positions of considerable power in government, industry, etc., and have seen nothing wrong in so doing. It appears that it is only when power is related to revolution that tender consciences manifest themselves. But while this is no doubt a valid debating point, the issues still remain and require further examination.

How then are we to understand power? Power is the ability to do something, to effect or achieve some result. The terms used in various languages indicate the extent to which the capacity to act is basic to this concept. In Greek the noun *dynamis* (power) derives from the verb *dynamai* (to be able), just as in Latin *potestas* comes from *possum*, from which the English word ultimately proceeds. In French likewise *pouvoir* is both verb and noun. All human beings therefore simply because they exist and have a capacity to act have power in a certain sense and to a certain degree.[2] Conversely, without this ability to effect some change or achieve some end, any individual ceases to be human. If the ability is impaired or drastically restricted, then to that extent the person concerned is dehumanized. It was an appreciation of this that led George Jackson, as reported in the previous chapter, to assert that he must have some control over his life in order that it may be invested with value and purpose. After all, human beings are only free to the extent that they can act as whole persons and have the possibility to transcend the given.

From this positive aspect, Christians have to recognize that power comes from the Creator God and indeed testifies to him in the world, as we acknowledge when we call him 'Almighty', i.e. all powerful. To speak of the divine omnipotence is to refer to that unconditional power whereby God is God. Human beings share in that power in so far as they have been granted dominion over the world (Gen. 1.26ff.). The exercise of power is then an essential part of what it means to be human and since it derives from God power in itself cannot be regarded as evil.

In one sense power is neutral because it is a necessary condition for doing either good or evil, but precisely because of this its exercise is never a matter of unimportance. While morally indifferent in theory, power is never morally neutral in the concrete situation, for power becomes human by reason of its agents, i.e. human beings, and therefore because it is integral to the human act it can never be outside moral concern.[3] It follows from this that power *per se* is necessary for Christians simply as human beings. Their problem relates to its exercise, for there is no doubt that it presents a temptation and may lead to corruption.

With unclouded vision, Jesus observed the way in which power functioned in the world of his day. 'You know that those who are supposed to rule over the Gentiles lord it over them, and their great men exercise authority over them' (Mark 10.42). This saying is not in itself a direct criticism; it is simply a statement of fact. Jesus then adds: 'But it shall not be so among you; but whoever would be great among you must be your servant.' In other words, in the Kingdom of God service is to be the true life style. This does not mean either that political power is not necessary here and now or that it cannot be wielded in a Christian manner, for, as I have previously argued, while a revolution is not to be absolutized and identified with the Kingdom, it may be a sign of the activity of the Kingdom and, to the extent that it is, the exercise of power as service is relevant to it. Indeed in this saying we have a complete reversal of values. Whereas in the ancient world every kind of service was regarded as inferior and even degrading, the affirmation that serving others is true greatness, that all authority is to be understood and exercised in the form of service, has a direct bearing upon the morality of power at the present day. In other words power is to be used for others. So the Dutch Bishops in their Lenten Pastoral for 1974, referring to this passage from Mark, declared that 'the cure of the almost inevitable corruption of power lies according to Jesus in this that it does not become an aim in itself, but is humanized in the *service* of many'.[4] To similar effect T. W. Ogletree has observed that 'if the human meaning of power is to be realized, it must finally be directed towards the emergence of an interdependent human community that has regard for the legitimate interests and aspirations of all men. It must, like the power of God, be used not to dominate or exploit others, but to empower them to participate in the direction of human life.'[5]

Power admittedly can corrupt, but to eschew power is to become ineffective for good. Christians then have to accept the fact of power and have to understand it positively, and this means relating it to love, justice and freedom. First: power and love. From one aspect love is the urge towards the reunion of the separated. Consequently when power supports such at-one-ment, it is performing the work of love. Indeed precisely because Almighty God is the source of power and is also love, power as power, when exercised under God, is one with love.[6] From the Christian point of view the indubitable reality of power points beyond itself to its source whose purpose should shape its exercise. So Solzhenitsyn remarks that 'power is a poison well known for thousands of years . . . But to the human being that has faith in some force that holds dominion over us, and who is therefore conscious of his own limitations, power is not necessarily fatal.'[7] Love, after all, is the motive for equalizing power and power is also to be used with a sense of responsibility for others. Human beings therefore have an obligation to seek power that will guarantee personal development, and they should seize power if they see it being misused. So love takes shape as an activity that aims to destroy the objective and subjective conditions of slavery, i.e. it seeks to be one with power in the service of others. Power then is not a concession that has to be made reluctantly to the contingencies of historical life, it can be a proper expression of love. Hence the National Committee of Negro Churchmen in the United States was absolutely right in declaring that 'we regard as sheer hypocrisy or as a blind and dangerous illusion the view that opposes love to power. Love should be a controlling element in power, but what love opposes is precisely the misuse and abuse of power, not power itself.'[8]

Already, in speaking of love as the motive for equalizing power, the relationship between power and justice has been indicated. Justice indeed should be the structure of power without which power is destructive, just as justice is the very essence of love, without which it would be mere sentimentality.[9] Justice requires the power to render to each person his or her due; justice imposes an obligation not to infringe the rights of others, but without power one cannot exercise any rights at all – they are only safeguarded or guaranteed by the sharing of power. Justice with love are indeed the moral determinants of power,[10] the purpose of which is to be defined in terms of the promotion and preservation of freedom. 'Power *exists*,' says Rahner, 'and it rightly exists, because it is the condition of the possibility of freedom. Power and freedom are mutually and dialectically interdependent.'[11]

It is of course true that power finds it difficult to make room for freedom and it tends to self-absolutization. In this sense it is weak. But this weakness of power is unmasked by God in and through Jesus. God 'chose what is weak in the world to shame the strong' (I Cor. 1.27), but declares that 'his power is made perfect in weakness' (II Cor. 12.9), i.e. power is greatest when it makes weakness powerful. Yet as this process advances, as the weaker members of society become stronger, there then emerge temptations of the same kind that were previously conspicuous in the strong at whose hands they had once suffered. Hence although the unmasking of the weakness of power can be at the same time its liberation, so that Christians may live by the power of the messianic presence in the midst of the world of human affairs, this is no safe option. It is no safe option because there is an ambiguity about power, which I have not previously stressed having been concerned to focus initially upon its positive aspect. This ambiguity rests upon the fact that power too has a compulsory side. When power takes the form of force it stems from sin, for if all human beings were one with each other in freedom, this type of power would never be exercised. Yet to acknowledge that power may be unreliable does not excuse Christians from accepting it as a task from God.* Nor must it be forgotten that this coercive aspect is only one element and power should not be simply reduced to it alone, otherwise it loses the form of justice and the substance of love. However this ambiguity reveals itself in violence and to this we turn in the next section.

Defining Violence

The first matter that has to be clarified, in seeking a definition of violence, is the extent to which the term is to be regarded as solely

---

* This statement reveals very clearly the contextuality of my own theological thinking. I speak from within a Western democracy where, as a Christian, I have – albeit within certain limits imposed by the system itself – as much chance as anyone else of attaining and wielding power. The situation of Christians in Eastern Europe is very different. In socialist countries, where atheism is the official policy, Christians have little opportunity to exercise power. There then emerges, in that context, a tendency to regard the Christian way as one of powerlessness, and some support is found in the thinking of Bonhoeffer, especially in his letters from prison when he was himself in a state of extreme powerlessness. If however circumstances altered, if, as a consequence of prolonged Christian-Marxist dialogue, believers were accepted as partners and involved in government, we should probably hear much less talk about powerlessness. I am not wishing to be cynical; I merely wish to stress that if one accepts contextuality, then one must also acknowledge that it is no longer possible to produce statements of an absolute character. It would be as wrong to glory in the West in the wielding of power as it would be to glory in the East in powerlessness. Neither power nor powerlessness *per se* are *the* Christian way. The question is how to use power, if it is available, or powerlessness, if there is no other choice, to serve God through the service of others. Just as it is false to absolutize revolution, so it is false to absolutize specific theological positions which are no more than a necessary practical response by Christians to their context.

descriptive or as both descriptive and normative. If it is the latter, then it functions as the description of something and at the same time has a moral overtone. What this means can be illustrated by reference to the words killing and murder. Killing is descriptive; it describes an act whereby someone's life is taken. Murder is also descriptive, in that it refers to the taking of life, but it also has a moral overtone because built into its definition is the judgment that it is unlawful killing with malice aforethought. In other words, murder, by definition, is unjustifiable. One may discuss in what circumstances killing may be a right course of action, but it would be out of the question to debate the possible rightness of murder. Similarly if violence is taken to mean doing injury or harm intentionally and without authorization against the will of the victim, there is already built into the definition a moral judgment implying that violence is *per se* wrong. The discussion would not then turn on the nature of violence but whether some aspect of a situation in which it was committed was sufficient to permit it as the lesser of two evils.

It may be that this is the nub of the moral problem, but it would be helpful at this juncture to examine further the relationship of force and violence, which as I have just suggested, has some parallels with that between killing and murder. Externally force and violence look very much alike and indeed the Latin *violentia* was derived from *vis* meaning power or force. Violence and force are often referred to physically identical actions: the arresting officer may be said to employ force and the resisting suspect violence. Nor is there much difference between the force exercised by a doctor to move a dislocated shoulder back into place and the violence of the ruffian who originally put it out of joint.

Force, in and of itself, is sometimes regarded as morally neutral, if it is understood to be 'the ability to work some change in the world by the expenditure of physical effort'.[12] Violence would then be the illegitimate or unauthorized use of force to effect decisions against the will or desire of others. The difference between them is not then to be discerned by observation but by means of a moral judgment. This will be more evident if we take a quite acceptable definition of violence and see if it can also be used of force. According to B. Gert, violence is an unwanted and intentional violation of five moral rules: do not kill, do not cause pain, do not disable, do not deprive of freedom or opportunity, do not deprive of pleasure. But precisely the same definition could be applied to force. Let us suppose that a policeman observes an IRA bomber about to throw an explosive device through the window of a public house. In order to prevent the outrage, he will have to exercise force, and in so doing he may well break every one of these five moral rules. He may have to disable him and cause pain, if not actually – though even this is possible – kill him, and he may intend to kill him if he sees no other way of restraining him. He will certainly take him into custody if he overpowers him and will thereby deprive him of freedom and of a certain amount of pleasure. The IRA man might regard the policeman as a perpetrator of violence, but most people in England would agree that he was employing justifiable force. The position is then that both may break the five moral rules, but this is insufficient to say that the one commits violence while the other uses force. One has to have other moral grounds for determining whether the force of the bomber was unjustified and therefore violence and whether the force of the policeman was justified and therefore was morally acceptable.

It would appear then that the distinction between force and violence is to be found in the possible legitimacy of the one and unfailing illegitimacy of the other. So Glenning Gray has contended that force is properly used 'only in the context of legitimate power and right and as a means to the achievement of communal ends. It may never be executed beyond the extent necessary to secure those ends, or else it becomes violence.'[13] Thus I may use force to disarm someone attacking my wife, but if, having rendered him helpless, I then shoot him there is violence and it is unjustifiable. Hence, in accordance with this line of thought, a legitimate government may properly use force to restrain a riot – the rioters themselves being guilty of violence. Conversely, citizens would be using force and not violence if they sought to overthrow an illegitimate government. Force is then to be applied to any action which is based upon the authority of just laws or possibly upon moral convictions and upon the desire for justice. In which case, if it could be shown that a revolution was opposing an illegitimate government or was prompted by well founded moral principles to seek to put right an evil situation, it could be said that the revolutionaries were using force and one would not speak of violence. The moral problem then is: in what situations is it right to use force to overthrow the existing structures of a society?

There is no doubt that much of the heat could be taken out of the contemporary debate about Christians and revolution if it were to be conducted in terms of force – a descriptive word – rather than of violence – a word which is both descriptive and normative and also emotive in that it produces immediate reactions without careful thought. There is much to be said for this, since the two nouns – force and violence – tend to predetermine what is still to be investigated and so foreclose the examination. The question would then be not force versus violence but how to differentiate the moral use of force from its immoral use. There is a further advantage too and that is that it would remove the whole subject out of the sphere of rhetoric – for the concept of violence can serve as a device for proscribing those political uses of force that one considers inimical to one's central interests. So the resistance of a slave can be condemned as violence, while the restraints imposed by the master are condoned as force. It all depends upon one's perspective. If one is an oppressor, then anything that tends to usher in the new or moves towards change is violence; if one is oppressed, then violence is that which denies one a future. In fact the former can be regarded on moral grounds as legitimate force and the latter as illegitimate. However it would be naïve to expect too much from this semantic clarification – people will still go on talking about violence, so let us analyse it further.

While in the past there has been a tendency to think of violence primarily as something physical, direct and personal, today the concept is being given a wider connotation. Even at the purely bodily level, we have to distinguish between biological and physical violence. The former, of which an example would be enforced starvation, reduces the physical capacity of the person suffering. The latter, of which flogging would be an instance, is a direct infliction of injury. Further, we have to acknowledge, side by side with physical violence, the possibility of psychological violence. A person subjected to brainwashing, to continual propaganda or to enforced indoctrination, would be a victim of this psychological aggression. Thus a black in South Africa could suffer physical violence, by being beaten up, but he is also faced with mental violence since apartheid so structures his life that his human dignity is constantly insulted and undermined. In addition to this, there is now widespread agreement – although some demur – that there exists what is called structural violence.

What then is structural violence? The Cardiff Consultation of the WCC declared that structural violence is present when 're-sources and powers are unevenly distributed, concentrated in the hands of a few who do not use them to achieve the possible self-realization of all members, but use parts of them for self-satisfaction for the élite or for purposes of dominance, oppression, and control of other societies or of the underprivileged in that same society.'[14] In other words, structural violence shows itself when resources and powers are unequally shared and are the property of a restricted number who use them not for the good of all but for their own profit and for the domination of the less favoured.

When a system, says Thomas Merton, without resort to overt force, *compels* people to live in conditions of abjection, helplessness, wretchedness that keeps them on the level of beasts rather than of men, it is plainly violent. To make men live on the subhuman level against their will, to constrain them in such a way that they have no hope of escaping their condition, is an unjust exercise of force. Those who in some way or other concur in the oppression – and perhaps profit by it – are exercising violence even though they may be preaching pacifism. And their supposedly peaceful laws, which maintain this spurious kind of order, are in fact instruments of violence and oppression.[15]

When violence is institutionalized in this way then law and order are put at its service. Structural or institutionalized violence therefore characterizes a system which results in exploitation and lack of freedom and deprives the oppressed of their livelihood or of a worthwhile human life. If people are starving, when this is objectively avoidable, then violence is committed and if that starvation is an effect of the existing social and financial system, then we have structural violence or alternatively violent structures. The adjective is as applicable in this case as it is to certain weapons of war. One speaks of an atom bomb as a violent weapon, meaning thereby that it possesses a quality that produces very marked effects in the way of injury. Structures can produce similar dire effects and can be properly called violent in that they possess a quality that produces very marked results in the way of injury. 'Violence,' said Ezekiel, speaking of the social conditions of his day, 'has grown up into a rod of wickedness' (7.11).

Five examples, briefly described, will serve to give poignancy to this concept. First, in the *Sunday Times* of 25 November 1973, there was a headline that read: 'A Famine that Left the Rich Richer and the Poor Dead'. This was an account of what happened in the drought-stricken Wollo province of Ethiopia. While thousands died of hunger and disease, wealthy landlords and village chiefs, able to withstand the effects of the drought, took the opportunity to buy land and cattle from peasants only too eager to sell their property for a pittance to obtain food. So in a country, which at that date was reminiscent of medieval England, with its landed barons and serfs, the rich increased their wealth and the lot of the destitute became even more desperate.

Second, in some countries recently decolonized there is to be observed a native élite co-operating with external forces and fostering serious exploitation at home. These alliances favour those political régimes, economic relations and development plans that accord with their own interests. They can result, sometimes in conjunction with a military élite, in a form of 'modernization' that is paternalistic, fosters dependence and puts a halt to the process of humanization. The decolonized then experience the violence of internal colonialism.

Third, one can instance a country in an earthquake zone where some of the inhabitants live in tremor-proof houses and others do not. When a disaster strikes, the latter die or are injured. While the natural calamity is unavoidable, if the differential in housing is avoidable and is simply a product of the existing system, then we have an example of structural violence.

Fourth, to quote J. Galtung, when one husband beats his wife there is a clear case of personal violence, but when one million husbands keep one million wives in ignorance there is structural violence. Correspondingly, in a society where life expectancy is twice as high in the upper as in the lower classes, violence is exercised even if there are no concrete factors one can point to directly attacking others, as when one person kills another.[16]

If any reader still doubts the existence of structural violence, let him or her consider what happens to those who oppose an existing system. How many of the freedom riders in the USA were badly hurt and even killed by those who included many staunch supporters of law and order? What was the fate of black African Nationalists in Rhodesia shortly after UDI?

The widespread adoption of this concept probably means that it is here to stay, but it has not been without its critics. James F. Childress, in an excellent preparatory paper for the Cardiff Consultation, opposed the idea on the grounds that it is simply a labelling as violent of everything that is viewed as evil or unjust and so violence becomes no more than a tag for condemnation or a way of attributing violence to a system so that counterviolence is seen as justified.[17] Yet it is difficult not to acknowledge that to starve some-one to death is nothing if not violence, but when this starvation is the result of an inequitable distribution of resources and when this injustice is embodied in and supported by existing structures, how can one avoid speaking of structural violence? Of course such violence is indirect and is frequently unintended and as such it is to be differentiated from direct and intentional violence. Childress incorporates 'intention' as a necessary element into his definition of violence and this definition then precludes structural violence since structures cannot be said to have intentions. But it is simply not true that intention is peculiar to violence; it is possible, for example, to intend harm and yet exercise justifiable force. Take an armed security guard at an airport. A terrorist opens fire with a machine gun; the guard shoots the terrorist. It is mere hair-splitting to say that the guard intended to stop the killer but did not intend to injure him. He quite clearly did intend to harm him and knew that this was the only way to stop further murders. Few people would say that such an action in defence of others was not right – it was therefore justifiable force. If this be correct, then it cannot be said that intended harm is peculiar to violence.

However, in the last analysis, all depends upon one's initial definition. If one produces a definition of violence that has built into it certain elements that cannot be applied to structures, then, by definition, structures cannot be violent, but then one must ask if the definition is adequate to cover all forms of violence. Gal-tung's definition, for example, is somewhat different from that of Childress. He says that it is present when human beings are influ-enced so that their actual physical and mental realizations are below their potential realizations,[18] i.e. when there is a discrepancy between what could have been and what is. Hence if resources are monopolized by a group so that the actual for all citizens falls below the potential, then, according to him, 'violence is present in that system . . . The violence is built into the structures and shows up as unequal powers and consequently as unequal life chances.'[19] So 'the general formula behind structural violence is inequality, above all in the distribution of power'.[20] Consequently one must accept the possibility of unintended and indirect violence. An example of this is the suffering endured by factory workers in England in the early years of the Industrial Revolution. There are few grounds for thinking that the owners deliberately intended to grind down their employees, but who can question that they did suffer harm?[21]

It can also be contended that to speak of structural violence is simply to employ a metaphor. This would appear to be the principal grounds for Paul Ramsey's attack on the concept. He dismisses it as a misleading category mistake or wrong use of terms that can confuse sound thinking.[22]* To appreciate this criticism one must understand how a metaphor works. A metaphor occurs when we take a word out of its original sphere and apply it to new circumstances.[23] Thus the verb 'to pursue' originally denoted 'to follow with hostility'. When the phrase 'to pursue a policy' was coined, it was initially metaphorical, but in time metaphors become part of ordinary language and then they are given an additional meaning that was not part of the previously established usage. So 'to pursue' now means both 'to follow with hostility' and 'to proceed in accordance with'. The bearing of this upon the concept of structural violence is as follows. If it be maintained that violence initially referred to direct, personal action and that to apply it to structures is to transfer it to new circumstances, then the question is: is it not an apt and natural metaphor? I have argued above that it is an appropriate usage, and, if the usage is accepted, the meaning of violence has to be and legitimately may be extended to apply to systems and institutions, especially as we have also to acknowledge that they can cause more suffering than personal violence. Galtung observes that 'the manifest structural violence in the Americas (and not only there) already causes an annual toll of nuclear magnitude'.[24]

Nevertheless Paul Ramsey would prefer to say of a system that it is gravely unjust, since 'injustice is a far worse thing than violence, and a far better justifying reason for an answering violence – if a justification of revolution was wanted'.[25] I doubt the force of this contention, because structural violence cannot so easily be dismissed as mere metaphor.[26] There are phrases, originally metaphorical, without which it is impossible to designate certain phenomena. So we speak of wireless waves – this is metaphorical, since in no literal sense are there 'waves' involved. But it is not a mere metaphor; there is no other way of referring to the phenomenon. Nor is the substitution of grave injustice for structural

---

* Ramsey also contends that the idea of systemic violence leads to an oversimplified justification of revolutionary violence. This is an abuse instead of a proper use of the concept.

violence adequate. Of course the latter is gravely unjust, but to use only this designation is not to lay bare the latent and covert violence that is present in a system, the effects of which can be both physical violence – starvation – and psychological – the creation of an oppressed consciousness.

To say of something that it is unjust is not to describe the nature of the injustice. Structural violence is both descriptive, in a way that grave injustice is not, and it is also normative, in the sense that it implies that it is unjust. There are forms of serious injustice other than structural violence. So, for example, there was an ecclesiastical canon that forbade the ordination of bastards. This is gravely unjust, denying to someone the possibility of serving God as a priest, not on the grounds of personal inadequacy but simply because, through no fault of his own, he was conceived out of wedlock. This injustice does not involve either physical force nor necessarily psychological, since the person concerned might calmly admit the right of the church to command his obedience. Disappointment there will be, but not violence; there is injustice, grave injustice, but violence is not involved.

The acceptance of the reality of structural violence is of value as a tool for analysing particular situations and it challenges those who see only those forms of violence that are consciously chosen, physical and disapproved by the guardians of established 'order'. It enables us to perceive that 'violence is very much reality in our world, both the overt use of force to oppress and the invisible violence (*violencia blanca*) perpetrated on people who by the millions have been or still are the victims of repression and unjust social systems'.[27]

Nevertheless one should not be so eager to discover structural violence that the necessary coercive role of the state is readily identified with it. We have seen, when discussing resistance to the state, that the state has to impose restraints upon evil doers in order to fulfil one of its functions. Any state to be viable has to have certain powers of compulsion and has to exercise a certain degree of force.

I have already stressed, in the opening section of this chapter, the ambiguity of power: it is now time to recognize the ambiguity of force. From one aspect, force, which is a form of power, is absolutely essential for human freedom. To regard it as reprehensible on principle and therefore to seek to renounce physical force of all kinds would be in itself immoral because it would involve renouncing liberty which is exercised in the material realm.[28] But force – let me repeat – is ambiguous: from its positive aspect it is good because it is necessary for freedom; from its negative aspect it may interfere in the sphere of others to act upon and change them without their consent. Wherever there is force in this second sense, there may be injustice, with a corresponding distintegration of love and power. But this disintegration is never complete, otherwise life could not survive. 'We live from the element of justice, which counterbalances the injustice implied in the use of force.'[29] No state, no social system, no humanly devised structures will ever be completely just, and so the contrast that concerns us in discussing the violence of revolution is not between force and unjustifiable force but between justifiable and unjustifiable force.

It was an appreciation of the ambiguity of force that led Luther to speak of compulsion as the strange work of love. He regarded the proper work of love as comprising self-surrender and mercy, while its strange work is killing and condemnation.

> What he meant, comments Paul Tillich, could be expressed in the statement that it is the strange work of love to destroy what is against love. This, however, presupposes the unity of love and power . . . In order to destroy what is against love, love must be united with power, and not only with power, but also with compulsory power . . . When does compulsion conflict with love? It conflicts with love when it prevents the aim of love, namely the reunion of the separated. Love, through compulsory power, must destroy what is against love.[30]

Force, then, from this aspect is instrumental;[31] it is a means to achieve certain ends and it may be justified if it is seeking to remove what is against love. But force which seeks its own interests and aims to dominate becomes unjustifiable and so spills over into violence. Hence the direct and justifiable use of force may be instrumental to social change, whereas structural violence is instrumental in preserving the *status quo*.

What then, finally, is there to be said by way of summing up this consideration of violence? We have seen that the concept has to be extended to include not only that which is direct but also that which is indirect. Further, that it must comprise not only the physical but also the psychological, and again that it relates both to the personal and to the structural. We have also seen that it is by no means easy to distinguish it from force and that it would probably be correct to speak of it as one end of a continuum that begins with

force. This means that the difference between force and violence is
in part a matter of degree, i.e. violence is an excessive use of force
greater than that required to reach acceptable objectives. Finally,
violence as excessive force cannot be justified, while the possibility
remains that force itself may be held to be morally right in certain
situations.

The Basis of Christian Moral Choice

In the preceding section I have used rather freely words such as
'justifiable', 'morally right' and so on. However I have not so far
indicated how one determines when an action is justified or unjustified. Consequently before considering the possible rightness of
using force for revolutionary ends, I have to say something about
the basis of Christian moral choice. How does the Christian set about
deciding what is right and what is wrong?

There was a time when the answer to this question was thought
to be relatively easy. All you had to do was to discover what Jesus
had said and then you acted in obedience to his command, confident that in so doing your behaviour was right. Nowadays we
realize that this was a simplification. Quite apart from the difficulty
of being quite certain exactly what Jesus did say, we now appreciate both the intricate problems involved in interpreting the words
attributed to him and the greatness of the gulf that separates the
first century from the twentieth.

The main burden of the message of Jesus – and there is little
reason to dispute this – was the preaching of the Kingdom of God,
coupled with a call to repentance and with the offer of forgiveness.
All else that he said, and this includes his ethical teaching, was
subordinate to this proclamation. To respond to him was to manifest the reality and meaning of the divine rule in one's life. The
consequence is that, from this standpoint, ethics are not regarded
as autonomous and there is no endorsement of their self-sufficiency
as the proper sphere of human purpose and endeavour. The primary question that Jesus' hearers were expected to put to themselves
was not 'how ought we to behave?', but 'how can we truly relate
to God?' Ethics then do not stand in their own right but are an
expression of the gracious relation with God which he has given
through Christ.[32] Such moral teaching as Jesus propounded then
consisted of a series of lightning sketches of how this new relationship with God was to be actualized in new relations with other

human beings – 'you will know them by their fruits' (Matt. 7.16).

This characterization of the ethics of Jesus means that the sayings are not to be understood as a series of either absolutes or of so many separate laws. To speak of an absolute is to say that something is right or wrong independent of circumstances. One who adopts this position will maintain, for example, that it is *always* wrong to kill a child. The effect of this *a priori* stance is to rule out moral debate, as will be evident if it is applied to the question of abortion. Apart from deciding exactly at what point during the pregnancy the embryo is to be regarded as a child, there is no place for further discussion. From that moment on, abortion is wrong. In certain circumstances this can lead to the death of both mother and child, instead of, if abortion is practised, the child only. By adopting this position, as an expression of reverence for life, the absolutist in fact allows two deaths instead of one. So, believing that there can be exceptionless moral rules, he does not take into account in reaching a decision the likely effects of his conduct. But, as D. Evans pertinently remarks, 'one ought not to set aside in advance the possible moral relevance of unmentioned possible consequences'.[33]

The absolutist may then seek to justify himself, falsely, on the basis of this approach to ethics or he may look for justification outside the realm of historical action, but it is precisely at this point that the Christian faith calls in question the whole procedure because it holds that God alone justifies us here and now. We cannot justify ourselves, not even in terms of our moral behaviour, which is rather to be regarded as a flowering of faith and not as a means of establishing our own righteousness. With reference to the title of this section – the basis of Christian moral choice – we have to set aside the absolutist method as unacceptable.

It is indeed this same question of justification that shows the fallacy, from the point of view of theology, of legalistic ethics. Human beings are prone to seek self-justification and are ready to make ethics subserve this end – legalistic ethics in particular can be readily used in this way. They lay down clearly and precisely what is right and what is wrong. If one does the former then one has a double satisfaction – that of believing both that one has done what is right and that one is justified in one's conduct by having observed the prescribed form of right action. This outlook is typified by the Pharisee in Jesus' parable who believed that his relationship to God was to be based upon his own achievements (Luke 18.9–14).

But Christians believe that God alone justifies human beings and that justification is by faith and not by works of the law (Gal. 2.16). Legalistic ethics leads all too easily to self-righteousness and that is neither the righteousness of God nor the righteousness of the Christian believer. Indeed as Bonhoeffer has so well expressed it,

> responsible action is a free venture; it is not justified by any law; it is performed without any claim to a valid self-justification, and therefore also without any claim to an ultimate valid knowledge of good and evil. Good, as what is responsible, is performed in ignorance of good and in the surrender to God of the deed which has become necessary and which is nevertheless, or for that very reason, free.[34]

> Moreover Christ is not the proclaimer of a system of what would be good today, here and at all times. Christ teaches no abstract ethics such as must at all costs be put into practice . . . What can and must be said is not what is good once and for all, but the way in which Christ takes form among us here and now.[35]

If Christ had set out to resolve all moral problems, he would have removed from all succeeding generations the responsibility of having to make their own moral decisions. After all, it is the right of Christians, as indeed of everyone, to be the subjects of their own actions and not mere functionaries implementing the will of someone else. To accept legalistic ethics is not to be provided with assistance in reaching a decision; it is to have the decision taken for us. The very idea of any ethical code, as I pointed out in the chapter on 'Law and Order' in the section headed 'Moral Choice', undermines an understanding of the individual as a moral agent and denied that moral responsibility is only meaningful if there is freedom to decide.[36]

A closer look at the ethical teaching ascribed to Jesus will also show how far it is from legalism. First, it is worth noting that if he intended to act as a legislator he singularly failed to provide clear directives as to conduct. Although, for example, he speaks of love of neighbour and of enemy, he gives few specifications of what should be done in relation to them. Second, many of the sayings which have been taken as laws cannot be so interpreted if they are looked at squarely. Take the saying 'if any one strikes you on the right cheek, turn to him the other also' (Matt. 5.39). If this really is intended to be a commandment having the force of law, it is ludicrously inadequate. A law must be applicable to specific cases and situations. These words would not be applicable to a blow on the *left* cheek or to a thump upon the back. If, however, it be suggested that this is a general law, then such slight precision as it does have renders it unsuitable as such. It would stand in stark contrast to accepted general laws by the very detail it contains. Thus, 'thou shalt not labour on the sabbath day' is an example of a general law. To apply it, the rabbis finally distinguished thirty-nine categories of work and further subdivided these. These categories are precise laws which spell out the application of the general one, but in no sense can 'turn the other cheek' be regarded as either. As J. L. Houlden observes: 'In Matthew, Jesus' teaching is such as to transcend the level of law: these commands cannot be kept in the way that a law needs to be capable of being kept.'[37]

But perhaps what is even more to the point – and avoids engaging in prolonged dispute about the authenticity of particular sayings – is the undoubted opposition between Jesus' ethical teaching and the legalistic morality of his day. The morality of Judaism was prescribed by the law and its basic concept was justice, in the sense of contractual justice, i.e. like for like, and this is summed up in the saying 'an eye for an eye'. Hence it was held that human beings have certain rights under the law which balance one another. To abrogate another's rights is to become liable to the abrogation of the same rights in one's own case. However, in such a context the relationship of human beings becomes a legal rather than a personal one. Obedience is rendered to the law and this regulates relations. But according to Jesus this is not enough and is indeed false; one should not determine one's response to another by some external legal requirement, especially when the requirement embodies a spirit of revenge. One should always go beyond what the law requires, according to Jesus, if true relations are to be established and maintained. He illustrates this by rejecting an eye for an eye in favour of turning the other cheek. He is not replacing one law by another; he is attacking the very foundation of the legalistic attitude to moral behaviour.

Indeed such legalism is life-denying. In the words of J. L. Walker,

> the anti-life individual suffers from the Ten Commandments mentality, attempting to fit life to categories which presume to cover every possible situation in life. He will not isolate or alter the code, even when the situation demands it.[38]

Legalism is then unfreedom, since the right done from a sense of duty is never the good, for merely to obey due to a sense of unwilling constraint is bondage – the bondage of sin. Consequently the basis of legalism is to be found in sin, in the fact that we are separated from God. The crucifixion of Jesus was the work of the highest form of ethical righteousness. Jesus was condemned for blasphemy, and the Pharisees were utterly and entirely sincere in believing that his death was essential to preserve morality. Thus the curse of legalism is revealed by the cross. Christian ethics cannot be the ethics of the law but of redemption, because Christianity is the revelation of grace. So William Blake could observe that 'the Gospel is Forgiveness of Sins & has No Moral Precepts; these belong to Plato & Seneca & Nero',[39] i.e. 'if Morality was Christianity, Socrates was The Saviour'.[40] It is an appreciation of the truth of this that led T. W. Manson to say, in words of which Blake would have approved, 'Christian ethics is certainly not a slavish obedience to rules and regulations. It is active living, and therefore it has the power to go to the heart of every ethical situation as it arises. It has the power to see what response is called for in terms of feeling, word and act, and the power to make that response, and make it creatively and effectively. In short, Christian ethics is a work of art.'[41] Solutions to moral problems cannot then be routine and mechanical; they must be creative. This means that there are no ethical laws requiring only to be applied to successive problems as they occur.[42] The conclusion to this argument is the same as that to our previous brief consideration of the absolutist position – an interpretation of ethics in terms of law is not the method the Christian should adopt in deciding between right and wrong.

If the ethical sayings ascribed to Jesus are not to be taken as either absolutes or laws, what are they? They are to be understood, as previously suggested, in the light of his proclamation of the Kingdom, i.e. Jesus came not to provide an amended set of moral commandments but to face people with God's sovereignty. This demand for obedience to God was given a specific content in the terms of his day in his ethical maxims. So his teaching provides 'perspectives, patterns and priorities and informs the Christian mind which then turns to the examination of contemporary issues'.[43] In other words, ethics are to be understood as part of human involvement with God, and Jesus' teaching may be regarded as comprising a summons which challenges, judges, and then exposes the need for forgiveness. It presents an obligation 'to reproduce in human action the *quality* and the *direction* of the act of God by which we are saved',[44] i.e. Christian ethics are not self contained nor self justifying but arise out of a response to the gospel. Jesus' sayings are a claim upon those who hear, yet their response does not involve the observance of some manageable code of behaviour, rather it involves the complete surrender of the human will to Christ in love and in the recognition that each and every situation provides an opportunity to serve God by serving our fellow human beings.

These claims have the character of ethical maxims; they can be accepted as working rules or guides to conduct. They are so many norms which are directives of action but are also subordinate to a basic principle that sets the direction of action, viz. the commandment to love.[45] If there is an absolute to be found anywhere in the teaching of Jesus, it is precisely here in the double command to love God and neighbour. This love, as illustrated by the parable of the Good Samaritan, is to be interpreted to the effect that neighbour-need determines the meaning of human obligation, that obedience means no more than love and that love fulfils every legitimate obedience.[46] Christian ethics as the ethics of love 'draw a man out of the citadel of the self into the world of another's needs'.[47] This is practical love, not some vague feeling or affection. This is the principle or ultimate norm of obligation that does not vary with the situation, as distinct from rules or contingent norms that are relative and do vary according to the context of moral decision.[48] Where the guide lines take the form of negative prohibitions, they are not to be isolated and understood as independent laws. Rather they exist solely to serve the positive commandment of love and they have to be interpreted accordingly.

In the normal run of everyday life, the relationship between principle and maxims presents few problems. Most ethical decisions are of the unheroic kind; the rules are readily applicable and moral conduct is almost habitual. We all accept, without question, that it is wrong to tell a lie because this denies our openness and love towards the person addressed. The difficulty arises in those situations where there is a conflict between what love requires and some particular guide line. There is always a prescription in favour of the latter, and they are not lightly to be disregarded, but there are circumstances when what love demands may involve such disobedience. So 'we may say of a particular action, such as telling a lie, that it is wrong, meaning by this, not that there are no circumstances in which it would be right, but that there is a more or less heavy burden of proof on whoever wants to justify it.'[49]

The moral dilemma arises when there appears to be no course that love can take that does not involve the overriding of a rule. So, for example, those who plotted against Hitler and were arrested had to decide what to do when interrogated. They could admit their complicity and provide the names of their fellow conspirators, leading to their certain death, or, to protect them and their cause, they could lie. Now the end to which truth telling is a means is an open relationship in love, while saving life may be said to be an end in itself (Mark 3.4). But what means may be legitimately used to save life? Under an oppressive tyranny, like that of the Nazis, even if Bonhoeffer and his friends had spoken the truth, the possibility of establishing a free relationship with those in power was virtually nil. To tell the truth in that situation would not have led to the end desired. Moreover if telling a lie will save lives – which was the case in this instance – then obviously lying was the right choice. But this does not make lying good;* the situation precludes any such justification. Love required the falsehood, but this does not make it good. In either case, by telling the truth or lying, they were guilty.

Although, therefore, one may decide that in a particular case a rule is not decisive, this does not mean that the rule is irrelevant. One may decide that it has to be overriden, but this does not turn wrong into good. Indeed, as D. Evans says, 'the *right* thing to do may sometimes be to do evil'.[51] I may decide to kill a police chief known for his inhuman torturing of political prisoners. This may bring a decrease in suffering and my motive may well be love for my fellow human beings, but the assassination does not thereby become good. I certainly do not show love towards the torturer by my action, however much my concern for others lies at the basis

* This statement rests upon a distinction between the categories of right and wrong and those of good and evil. I have attempted in my use of terms to preserve this distinction throughout the text and a word of explanation is needed. Right and good are not synonyms. It is not a good act to kill, but it may be right to do so on occasion. It is even doubtful if one can speak of actions in themselves as evil apart from accompanying circumstances, e.g. intercourse and adultery are the same act; it is the circumstances of the parties concerned that alone enable a distinction to be made between them. So, to illustrate my usage further, I would agree with N. Micklem when he says: 'we may never do wrong that good may come. But if under the tragic circumstances of the hour war is, of all possible actions, the best, then it is also right'.[50] This does not of course mean that war is ever good.

of what I do. When love as a principle is opposed to loved embodied in a maxim, there is no easy way out, for in these cases one is faced with a borderline situation, where there is genuine conflict about what love requires.*

A borderline situation may be defined as one involving a struggle against injustice, although the struggle may not be a personal one against an individual adversary. It is one that aims to preserve values and prevent perversion. Further, the situation is such that the struggle can only be effectively carried out if, to a certain degree, one is prepared to use some of the methods of the opposing power. This in itself will incur guilt and is unavoidable. Finally, where the Christian is concerned, his or her endeavour must be without hatred and this means that the opponents are not to be regarded as agents of evil but as children of God bound by the chains of evil.[53] In other words, a borderline situation is one of sin – and here we see further how Christian ethics cannot be autonomous but operate within an interpretation of the human condition. Whatever is done in such a situation carries guilt. Again this can be illustrated from the plot to assassinate Hitler.

Here we have to recognize that those implicated were already guilty men in that they had failed to stop Hitler in previous years. Failure to act in an evil situation is to be guilty of a sin of omission. Further, not to proceed with the plot and so to do nothing to prevent the continuing destruction of countless lives would also have been a sin of omission. Yet to blow up Hitler was to be guilty because it involved the taking of a human life. What then was the right course of action? The Christian is called to loving service of others not to concern about personal salvation, just as Paul was prepared to say: 'I could wish that I myself were accursed and cut off from Christ for the sake of my brethren, my kinsmen by race'

---

* It will be apparent from this that I do not accept situation ethics as propounded by J. Fletcher.[52] While much that he says is of value, he fails to recognize the proper agony of decision in borderline situations. Since, according to him, love is all and the maximization of love is the supreme goal, one can calculate accordingly and if one's decision is indeed a means of increasing love, then what one does is good. Whether one breaks a moral rule or not does not matter; the decision and action are good – guilt does not arise. Hence the plotters against Hitler should have made their calculation and then acted in the knowledge that they were pursuing the good, but to have done so would have been to have revealed a superficial analysis of their borderline situation and a failure to appreciate the function and value of moral rules.

(Rom. 9. 3). It was neither their guilt nor their lack of it that was the primary consideration, but their answer to the question: what does love of my brethren demand here and now? Their decision was to kill, and one may say that this can be justified, in the sense that it was the *right* course and not in the sense that thereby the plotters would be justified. In other words, one cannot justify assassination, but in such a borderline situation the decision to kill can be taken in the knowledge that 'the guilt thus assumed for the sake of others cannot separate from the love of God, and that thus there may even be hope of forgiveness'.[54] Indeed it is only awareness of the possibility of forgiveness that allows recognition of the guilt involved. There is always a considerable danger of moral decadence for anyone who sees no problem in assassination. But whoever accepts the guilt in the name of forgiveness, whoever acts *in re* within the nexus of sin, that person may go forward *in spe* towards the future.

It does not follow from the above that Christians can do absolutely anything in the bland assurance that forgiveness will be forthcoming. Love must control what we may or may not do. We cannot say: we will manifest love as far as we can and to the extent that circumstances permit. The love commandment is unconditional and this does not allow of exceptions. So this command is also a declaration of judgment upon human society warped by sin – compromise is the only possibility between the divine requirement and what can be achieved in a corrupt world, but any necessary compromise falls short of the ideal. This is unavoidable. Christian ethics are indeed to be a witness to the life of the Kingdom, but precisely because the Kingdom is already but not yet, the witness cannot attain absolute perfection. The study of ethics then cannot remove the task of decision; ethics cannot solve problems beforehand; they cannot casuistically prejudge issues. They can clarify them; they can give some guidance but they can never remove from human beings their responsibility within history for history, a responsibility which, if freely exercised, includes a readiness to accept guilt.

To sum up. Christian ethics, because it is not concerned with absolutes nor laws, does not provide any easy solutions to what is right and what is wrong in specific circumstances. It is only in the situation that such a decision can be made, using the guide lines provided by Jesus and seeking to respond to the love commandment, in the knowledge of guilt and in the hope of forgiveness. What this means in relation to revolution – itself a borderline situation – is to be investigated in the next two sections, but before proceeding to do so, there is one matter that remains for brief consideration and that is the idea of the imitation of Christ.*

To some the living of a moral life means taking Jesus as the model; it is then this model that determines what is right and wrong. There is no doubt that from the earliest times this understanding has had a place in Christian thought. Within the New Testament itself we find Paul exhorting the Corinthians to 'be imitators of me, as I am of Christ' (I Cor. 11.1), and the author of I Peter refers to Christ as an example (2.21). This has been taken to mean that how Jesus behaved is how we should behave; if our actions copy his they are right, if they deviate they are wrong.

Although some have thought otherwise, most would agree that whatever the imitation of Christ may mean it does not refer to an exact copying of the historical life of Jesus. After all, Jesus was unmarried; he lived the life of a peripatetic preacher, dependent upon the charity of others. Literal imitation would require Christians to abstain from marriage, to give up a settled home life and to spend their time like Franciscan friars. No one questions that some people may serve God in these ways, but it would be absurd to suggest that this is required of all; it would be a moribund archaism. Rather, the call to imitation is 'not an endeavour to copy the historical Christ but a case of the Holy Spirit moulding the life of the Christian into some likeness of Christ . . . The difference between a slavish imitation and one that is creative is that the latter produces ever new patterns according to the personality concerned, that have a genuine individual stamp within a genuine likeness.'[55] In other words, the following of Jesus does not mean becoming a Jesus oneself. Rather our discipleship is to be pursued in our response to the mission of Christ at the present day. One cannot therefore solve ethical problems by asking: what would Jesus have done? Our choices are not the same as his. Each fresh situation that confronts us is unique and demands a unique response. As Hans-Ruedi Weber asked – implying a negative reply: should we look to 'the living Jesus who again and again astonishes us and corrects our imperfect and wrong understandings of him, or to a once-for-all fixed image and model?'[56]

Above all, however, we must never forget the uniqueness of

* I have examined this subject earlier in connexion with the argument that since Jesus was apolitical we, as imitators of him, must keep apart from politics.

Jesus himself, which was rightly stressed by Kierkegaard, at the same time as he took him as a model: 'in one respect no one can be like it, nor even think of wishing to imitate it (that would be blasphemy), in so far as the model is our saviour and atoner'.[57] What became the redeemer does not settle or predetermine our behaviour. Neither by his example nor by his teaching does Jesus remove human responsibility and freedom.

Justifiable Force

It is now my concern to bring together what has been said previously about force and about the basis of moral choice in order to illuminate the problem of violence and revolution. This is to use the commonly accepted terminology, whereas I have suggested that violence is the unjust and excessive use of force and consequently by definition cannot be justified. Rather, the question is whether it is ever right to use the force necessary to carry through a revolution. It is in these terms that I shall examine the subject, although certain of the quotations I shall give from other writers will necessarily include the word 'violence'.

Most Christians regard the use of force in certain circumstances as legitimate. This position rests in part upon their understanding of the state, which was investigated in chapter 3. There we saw that the state has to have a certain coercive power. This does not mean that the essence of the state is to be identified simply with the use of force – which was the view of both Marx and Tolstoy. The state exists not only to maintain justice and preserve order and security (which may require force) but also to promote freedom and welfare. Nevertheless, as G. E. M. Anscombe rightly affirms: 'Society without coercive power is generally impossible',[58] because of the need to restrain evil. Through the exercise of just laws and their enforcement, life without violence is made possible, i.e. force, which is accepted as legitimate, serves to minimize force that is illegitimate. Of course we have to recognize the tragic nature of this coercion because it involves treating persons as things. Yet, says Paul Tillich, 'we have to apply force, otherwise we would sacrifice the power in which love is embodied; we would sacrifice the justice which is the principle of form of all social life.'[59] This is the sadly avoidable way of love to conquer what is against love.

Human beings then do not have a choice between two worlds: one where coercion is necessary and one where love reigns supreme. There is only one world, where love and power may and do conflict and where order has to be preserved by coercion and where the persistence of sin makes resistance and war necessities of justice. Consequently, the majority of Christians throughout the ages have accepted, with reluctance, that the use of force, even to the extent of killing others, may be right and even morally necessary.* Indeed there is little reason to doubt that if, tomorrow, without provocation the United States were to be attacked by communist China or England were to be invaded by fascist Spain, the majority of sincere believers would consider it their duty to fight in defence of their country.† Why then should many of these same Christians, if a revolution is in question, then begin to talk of Christ the Prince of Peace and argue that in a situation of grave injustice passive obedience, or at the most nonviolent resistance, is the only way? Of course, not every war can be regarded as just and the selective conscientious objection of many Americans to the Vietnam engagement was testimony to this. Many of these protestors did not regard all possible wars as wrong, but instead asserted their right to reach their own moral decisions in relation to that particular conflict. Their conduct, not based upon any absolute which foreclosed decision, was determined by the view that it constituted an unjustifiable aggression on the part of the United States. If Christians, who accept the possibility that some wars may be just, are to be consistent, they must also admit that the use of force, including killing, may be right in relation to revolution – here too decision is not to be foreclosed. There is indeed much force in the argument of John Milton that if it is right

---

* Once recognize this and the fallacy of J. Ellul's argument that 'violence' is of the order of necessity which Christians must reject in order to be free becomes apparent.[60] Indeed the argument from necessity can be turned round and opposed to his own position. Christian hope enables us to realize that we do not have to think and believe as functions of a given system. This is the freedom of the Christian and his hope may lead to revolutionary activity. Thus Ellul's contention that force is of the order of necessity and that only Christ can liberate us from it is to be countered by the argument that to endure oppression passively without hope in human action, as instrumental to God's purpose, is to belong to the realm of necessity from which force may liberate us.

† The question of nuclear war, as distinct from one with conventional weapons, raises totally different issues. I believe a case can be made for conscientious objection in relation to such a conflict[61] but that is not relevant here.

to resist a foreign monarch who invades a country with the intention of enslaving its people, it is equally right to resist one's own government if it is intent upon tyrannizing the populace: 'the Law of civil defensive war differs nothing from the Law of foreign hostility'.[62]

If those who do accept the possibility of war and yet reject that of revolution are inconsistent, absolute pacifists* are entirely consistent. In no case will they resort to force or engage in acts of resistance or go to the length of killing anyone. That which, in their view, rules out participation in armed combat makes it always wrong, whether the situation be one of war between states or an internal struggle to transform society.

This is not the place to undertake a full scale examination of the pacifist case, but some brief observations are obviously necessary. I cannot accept absolute pacifism as *the* Christian position and this for a variety of reasons.

(*i*) It confuses personal with social ethics.[64] When Jesus radicalized the sixth commandment and extended it to every act of hatred (Matt. 5.21f.), he was clearly thinking of interpersonal relations and not of the phenomenon of war, to which, in any case, there is no direct reference in any of the teaching ascribed to him, neither to the appropriate behaviour of a political community threatened by aggression nor to the conduct of the oppressed in conditions of structural violence.

(*ii*) The ethics at the basis of this kind of pacifism are both absolutist and legalistic. Having rejected this understanding in the previous section, there is little need to say more, apart from remarking that if it is false to characterize the ethics of Jesus as a series of absolutes or laws, then this approach to the moral problem of the use of force is invalid. After all, ethical decisions arise from the discrepancy between what is and what ought to be, i.e. between the present where the Kingdom is already operative and the future of its not yet realized perfection. It is unrealistic to attempt to live as if the Kingdom were already consummated.

---

* I am using the term 'absolute pacifists' to distinguish them from those who practise selective conscientious objection and from those who adhere to a pacifist position but feel that revolutionary force may be the only road in Latin America or South Africa. They are also to be distinguished from those who are prepared to support revolution, because of the established disorder in some countries, but will do so not by carrying arms but by acting as medical officers, etc.[63]

(*iii*) Equally invalid is the supposed literalism entailed in this way of using certain passages of scripture. For example, the sixth commandment is concerned with murder and cannot be held to condemn killing in general, since the Old Testament explicitly sanctions both war and capital punishment. To suppose otherwise is to be guilty of a naïve biblicism, which itself conceals a legalistic approach. A verse is used to deduce from it directly a rule of action. Little account is taken of the context and there is no recognition that certain statements relate to specific circumstances. Many of the sayings attributed to Jesus are concerned to testify to the redemptive action of God and are not to be transformed into universal rules constituting a system of social ethics. Let us take as an example the saying that 'all who take the sword will perish by the sword' (Matt. 26. 52). It can only be pretended that this is an injunction to absolute pacifism if the words are removed from their setting and if the intention of Jesus, at the moment of uttering them, is disregarded. He was simply saying that at that hour he had no need of armed support. In no sense were these words uttered in a political situation which is constitutive for the problem of war but in relation to the prevention of Jesus from pursuing his path of suffering.

However, I have deliberately qualified literalism above with the adjective 'supposed', because on occasion the meaning that some pacifists find in biblical passages would seem to rest upon faulty exegesis. In particular this would appear to be so in relation to their interpretation of turning the other cheek. I have already pointed out, in the previous section and in the chapter on resistance to the state, that this saying is to be understood as a rejection of the *lex talionis*. It is primarily concerned with asserting that Christians in their conduct must not be motivated by a spirit of revenge. As such it has no bearing upon an overt act of defence. It is possible to use force to protect others without a feeling of hatred. This saying certainly does not rule out the possibility of preventing one's neighbour being the victim of a criminal attack by resisting an aggressor. For love to be effective action it may be necessary to employ force. No Christian will eagerly resort to arms, but love and the repudiation of vengeance do not allow us to close our eyes to the suffering of other human beings. Moreover even if this saying were taken to mean that one of Jesus' followers should literally turn the other cheek in his or her own case, it does not enjoin that the disciple should lift up the face of another oppressed person for the blow to be received on his or her cheek. It is not part of the work of love to allow this to continue to happen. 'Instead, it is the work of love and mercy to deliver as many as possible of God's children from tyranny . . . When choice *must* be made between the perpetrators of injustice and the victims of it, the latter may and should be preferred.'[65]

But even this is probably to be too literalistic. Jesus in effect was saying that the *lex talionis* allows an identical reflex to an aggressive action. In opposing this, he intimates that if you really give up a spirit of vengeance, you will not return like for like, and he forces this home with the relevant and vivid picture of turning the other cheek. He could equally well have used a different illustration – though less apt in terms of the actual wording of the law – and he could have suggested that if someone takes your purse, you should give him the money he has missed in another pocket. It would be as absurd to universalize from this as it is from the existing imagery.

However, if Christian action is to be based, not upon a literalistic, supposed or otherwise, interpretation of Jesus' teaching – which was the mistake of Volusianus quoting the very verse which I have just considered[66] – but upon love, then one can ask whether or not the pacifism practised by the first Christians (which is not to be disputed) was morally higher than the later concern for responsible participation in public life. Paul Ramsey has contended, with good reason, that it was out of love that Christians assumed the task of involvement in the political life of the societies in which they lived and were prepared to defend them with arms.[67]

Absolutism is no less evident in the presentation of Jesus as the perfect model of behaviour that is to be copied literally – here an absolute model is substituted for a series of absolute moral laws. I have twice previously criticized this position – first in chapter 2 when considering how far the 'apolitical' Jesus is to be taken as a pattern of conduct that rules out political involvement, and again at the end of the previous section of this chapter when considering how far the imitation of Christ can be regarded as a basis for deciding what is right and wrong. I return to it here a third and final time because it has been used to support a powerful argument against the use of force for the purpose of revolution.

In a series of reflections upon the events in Paris of May 1968, M.-J. Le Guillou expressed himself scandalized by certain Christians who were prepared to approve the possibility of 'violent' revolution. To him this was '*une trahison du mystère de Dieu par de trop nombreux clercs*'.[68] Le Guillou then affirmed that the foundation of Christian living is the *imitatio Christi*,[69] that Christ was the Suffering Servant who rejected the devil's temptation to pursue 'the road to triumph by means of force and violence'[70] and that Christians must 'reproduce the traits' of the Suffering Servant in their lives – 'the attitude of the Suffering Servant must be the norm of Christian behaviour'.[71] He rested much of his case upon I Peter 2.19–25 which speaks of the need for slaves to be submissive to their masters even to the extent of suffering unjustly, just as Jesus suffered and left an example 'that you should follow in his steps'.[72]

It is perhaps not a point of substance to remark that nowhere in the accounts of the temptation in the wilderness is there any reference to force or violence, although it is worthy of note that 'the "cross" of the murdered prophet is not the same as the "pain" of the oppressed poor'.[73] Nor is revolution itself without suffering for those who take part. Cromwell, it will be recalled, distinguished between passive and active principles. He refused to sit in judgment on the former but had no hesitation in declaring that the latter also involved suffering and even death.[74] But what is above all important is to recognize, in relation to Le Guillou's position, the uniqueness of Christ's role. The general thrust of his argument runs counter to the orthodox belief that Christ was the saviour of the world and that his suffering and death constituted the sacrifice which overcame the separation of humankind and God and destroyed the power of Satan. This can be said of no other person. His role as the Suffering Servant, which is *par excellence* a redemptive role, is the necessary corollary of his being the saviour. But Christians are not themselves individual redeemers. The sacrifice of Christ, according to the New Testament, is complete, once and for all. We Christians cannot repeat it. The contention that our discipleship is to be an exact imitation of Christ as the Suffering Servant fails precisely because it compromises the uniqueness of Christ and of his act of liberation.

It is, of course, not to be denied that Jesus did not put himself at the head of a nationalistic freedom movement, employing forcible means to secure liberty, but this has nothing to do with the question of violence or nonviolence; it was the logical result of his refusal to regionalize the Kingdom of God. As the agent of the inbreaking Kingdom, Jesus would not reduce its totality to one particular province or part of this world.[75]

Nor can Le Guillou's literalistic approach to I Peter be taken to carry much weight. The passage in question is devoted to advice to slaves in their relations with their owners. It is faulty hermeneutics to assume that these admonitions can be applied directly to other categories of persons, for this is another example of removing words from their context and attributing to them an absolute value they cannot possess. Of course, it may be argued that while the verses originally concerned slaves, there are today other groups of oppressed who can be regarded as enslaved. But such a procedure masks a shift in interpretation. First it is admitted that those in I Peter and the 'enslaved' today are not the same people in identical situations and that the oppressed in the twentieth century can only figuratively be regarded as being in the same condition; but then the supposed advice about non-resistance is taken quite literally. But if one part of the passage is given an interpretation that is not that of its original meaning, why should the other part be pressed *au pied de la lettre*?

However Le Guillou also fails to appreciate that this very passage does stress the uniqueness of Christ's role. 'The writer's plea,' comments J. N. D. Kelly, 'is not that slaves should attempt to reproduce all the particular details of Christ's passion which he is recapitulating. That is in any case excluded since "he suffered for you", "bore our sins", etc. Rather it is that they should expect to have to suffer, and to suffer without having in any way earned it, and that they should be ready to exhibit the same uncomplaining acceptance.'[76] To universalize from this and to assert that all Christians, no matter what their circumstances, *must* accept suffering rather than do anything to bring about change, is simply not legitimate exegesis. In its original context the advice was sensible and realistic – given the first-century situation, the only feasible course of action was non-resistance; when different circumstances obtain, the advice is no longer necessarily valid. Each situation has its own problematic circumstances which require believers to think through each act of obedience without any absolute ethics upon which to reply, either in the form of laws or of personal example. To look for such an absolutism is to deny Christian freedom.

If absolute pacifism has doubtful support in the Bible, and in the New Testament in particular, it may appear that rationalistic humanism may come to its support. It is Karl Popper especially who has maintained that there is an absolute antithesis between reason and 'violence'. If there is a difference of opinion, so he contends, it can be resolved in only one of two ways, either by argument, involving give and take and a certain degree of intellectual humility, or by the use of force. The former is the only reasonable course of action to adopt, and the latter is to be condemned as irrational.[77]* One of the principal weaknesses in Popper's case is his facile identification of reason with argument or discussion, which enables him to suppose that when force is used instead of argument, reason (i.e. argument) has gone out of the window and the behaviour is therefore unreasonable. This is in fact circular reasoning.[78] It is perfectly possible, in opposition to this, to conceive of situations where force is reasonable. Let us suppose I discover a burglar who has broken into my house. His choice of profession may be eminently reasonable in that he has weighed up the chances of detection and decided that the risk is worth it in view of the possibility of a rapid improvement in his finances. He will not wish to be detained if caught in the act, quite reasonably as this could result in his arrest and a prison sentence, and so he resorts to force to prevent my apprehending him. He chooses 'violence' rather than argument, but who can doubt that according to his premisses his behaviour is reasonable? Conversely, if I use force against him, will not this be the act of a reasonable man, taking steps to avoid seeing some of his treasured possessions disappearing for ever through the window?

Alternatively, one may take as an example an interracial struggle. This is always to be deplored, but it is not necessarily irrational; it is the logical and rational consequence of racism. Moreover, 'violence, being instrumental by nature, is rational to the extent that it is effective in reaching the end that must justify it'.[79] Force may minimize misery and to the extent that it does it is reasonable to make use of it and so, if not morally mandatory, it is morally in order. Hence in a revolutionary situation the use of force can be the greatest tribute to reason and justice, for, as Ortega y Gasset points out, 'this form of violence is none other than reason exasperated'.[80] Indeed my main quarrel with Popper does not centre in the circularity of his reasoning but in his concept of

* In order not to misrepresent Popper, I should point out that he does hold that there are limits to tolerance and that he was in favour of war against Nazi Germany. Popper is therefore not an absolute pacifist as such, but since his position is directed against revolution it has to be reviewed.

human nature. Implicit in his thesis is the presupposition that human beings are rational animals; to use force is, to him, to lose this attribute of rationality and so to become no more than animals. But human nature consists of much more than pure reason: it includes memory, imagination, consciousness and conscience. To be human involves achieving personality through meaningful acts (not just by a process of ratiocination) and through attaining freedom, i.e. attaining the power to act. One of the root causes of the use of force for revolutionary ends is the difficulty of acting effectively as distinct from merely behaving or reacting. If, through rebellion, human beings engage in meaningful acts, achieve greater freedom and so do act effectively, then they are conducting themselves rationally and the supposed antithesis between reason and force is shown to be false.

In fairness to the pacifist position, which I do not wish in any way to misrepresent or underestimate, it has to be acknowledged that this does not necessarily require complete passivity in the face of suffering and oppression. John Ferguson rightly points out that the word pacifist derives from *pax* and *facere* and it therefore means 'peace maker', i.e. the pacifist is not the one who just says 'no' to armed conflict but one who also says 'yes' to peace and works to that end.[81] Indeed no Christian, pacifist or not, should adopt a role of acquiescence. 'Keeping aloof,' say the Catholic bishops of the Netherlands, 'may ultimately become complicity.'[82] There is no position of neutrality. By refusing to act, Christians become accomplices in the exploitation of the many through the instrumentality of unjust social, economic and political structures. Passivity can place one in the ranks of the oppressors. At certain times and in certain places evil assumes such proportions that to tolerate it is to contribute to its increase. Nonviolent acquiescence may be no more than an abstract victory of principle – a Pyrrhic victory for Christ! 'There is no glory,' says Bonhoeffer of pacifism, 'in standing amid the ruins of one's native town in the consciousness that at least one has not oneself incurred any guilt.'[83] There is no glory in living in an unjust society believing that one's non-resistance has preserved one's purity.

Indeed it cannot be denied that in certain situations of massive oppression the absolute pacifist may be unwillingly reduced to a position of passivity, in that nothing he or she can do can contribute to the making of peace. Where such is the case, the positive aspect of pacifism – working for peace – is negated and there remains only the ineffectual refusal to resist. For this reason some pacifists would accept the necessity for non-violent resistance. In so doing their absolutism and consistency are compromised. There is no justification for taking 'turn the other cheek' literally as an absolute and disregarding the first half of the same verse with its injunction not to resist evil. Of course I have argued previously[84] that Matthew 5.39a is to be understood as forbidding vindictive harm and is not a universal rule condemning all opposition to evil. If this be accepted, then the question at issue is not: should I resist in order to effect change? but: what form is it proper that my resistance should take?

While most Christians would agree that the path of nonviolence is preferable, here again this is not to be elevated into an absolute. Its limitations have to be taken into account. In particular it has to be appreciated that its successful use presupposes the existence of compassion and a sense of justice on the part of the adversary. The case of Gandhi is here very apposite. Gandhi himself was neither a systematic thinker nor an absolute pacifist. He accepted killing in self defence. While preferring *satyagraha* (force borne of truth and love or nonviolence), he advocated violence rather than cowardice and he eventually sanctioned the use of armed might against the axis powers in World War II.[85] Moreover the popular view of his achievement is both an oversimplification and probably a misreading of history. According to this understanding, India achieved freedom under the leadership of Gandhi through a nonviolent struggle that demonstrated the power of love. In fact *satyagraha* was neither understood nor tried by the majority of Indians. Further, violence did play a part in the ultimate achievement of independence and the British withdrawal was the result of a whole host of different factors and would almost certainly have taken place eventually even if Gandhi had not appeared on the scene.[86] Above all, such success as Gandhi did have was due to the fact that the British had a conscience. Put him in the Rome of 1925 or the Berlin of 1933 and not only would he have been arrested but no more would ever have been heard of him.

Moreover for a realistic appraisal of the subject it should be recognized that the difference between nonviolence and violence or force is one of degree, since the former can involve coercion, restraint upon liberty and even destruction of life and property.[87] So, for example, there was more violence after the Freedom Riders began their activities than there was before. Of course one may seek to justify this by pointing out that the amount of violence was insignificant compared with the amount of justice won, but one cannot escape the fact that violence had been provoked by these nonviolent means. Further, the consequences of nonviolent action may be more harmful in the long run than the use of force, and, in any case, nonviolent methods may be entirely ineffective or effective only at a price that is morally unacceptable by comparison with some form of forcible resistance. Indeed the use of force is not necessarily in itself an indication of a failure to acknowledge the general moral obligation not to harm others because one may use force to protect others. It is a reasonable conclusion, therefore, that one should not draw a distinction between the absolute rightness of nonviolence and the absolute wrongness of 'violence' or force, since the difference between them *is* one of degree. This difference is however important in making moral decisions. Christians should be prepared to assign a moral priority to nonviolence and acknowledge that the use of force requires justification, but they should not at the same time accept nonviolence as an absolute. Instead it is to be taken as a guide line, and this means that while force is *prima facie* wrong, its use may actually be right when other claims, such as the protection of the innocent and the establishment of justice, are taken into account.

In a world where force is continually operative, nonviolence can only be relative. This relativity implies not only that there will always be a limit to the integrity of any given action, but also that any action will have to include some measure of force. 'What is vital is that this "violence" should be truly and unavoidably required by a love which would fail in its obligations if it did not have recourse to it.'[88] Christian love requires the acceptance of the possibility of force in limit-situations, where everything else fails, i.e. resort to force may be acceptable as an ultimate recourse in extreme circumstances.

Yet to many nonviolent social change is a contradiction in terms and it would be unethical to limit the possibilities of the oppressed by removing from them the option of revolution. This would be to use one interpretation of Christian ethics to support the *status quo* and to fail to perceive that nonviolence may be a luxury that the destitute cannot afford. Too often the cross of Christ has been regarded solely as a symbol of passivity and of the acceptance of suffering, and this has obscured the fact that the cross is also a symbol of power. 'Power, however dangerous this assumption may be, is thought in New Testament faith to be – within limits –

usable in a perspective of *agape* as symbolized by the cross. Revolution, in the sense of planned overthrow and capture of the power structures of society, may be included in the active concern of love.'[89] Here, in more modern terms, we encounter the valid distinction drawn by Oliver Cromwell between the active and passive principles of suffering.[90]

If neither absolute pacifism nor nonviolent resistance are the only options open to Christians, what can be said of the option to use force? Christian ethics have generally recognized the right to self defence and to assistance when attacked. Indeed one can go back to the seventeenth century to find Samuel Rutherford advancing precisely this argument to the effect that as an individual may protect himself so a proportion of the populace, suffering injustice, may do likewise.[91] Certainly love of neighbour may on occasion require the use of force if the oppressed are to be given any help – force in this context is essentially defensive force. But love of enemy can also be the motive for taking up arms. So Paulo Freire can say:

> It is – paradoxical though it may seem – precisely in the response of the oppressed to the violence of their oppressors that a gesture of love may be found. Consciously or unconsciously, the act of rebellion by the oppressed . . . can initiate love. Whereas the violence of the oppressors prevents the oppressed from being fully human, the response of the latter to this violence is grounded in the desire to pursue the right to be human. As the oppressors dehumanize others and violate their rights, they themselves also become dehumanized. As the oppressed, fighting to be human, take away the oppressors' power to dominate and suppress, they restore to the oppressors the humanity they had lost in the exercise of oppression.[92]

These observations enable us to appreciate the threefold reference of love in a revolutionary situation. There is, first, love to the oppressed which may lead us to defend them by force. There is, second, love for the oppressor which may lead us to use force to remove him from power as a step towards his own liberation and greater humanization. There is, third, a denial of love if I have to kill an oppressor. It is vain to suggest that such an act can reveal my love towards him. Killing in this situation is always a partial denial of love. Love for the oppressed may strive against love for the oppressor and there is no way out of this dilemma whereby I can be justified. I have to accept the guilt without cowering behind the pretence that it has not been incurred.

The value of Freire's discernment is, further, not only that it enables us to perceive how love of enemy may itself involve force, but also the extent to which a situation of oppression is itself already one of violence. Here we return to the subject of structural violence previously considered. If this be accepted as a reality, then it becomes apparent that Christians have little choice – their decision relates to the extent to which revolutionary force is less or more deplorable than the violence perpetuated by the existing structures. In this way, they will avoid falling into the pitfall of accepting a double standard, which asserts that violence is acceptable when it maintains the *status quo* but is wrong when it is used to change it. In other words revolutionary force can be understood as counterviolence, i.e. as the force that breaks the old violent structures in order to bring liberation and establish the possibility of freedom. Too often the preservation of what is is not looked upon as wrong, while the attempt to alter it is so regarded. This is a fallacy. Moreover the force needed for revolution will depend upon the form of repression adopted by the ruling élite. As John F. Kennedy said: 'Those who make pacific revolution impossible, make violent revolution inevitable.' If a revolution is for a just cause, those in power are morally bound to give way; only when it is not for a just cause has the government the right to be defended. But if it is for a just cause, then the oppressors themselves are largely responsible for any violence that may ensue.

At this point in our discussion it is as well to note that the problem of force and revolution is not solely a moral one; it has a theological dimension which is related to the question how far God is the kind of being who will encourage revolution, even when it involves the use of force. Several of the points made in the previous chapter lead to an affirmative reply to this enquiry. Thus we saw that, according to the Bible, God is not one who is concerned to preserve things as they are; rather his will is to transform de-humanizing structures. To similar effect is the emphasis upon God's fight for freedom and justice; he is the one who 'breaks the rod of the oppressor' (Isa. 9.4). A revolution indeed may be a sign of the Kingdom, that God is at work putting down the mighty from their seat. This God is one who wields power. The Assyrians – not remarkable for their restraint in battle – are the rod of his anger (Isa. 10.5), while the Babylonians represent the divine 'outstretched hand and strong arm' (Jer. 21.5). It is however no argument against the use of force to acknowledge that God is the one who avenges the misery of the poor and then to say, with Jacques Ellul, that it is he alone who sweeps aside oppression.[93] How does God accomplish this? I know of no action attributed to God in history that is not at the same time the action of human beings believed to be his agents, and 'if we have the honour to be God's instruments,' proclaimed Edward Corbett in the House of Commons in 1643, 'we must do the office of instruments and be active . . . we must go along with Providence.'[94]

Does God then say use force? Apparently yes, but at the same time he bears the force in himself. According to the New Testament, God is one who accepts force, even violence, as directed against himself in the person of his Son. Further, if human beings are made in the image of God and if God requires the exercise of force, then every act of force against another is against God. He is at the beginning, within and at the end of the process of force. If right conduct is acting according to the will of God, who can say that he will never demand force? To exercise it is to incur guilt, but here again God bears the cost of forgiving that guilt, having paid the price of reconciliation on the cross. Christians who opt for force enter upon an ordeal which divides them to the very depths of their being; they engage in a tragic existence wherein they bear the burden of sin. They should not seek to defend their actions on spurious grounds and advance vain excuses, suggesting they are involved in a crusade or holy war. Christians know that guilt is inescapable. To tolerate evil is to be as guilty as to react effectively against it. If by doing the latter, we risk the loss of our souls, by putting force at the service of pity and love, we can still ask ourselves, with Ernst Bloch: 'What does the salvation of souls really matter?'[95] But it is 'precisely in the responsible acceptance of guilt that a conscience which is bound solely to Christ will best prove its innocence'.[96]

In no sense is this to romanticize violence or the use of force. It is absurd to pretend that it is beneficial in itself or that it is renovating and purifying.[97] It is with the name of François Fanon that this hollow idealization is most associated. Faced with the horrendous struggle of the Algerians for freedom, he spoke of violence investing its perpetrators with positive and creative qualities and as a cleansing power restoring self respect.[98] He was followed by J.-P. Sartre who, in his introduction to *The Wretched of the Earth*, could say that 'this irrepressible violence is neither sound and fury, nor the resurrection of savage instincts, nor even the effect of resentment; it is man recreating himself'.[99] This is a confusion of power with violence. To be a human being, as I have previously suggested, is only possible if one has the power to act. In revolutions people reassert themselves and claim that power and, in the process, recover their self respect, but when the means to this end is force, even justifiable force, then guilt must be borne. Force cannot be sanctified; its exercise may be forgiven.

All this means that the Christian is inevitably a reluctant revolutionary and, in particular, he or she is very loath to go to the lengths of taking life. Typical of a valid Christian attitude in this respect is that manifested by Oliver Cromwell, himself a man of faith, convinced that it was the divine will that he should engage in rebellion. In his first speech before the Little Parliament on 4 July 1653, Cromwell declared:

> The thinking of an act of violence was to us worse than any battle that ever we were in, or that could be, to the utmost hazard of our lives: so willing were we, even very tender and desirous if possible that these men might quit their places with honour.[100]

None of this means that Christians will support any and every revolution. Oppression can be challenged by forms of resistance that are nonviolent or involve force or some combination of both. Which is adopted is a question of strategy. At one time they may say 'no' to any participation, at another 'yes'. Hence Christians do not have to repudiate all revolutions which, in any case, have a contingent nature in that they have a necessary context in a specific social system. All that I am affirming is that Christians must be held to be free *vis-à-vis* this question and that the choice of force is not to be excluded *a priori*.

It is not to be expected that Christians will all be of one mind about this problem. Such a great fighter for social justice as Helder Camara has repudiated the use of force for himself, while respecting those, like Camilo Torres, who have accepted it.[101] In any case, moral issues are seldom clear cut; different Christians will deal with different issues in different ways, especially if they are convinced that they have no infallible guide miraculously dropped down from heaven. But at least it may be accepted, on the basis of this discussion, that just as the church has accepted the validity of the pacifist witness, while refusing to hold that it is incumbent on all, so it is time that it accepted the possible validity of the witness of the revolutionary Christian, while equally refusing to universalize this form of discipleship.

Not only will all Christians not agree on this matter, even those who do agree with Marxists in positing the need for revolution will find themselves differing from them in their moral position. No Christian could agree with Engels when he said: 'Any means leading to the goal is suitable to me as a revolutionary – both the most violent and that which seems the most peaceful.'[102] While Christians live in hope out of the future, they do not regard the present as lost. This is the error of some revolutionaries who regard the present as only existing for the future; the present is then denied and becomes a time of absolute negation. So human beings can be absolved from inhumanity now as the time of transition. Here we see the stark antithesis between the Communist on the one hand and the pacifist on the other. The Communist sets justice above compassion and is prepared for violence and bloodshed; the pacifist sets compassion above justice and will have nothing to do with violence and the spilling of blood. Many Christians, who are open to the possibility of using force in a revolution, can accept neither of these extremes; although they do have to consider the question of ends and means, which the Marxist raises so forcibly. It is to this that we turn finally as we come to the conclusion of this section.

The case against the use of force in revolution is frequently presented in terms of ends and means to the effect that the latter affect the former. Evil means, we are told, corrupt good ends.[103] Force/ violence is reciprocal and perpetuates itself and can never result in the establishment of justice. Means will only issue in certain ends if they are both of the same nature; so the pacifist will contend that 'peace is not only the goal, it is also the way'.[104] After all did not Paul condemn the view that one should do evil in order that good may come (Rom. 3.8)? This is an impressive case, but it is doubtful if it can really stand up.

It is simply not true, as Antony Flew has emphasized,[105] that evil means can never lead to good ends. Few Christians would deny that the crucifixion of Christ was an evil act, but equally they would not question that out of this came immense good. Again, to take a modern example, the recent Portuguese Revolution involved the use of force and a certain number, though not very large, of people were killed. Whatever the future course of events in that country, the independence granted to her African territories has terminated the bitter guerrilla warfare that had cost already many lives and, if it had continued unabated, would have led to more bloodshed. There was truth in the speech of Agostinho Neto, chairman of the People's Movement for the Liberation of Angola, when, in a speech at the signing of the independence agreement on 15 January 1975, he said: 'Today the trigger has given way to dialogue, and the right has been recognized of both peoples to independence and liberty, and embraces and fraternization have taken the place all of a sudden of violent confrontation.'[106] A refusal to risk killing through the army uprising would have meant that repression would have persisted in Portugal and lives in Angola would have been sacrificed. In other words, it is impossible to maintain that good ends can never be achieved by so-called evil means. Nor can Paul be properly cited to the contrary. To do so is to perpetrate another example of naïve biblicism. He was not enunciating an eternal principle. He was simply dealing with a current misunderstanding of his gospel of grace, which had led some to argue that if the goodness of God is revealed by his gracious forgiveness of evil deeds, then we are free to commit more and more moral misdemeanours because they will provide occasions for and demonstrate the continuing divine mercy. The theoretical question of ends and means was far from the apostle's thought.

There are indeed two erroneous ways of evaluating ends and means. The pacifist absolutizes the means, while the Communist absolutizes the ends. Both positions underestimate the moral complexity of the problem. The one evades it by treating maxims as laws and holding that, for example, it is *never* right to lie, steal or kill – and this is demonstrably false. The other evades it by holding that one can forget the question of right and wrong here and now in the name of the end – and this is to surrender moral discrimination. The first is an instance of legalistic moralism; the second rests upon the false premiss that the end always justifies *any* means. This is not to say that the end never justifies some means, but clearly if certain means are contrary to a moral guide line, only a very special end would be held to justify them. One has to apply discrimination, whereby one decides what is morally tolerable in the light of the proportion between possible just and evil consequences.[107] So the killing of an enemy in battle is such a *prima facie* violation of love that it requires justification in terms of the countervailing requirements of love. To kill someone is never good, but it may be the right course of action depending upon the circumstances. Christians may have to accept the guilt of killing in the name of forgiveness and only in this way will they be preserved from moral indifferentism.

To a certain degree this preceding discussion has been theoretical and has obscured the fact that in some situations there are not a variety of means from which to choose in order to attain a specified end. When massive oppression obtains, nonviolence may not be an effective means to achieve liberation. So we have to recognize that in specific circumstances the means to be employed are affected by the situation itself. To think otherwise is to suppose that means can be viewed ahistorically. There are no such things as means *per se*. There are only means conditioned by a situation. To seek to define the sanctity of ends and the purity of means is to be guilty of an abstraction. 'Anyone,' says Hugo Assman, 'who always knows *a priori* how to act in a situation which does not yet exist takes an immoral decision precisely because it is abstract and non-historical.'[108] Hence my concern in this section has been to establish that the use of force for revolutionary purposes may be regarded as a possible option for Christians and is not to be ruled out *a priori*. We now have to consider more closely the circumstances in which the choice of such a course of action may be deemed a right one.

Just Revolution

Although many Christians, particularly in the affluent West, may look askance at the conclusion of the previous section, viz. that there is an open possibility for believers to use force for revolutionary ends, I have in fact done no more than present a series of arguments that supports the conclusions of many church leaders and representative ecclesiastical bodies. It would be tedious for the reader to be subjected to a plethora of quotations in support of this observation, but a few are necessary to place it beyond question.

According to Pius XI, in his encyclical *Nos es muy*, addressed to Mexican bishops on 28 March 1937:

> If a situation arises when the duly constituted authorities oppose justice and truth to the extent that their destructive acts affect the very basis of authority, one cannot see how one should condemn those citizens who unite to defend the nation and themselves, by legitimate and appropriate means, against those who take advantage of their power to lead the country into ruin.[109]

Paul VI, in *Populorum Progressio*, paragraphs 30 and 31, condemned injustice and warned against the dangers of revolution,

except in the case of manifest and prolonged tyranny which attacks fundamental rights of the person and endangers the common good of the country.

In the light of this it is understandable that a Brazilian bishop, Dom Jorga of S. Andres, could declare on television that

armed revolution by the people is justified when oppression rules and famine wages obtain.[110]*

Then we may cite the Zagorsk consultation on 'Theological Issues of Church and Society' to the effect that

we must realize that some Christians find themselves in situations where they must, in all responsibility, participate fully in the revolution with all its inevitable violence.[111]

The Report *Violence in Southern Africa* contained this conclusion:

It is too late to insist that our support should be confined to those pledged to non-violence. To urge their subjects to avoid violence furthers the ends of the governments of these five† territories, who themselves habitually employ violence to repress any move that would upset the rule of privileged minorities. *The time has come to show our solidarity with those seeking radical change and struggling for freedom in Southern Africa.*[112]

These statements, and many others like them, tend to be a little grudging in their formulation – 'we would not condemn' rather than 'we think it right' – and they only provide a few indications of when a revolution might be considered just. To a more detailed analysis of this we now turn.

A revolution, involving force, can be defined as an internal war directed towards changing a government's policies, rules and organizations and transforming the social and economic structures. Consequently recourse has been had to the long standing theory of the just war in order to shed light on the question of the just revolution. There is no need to trace the history of the former concept, starting with Augustine, and passing via Aquinas and Suarez up to the present day.[113] Rather we need to know simply what the theory was intended to achieve and what its main elements were.

The theory was originally devised as an attempt by the church to

---

* Indeed many Latin American bishops took the words of Paul VI to justify revolution, although, despite what appears to be the sense of the text, he later, in a speech in Colombia, denied that this was his intention.

† The report was written before the Portuguese actions in Angola and Mozambique reduced these five to three.

limit wars and to decrease their brutality. This justification of some wars was not in terms of possible exceptions to Christian conduct, rather it was an expression of the Christian understanding of moral and political responsibility. In its most developed form the theory laid down six conditions that had to be fulfilled for a war to be just.

1. It has to be declared by a legitimate authority.

War, in other words, is to serve public, not private, ends, and the highest public authority is the one to decide this.

2. The cause must be just.

Such a cause covers defence against aggression or against the suppression of basic rights. The situation has to be extreme to permit recourse to arms.

3. It must be undertaken as a last resort.

Only when all other means of defending one's cause or achieving one's legitimate aims have been tried can war be deemed right.

4. It must have just goals.

It must aim to achieve a fair and just settlement. Under this heading wars of aggression stand condemned.

5. The means employed must be just.

This factor relates both to the immunity from direct and intended attack of the innocent and noncombatants and to the proportion between the means and the goal. It would, for example, be wrong to destroy a whole village simply because an enemy were sheltering in a single house.

6. There must be a reasonable chance of success.

This applies to success both in the military sense, i.e. the prospect of victory is relatively certain, and in relation to goals, i.e. the prospect of realizing the original goals is favourable. There must therefore also be a strong possibility that the good achieved will be greater than the evils combatted.

In recent times, particularly in the United States with its engagement in Vietnam, this theory has been very carefully scrutinized. It has been recognized that it may help to limit the evils that war entails and to humanize its conduct to a certain extent. It has been appreciated that it provides tools for the analysis of a conflict using conventional weapons.* It has provided a basis for moral

* It could equally be applied to a nuclear conflict but with the strong possibility that it would condemn such a war as unjust.

discrimination and for moral objections to specific wars. Without facing these questions, with the assistance of such a theory, Christians would be opting out of history; they would be denying their traditional view that political society is necessary for human good on earth, and they would have simply nothing to say of any relevance in those situations where war may obtain.*

In the sixteenth and seventeenth centuries, the theory of the just war was regarded as having implications for domestic politics and the step was taken of defining the necessary conditions for engaging legitimately in a civil or internal war. Rebellion against a tyrant was regarded as justified whenever it fulfilled at least three of the requirements of the just war. It had to be undertaken at the command of a legitimate authority; it had to have a just cause and its means were to be just.[116] In effect, the first of these conditions was variously interpreted, as we have seen in chapter 3. Calvin, for example, defined legitimate authority as the magistracy, while John Knox declared that every citizen had the right to instigate an uprising against an unjust government. As regards the second requirement, this was understood primarily in terms of defensive action, i.e. resistance was just if it involved defence against aggression on the part of one who ruled contrary to the established legal or moral order. The third element comprised restraint and condemned such violent activities as pillage, rape and unnecessary killing. These considerations were not, of course, applied to revolution in its modern sense, as a complete social and economic transformation. They were largely directed towards justifying the forcible removal of an unjust ruler and his replacement by someone else. However it is not a great step from this position to current analyses of the concept of the just revolution. This is also a necessary step in the logic of this present study. Having established previously that Christians

---

* Ellul, in cavalier fashion, discards the just war concept as irrelevant to the present day; in so doing, he ignores completely the important role it has played in ethical thinking in contemporary America. The one objection he briefly mentions is to the effect that in modern warfare noncombatant immunity is impossible.[114]. Against this it can be said that the theory does not stand or fall by the retention of this element, since it was not part of Aquinas' original theory. But, in any case, to say that the distinction between combatant and noncombatant is meaningless is, according to G. E. M. Anscombe, 'pure nonsense; even in war, a very large part of the enemy population are just engaged in maintaining the life of the country, or are sick, or aged, or children.'[115]

are free to choose force for revolutionary ends *in certain circumstances*, it is precisely by an investigation of the just revolution that it becomes possible to define what exactly those circumstances may be.

The Sodepax Report, entitled *In Search of a Theology of Development* (1970), affirmed:

> There should be no veto of revolution arising either from a theological rejection of resistance to established authority or from an absolute pacifism that rejects all use of violence. The pacifism of individual vocation can play an important reconciling role in any situation, but there is need for the concept of 'just revolution' in political decisions.[117]

So, taking the six elements of the just war theory, we must now look at each in turn in relation to revolution.

1. *Legitimate Authority*

Of all the six conditions for a just war, this is the one that appears least applicable to a just revolution. The word legitimate ultimately derives from *legitimare*, meaning to declare lawful, and so it has close association with the concept of legality, e.g. a legitimate child is one having the status of being lawfully begotten. In this sense no revolutionary group can be regarded as legitimate, since no country's laws allow for their existence. In effect, strictly speaking the only legitimate authority in a country is the existing régime and its officers, and hence, if this requirement were pressed literally no revolution could ever be right. Of course a government may be held to have lost its legitimacy if it behaves in a totally unjust manner, but this does not *ipso facto* legitimize anyone else.

However it can be argued that in times of dire necessity, such as constitute a just cause for revolution, all authority reverts to the community, but it is still difficult to conceive of any possible means whereby the people could actually authorize revolution in such circumstances. Again, in the line of John Knox, it may be contended that a private individual may lead a rebellion as long as he acts in 'a magisterial capacity', i.e. on behalf of society as a whole, as does anyone carrying out what is known as citizen's arrest. There is some substance in this. Once it is accepted that it is the people that have the supreme authority, then they must also be accorded the right to depose those in power and change the structures of their society and they may take the necessary steps to effect this. But revolutions seldom start as movements of the whole population, not even with the support of the majority. Their spearhead is rather a revolutionary élite and so R. J. Neuhaus has suggested that such a group may anticipate, although not currently reflecting, what the will of the people will be when they have been liberated through revolution.[118] Here however the legitimization is really *post factum*.

The existence of such a group may be said to have some justification in that it performs a symbolic function and is instrumental in the process of conscientization. Since this increase in awareness, as I have previously suggested, is an indispensable element in leading to a successful revolution, it may be held that, before the resort to force, conscientization must be undertaken and that when, as a consequence, the resistance enjoys the confidence of a sizeable proportion of the people, then it becomes invested with legitimate authority.

For Christians however there is a further matter to be taken into account. They believe that they must follow their consciences and that their ultimate authority is God himself. Although the concept of legitimate authority was originally centred in the idea of lawful human power, it is not stretching the subject too much to suggest that, since 'we must obey God rather than men', the final legitimate authority must be said to rest in the divine being. If after careful analysis of a situation, Christians reach the conclusion that it is a work of love to strive against love, who can say that their choice is wrong?

2. *Just Cause*

The function of this requirement is to serve as a limiting factor, i.e. recourse to force is not to be undertaken simply for any grievance whatsoever. We are talking solely about limit-situations where conditions have reached an extreme. Hence the presence of structural violence is not sufficient in itself to justify counter-violence. To reject the *lex talionis* – as Jesus certainly did – and so to repudiate the returning of like for like, means that counter-violence is not *per se* condonable. It is the degree of violence that is the important factor. We are concerned with what Neuhaus calls 'revolting levels'[119] or alternatively one might speak of levels of toleration. These are obviously impossible to quantify and indeed no theoretical answer is possible. It is simply astonishing the amount of suffering human beings can bear – whether they ought to continue to endure it, if it is avoidable, is another question.

However the general characteristics of those circumstances that may constitute a just cause are not difficult to sketch; they may be summed up under the heading *salus populi*, employed by Oliver Cromwell.[120] Obviously there are grounds for action when a government has become tyrannical, i.e. '. . . if it fails to take any steps to remove injustice, and if it inhibits any form of criticism and organisation within the State aimed at removing injustices. These injustices may be concerned with racial discrimination, economic disparity and poverty, or cultural, religious or educational life – or any combination of these.'[121] Where there is not only deprivation of civil liberties but brutality in the form of wilful killing, torture, psychological violence and inhuman or degrading treatment – there we have a tyrannical government. There is, says Yoskiaki Iisaki, 'no moral ground for saying that tyranny is always preferable to anarchy, or that patience to endure the wrongs of tyranny is always a greater Christian virtue than courage to resist unjust powers'.[122]

Further, just cause is applicable to a society where the political life has become disordered. 'The right to revolt,' according to Berdyaev, 'is morally justifiable when the wrongs of the old régime have grown outrageous and its spiritual foundations have crumbled away.'[123] Consequently revolution is just when there is societal failure and when the state of a community is so dire ·that it is indeed worse than an armed conflict that seeks to transform it. Revolution is then an *ultima ratio* in a situation where, owing to the action or the failure to act of an oppressive régime, it is more harmful for human beings than an uprising would probably be. A glance back at the previous chapter where I described certain 'sinful situations' will provide further evidence of the kind of circumstances envisaged, circumstances in which Christians have to accept the view that mere biological survival is not the supreme value in human existence.[124]

The borderline situations I have in mind are also to be described as those where the oppressors are exercising violence and are inflicting suffering and death and where these will continue unless they are effectively challenged. The presence of such violence may also be understood as 'a sign of the imminent breaking in of the divine judgment upon an established order of power and life which has been weighed in the balance and found wanting'.[125] Such existing violence reveals the dehumanizing dynamics of a society in which unjustifiable force has become endemic. So I am talking of that which may be deemed to be an irrevocable perversion of justice and freedom against which no other action than the use of force is conceivable. Such force is to be employed for the neighbour in a defensive struggle against aggression; it arises out of concern for the justice of God and obedience to his will.

Yet there is a proviso to be entered here. Sometimes just cause may refer not to an existing situation but to one that may be confidently predicted. The obvious instance of this is Germany in 1933 when Hitler assumed power. It was only when the violence of the Nazis had assumed demonic proportions that some Christians decided they must act. This delay certainly added to the sum of suffering. Tens of millions of people died because Hitler was not stopped when he first gained control. Yet in *Mein Kampf* he had very clearly set out precisely what he intended to do. Not all wouldbe tyrants are so frank, but those who would find just cause to halt a movement of oppression by resorting to force have to take the risk of reading the signs of the times. This is indeed a very difficult task; it is so easy to be wise after the event. Solzhenitsyn raised this very question about when to resist in *The Gulag Archipelago* and suggested that if, instead of meekly accepting oppression and arrest, the people had opposed the security forces in the USSR then 'notwithstanding all of Stalin's thirst, the cursed machine would have ground to a halt'.[126]

This requirement of just cause cannot be separated entirely from other conditions for a just revolution. A cause is also rendered just if all other ways of changing a situation have been pursued without success and if there is a realistic prospect of introducing a better order and greater justice than those that obtain in the present. The former of these considerations directs attention to the next requirement, while the latter will be reviewed as the sixth item.

3. *Last Resort*

Christians, as I have suggested previously, must always be reluctant to kill; consequently they should not be over hasty to engage in armed revolution until they are reasonably convinced that no other way of improving an extreme situation is possible. If all means of legal criticism and legal action have been tried courageously and patiently without success, if every effort to seek a solution by negotiation and conciliation has come to nothing, if an important section of the community has found its most cherished and vital ends and interests thwarted and denied through political channels, then resort to force must be regarded as just, if the cause is just. Even Jacques Ellul is prepared to allow that 'while I cannot call violence good, legitimate, and just, I find its use condonable

(1) when a man is in despair and sees no other way out, or (2) when a hypocritically just and peaceful situation must be exposed for what it is in order to end it.'[127]

In particular, if it has become apparent that the language of force is the only one understood by the oppressors, those who wield force against them may reasonably claim that they do not want it but cannot avoid it if they are to be free human beings, recovering and affirming their dignity as they stand on their own feet. The questions to be faced are: can we, or must we, seek to attain our aims now, or can we afford patience and evolution? Can we achieve our goals within the legally sanctioned system of conflict resolution – if such exists – or must we operate outside the law?

To decide that resistance is necessary is not immediately to define the means. In certain situations nonviolent resistance may be feasible and right; in others force will be the only way to gain redress. It is not a matter of either one or the other, irrespective of circumstances. It is only by a careful analysis in the situation that the basis of choice can be laid.

4. Just Goals

Just goals are the necessary corollary of just cause, for if the latter embraces, e.g. oppression then the aim must be freedom, or if starvation and malnutrition are grounds for revolt then its goal must be a fairer distribution of available resources.

Just goals also refer to right intention, i.e. to the purpose to suppress disorder and evil and ensure peaceful conditions in which what is good and righteous may flourish. Consequently a revolution that is entirely negative in its aims, seeking no more than to tear down and destroy, could not be regarded as just. In so far as a movement has little idea of the shape of the projected new society, it is self-defeating. It organizes itself in response to the dominant structures of power and risks preserving, as if in a photographic negative, the very shape of the power it wants to abolish. 'Negation,' says Rubem Alves, 'may expel an evil spirit, but it cannot create a positive reality.'[128] Not to have a programme for revolution but simply to regard being a revolutionary as all important is to engage in an action which is anti-intellectual and irrational. Speaking in 1968 of the current protest movements, the Solicitor General of the USA, E. N. Griswood, observed with regret that 'most protest seems reflexive rather than cerebral, motivated by a desire to reject established positions and policies than by deliberate preference for some alternatives.'[129] Equally to be repudiated is an anti-institutional stance. If a revolution is for gaining and using power, how can it operate without organizations and institutions? A purely destructive approach is really *laissez-faire* since it assumes that to destroy what exists will of itself bring about progress.

Christians in the past have stressed the dangers of disorder more than those of oppression, but, while this is a mistake, it would be irresponsible for them to engage in a revolution against an existing order unless they had some clear vision of a new order to replace it. In other words, resistance has to be offered in the name of something positive that will succeed what is to be overthrown. This does not mean that some perfect blueprint is to be devised, because once a revolution is in train there is an inescapable fluidity; hence any plan has to be flexible and adaptable to changing circumstances, but to have no plan whatsoever is to have no justification.

Of course such feelings as envy and greed will survive a revolution, but 'this truth', comments Berdyaev, 'does not exclude the possibility, nay the necessity, of enquiring what social régime is likely to bring the most equitable and least prejudicial results to human souls.'[130] Just goals therefore require some preplanning with the intention of changing social conditions and establishing greater justice for all. One participates in the knowledge that the revolution will not usher in the millennium, for it is directed towards a practical future, involving an attempted fusion of the old conflicting forces and the production of a new synthesis in society – to say this is to point to what is human, fallible and short of the absolute. Yet unless there is a constantly renewed concern for the establishment of peace and reconciliation, no revolution can be regarded as a sign of the Kingdom of God.

5. *Just Means*

The original purpose of the theory of the right to go to war (*jus ad bellum*), it will be recalled, was to limit war – by emphasis upon just cause, last resort and just goals – and also to decrease brutality – by emphasis upon just means (*jus in bello*). This particular requirement therefore is essentially one that aims to set limits to what human beings may justifiably do to others. As Paul Ramsey observed of the just war, 'the justification of participation in conflict at the same time severely limited war's conduct. What justified also limited.'[131] Although ends, to a certain extent, justify means, they do not, *pace* certain Marxists, justify *any* means. Morality does not go on holiday when armed conflict breaks out. To engage in a revolution is not to say that anything goes. Force may be called for, if there is just cause, e.g. defence of neighbour, but the elementary rules of humanity have to be observed. Even in the very act of using force, it must be questioned. Force is to be undertaken and only exercised within an action that is obviously inspired by justice and peace. The injustice of the opponents' aggression does not exempt anyone from controls and norms.

Consequently it should be recognized that there has to be a proportionality of means to end and also a discrimination between means. If force is allowed to go unrestrained, it can go beyond its specific military purposes. In this connexion the principle of double-effect should be noted. This is based upon the distinction between the intended and merely foreseeable effect of a voluntary action. Suppose I go to the defence of someone who is being mugged. I will not intend to kill the assailant, but if I have time to reflect I may foresee that his death could result. If, in the struggle, I do actually kill him, I am not guilty of murder. Yet the means employed may on occasion be such that it would be nonsense to suppose that the effect was not intended. If I drop an atom bomb on a city, saying that it is simply to destroy a munitions factory, I cannot but be aware that the result will be the obliteration of an entire area. Hence one must not use the principle of double-effect in an attempt to justify what is clearly foreseeable as wrong. The saturation bombing of Cologne in World War II was clearly a wicked act and no amount of juggling with the principle of double-effect will justify it. However if a plane is sent to destroy a rocket factory and through unintended lack of accuracy the bomb, of restricted power, falls on a nearby orphanage, the principle of double-effect does permit one to say that the crew of the aircraft are not guilty of murder.

For revolutionaries to engage in a welter of destruction is certainly wrong and they cannot plead double-effect on their own behalf. What is the point, in any case, of destroying large areas of a country one wants to liberate? Where is the good in alienating public opinion by acts of mass terror when the aim should be to promote revolutionary consciousness? It may be possible to define morally legitimate targets, such as a doctor who is known to have assisted in torture, but this selective action is essentially different from indiscriminate attacks, which do not differentiate between combatants and noncombatants. This is the basis for declaring

IRA bombing to be wrong – to leave explosives in railway stations or public houses, without as is frequently the case any warning at all before they are detonated, is just hitting out at all and sundry to the complete ignoring of the need to discriminate. Hi-jacking belongs to the same category. When the travellers in an aircraft belong to neither side in a particular dispute, noncombatant immunity has gone out of the window and *jus in bello* has departed with it.

No Christian can agree with the attitude of certain revolutionaries who are prepared to say that 'what we affirm is that we must follow the road to liberation, even if it costs millions of atomic victims'.[132] No Christian can endorse the sentiments of Che Guevara when he upholds 'hatred as a factor in struggle; intransigent hatred for the enemy, which impels one to exceed the natural limitations of the human being and transforms him into an effective, violent, selective and cold killing machine'.[133] It is no doubt easier to bring oneself to kill if one hates, but it is possible to kill without malice or a spirit of vengeance. After all, according to Marxist analysis, which in this particular is very apposite, oppressors are not just to be envisaged in individualistic terms as the enemy. They are as much victims of the system as those they keep in subjection.[134] They are as much in need of liberation as anyone else. When love strives against love, then such oppressors, if they resist, may have to be killed, but this is to be done in a spirit of repentance.

Failure to perceive and act upon this truth means that one has not appreciated the dialectical relationship of means and ends. 'The end,' says H. Marcuse, 'must be operative in the repressive means for attaining the end.' Moreover, to continue to cite Marcuse, 'no matter how rationally one may justify revolutionary means – in terms of the demonstrable chance of obtaining freedom and happiness for future generations, and thereby justify violating existing rights and liberties and life itself, there are forms of violence and suppression which no revolutionary situation can justify: they negate the very end for which the revolution is a means. Such are arbitrary violence, cruelty, and indiscriminate terror.'[135]

It is only when they have a total respect for human beings, joined to a profound love of peace, that Christians may engage in revolution and seek to differentiate between the means they employ. Very relevant to this consideration is a statement in *The Times*' leader of 10 December 1974:

Most Christians are not pacifists. They believe in the right of an oppressed or attacked people to take up arms in its own defence. But it is the special role of the clergy to keep alive the virtue of compassion in the nation at war, to remind the fighter that his enemy is also his brother and that public peril cannot justify private hate.

It should perhaps be added that this is not only the role of the clergy but of any Christian when a revolution is under way.

Yet Christians cannot escape a certain tension which can be indicated by a question: if collective resort to conflict is undertaken, how can one ensure the preservation of human values in the course of hostilities? Christians can never be certain that they will be successful in this and they may be unfaithful to the gospel, but they have to assume their responsibilities. They may have to choose and act in a way that appears right and with the hope of forgiveness.

It is precisely here that pacifism appears to have played an unfortunate role. Because of its refusal to distinguish between the shedding of innocent blood and the shedding of any human blood whatsoever, it has, in the view of G. E. M. Anscombe, 'corrupted enormous numbers of people'.[136] It has done this because, although many people do not accept absolute pacifism, they have accepted the pacifist view that there is no distinction to be made in the shedding of blood and so they hold that when a war has broken out there are no limits to what may be done to achieve victory. But if one is to speak of just means such a surrender of discrimination cannot be endorsed. Force should be controlled in the interests of morality. Because conflict and the exercise of power are unavoidable in a revolutionary situation, this does not mean that we cannot examine what forms of force are unjustifiable and when they are disproportionate to just goals.

Those who have studied guerrilla warfare are aware that threats and terror are not their normal weapons *vis-à-vis* the population as a whole. 'No guerrilla,' observes R. Tabor, 'can afford to use it against the people on whose support and confidence he depends for his life as well as for his political existence.'[137] The guerrilla, in Mao's famous phrase, is like a fish in the sea; if he fouls it and turns it into a hostile environment he cannot survive. This necessary limitation of violence, if just means are to be employed, can be best illustrated by a consideration of torture.

According to the *Oxford English Dictionary* torture is the infliction of excruciating pain, as practised by cruel tyrants, savages, brigands, etc., in hatred or revenge or as a means of extortion. It is especially used to force a confession or to compel an unwilling witness to give information. It is closely associated with anguish and agony and the verb itself implies acting violently. The term derives from *torquere*, to twist or bend, and so built into it is a description of some of the methods employed for either physical or psychological torture. Yet torture is to be understood as not only descriptive but also normative. It is a method of interrogation. It can be said that as killing is to murder, as justifiable force is to unjustifiable force, so interrogation is to torture. It is by its very nature violent and therefore it involves the use of unjustifiable force.

Attempts are made to justify torture in certain circumstances on the grounds that it may succeed in extracting information about the enemies' movements or plans and so help to decrease loss of life and lead to more swift success. Here the ends are being used to justify any means and in fact the supposed advantages have to be balanced against certain adverse effects. These may be illustrated from the Algerian war of independence. Whatever the short term benefits of torture, in the way of obtaining the names of other activists, in the long term it certainly increased the alienation of the natives from the French.[138]

There are other effects, inseparable from torture, that have to be taken into account. Torture brutalizes the torturer and dehumanizes the victim. So Fanon, despite his romanticization of violence, concluded *The Wretched of the Earth* with forty-eight pages of case histories to show how torture produces mental disorders.[139] He himself was strongly opposed to it and demanded that discipline should be exercised against those revolutionaries who acted contrary to the rules of war. He condemned the adoption by them of the methods of their adversaries.[140] Torture is so evidently cruel that it denies human values and its exercise impedes the practice of those values during a period of armed strife. This in turn decreases the chances of eventually arriving at a settlement that embodies these values. It is by considerations such as these that some limits must be placed on the barbarity of man to man once the revolutionary struggle has been undertaken. Without such limitations, without the constant application of moral maxims within the situation, the means employed may pass beyond all possibility of justification and so impair the justice of the revolution itself.

6. *Likely Success*

Common sense, quite apart from moral considerations, dictates that there should be no resort to armed conflict without a reasonable prospect of success. Success, in this context, has three aspects: (*a*) victory must not be gained at such a price that the suffering it involves is greater than the existing suffering that might otherwise be held to justify the rebellion; (*b*) there must be a good chance of eventual military victory; (*c*) there must be a strong likelihood that the just goals of the revolution will be attained. These three aspects of course are closely interrelated. There can be no achievement of goals without military victory, while the suffering entailed in the uprising is clearly connected with the struggle leading to victory.

(*a*) Rebellion, involving bloodshed, undoubtedly breaks certain Christian moral guide lines. If I kill someone, even in defending others against aggression, I cannot call that act of killing a work of love towards the person concerned. These rules are to be observed in normal circumstances in order to avoid the unwanted evils that result from disregarding them. Nevertheless, B. Gert has rightly emphasized that there is a point at which the amount of evil to be prevented by keeping a rule is so much more than the amount of evil caused by breaking it, that one ought to break it.[141]

There is frequently more distress and suffering caused by economics than by military battles. There are situations in which the injustices do outweigh the evils of armed struggle. Hence one has to calculate the chances of a future society against the chances of an existing one. Such a calculation must take into account the sacrifices exacted from those living under an established order, the number of victims it claims and the possibility of revolution improving those conditions. Planned revolution is called for and not blind rebellion. The outcome of an unsuccessful uprising can be more violent than if it had not been undertaken. Thus in the violence of 1948–58 in Colombia, 200,000 peasants died – to no effect.

Yet a successful revolution is usually less destructive than an existing unjust *status quo*. So the costs in terms of personal violence were almost certainly lower in the Cuban Revolution than the gains in the reduction of structural violence that had obtained under Batista. Indeed Fidel Castro was not in error when, addressing a congress of doctors in February 1966, he declared: 'In reality, it is not the revolutionary struggle which costs the greatest number of lives but misery and exploitation.'[142] He was of course speaking against the background of a revolution that had overthrown the previous corrupt régime. The chances of military success have therefore to be taken into account in assessing the extent to which the evils of a civil war are less than a patient endurance of existing evils.

(b) In calculating the chances of military victory, absolute certainty is impossible. The future is never sure; the unforeseen may happen. Because of this inescapable unpredictability some, such as Karl Popper, would regard the use of force as unjustifiable. But consideration of possible consequences does provide data relevant to moral choice; if this were to be ruled out because complete foreknowledge is not attainable, then the conservative supporters of the *status quo* would be left in an impregnable position. Neither the English nor the French nor the American Revolutions would have taken place if this argument were held to be binding. Yet, as Marcuse has stressed, each led to a demonstrable enlargement of the range of human freedom. The concept of the rights of man came out of the French and American Revolutions and that of the value of tolerance was the product of the English Revolution.[143] Moreover they did bring about a redistribution of social wealth and this remained true despite later reaction and restoration. The countervailing argument that this would have happened in any case is not valid. There is no possible foundation in fact for such a speculation. We can only say with confidence that 'there is the fact of moral advance for humanity brought on by these great revolutions, and no adequate grounds have been given for believing that in those circumstances – those great turning points of history – advances could have occurred in anything like a comparable way without the use of force against the old order.'[144]

However ethical justification after the fact is no help in making moral judgments in a situation. But in any and every situation, let alone a revolutionary one, moral choice has to be made without certainty about the eventual outcome.

> In any kind of action, says Staughton Lynd, where one does involve the whole of oneself, the element of unpredictability or lack of control over the whole situation is very much a part of the nature of such action. And *something* like that, I think, is intended by the language of the New Testament about losing one's life to find it.[145]

Yet it is in the situation that the calculations have to be made and this is by no means as uncertain a procedure as some would have us think. We are not solely in the area of guesswork. For a revolution to succeed it must have a monopoly of social force. This can be expressed in the form of an equation:

$$\text{Social Force} = \text{Organization} + \text{Propaganda} + \text{Agitation}[146]$$

By organization is meant the support of the populace sufficient to ensure bases, means of escape, recruitment, etc. Propaganda refers to conscientization whereby the people are enabled to appreciate their plight and their sympathetic understanding of the struggle is engaged. Agitation refers specifically to armed insurrection, properly so-called, whether in the form of guerrilla activity or companies of troops.

An alternative, but complementary, analysis of the conditions for success is the following:

(i) There must be an unstable political situation, marked by sharp social divisions and usually, though not always, by a stagnant economy.

(ii) There must be a clearly defined political objective, based on firm moral grounds, that can be understood and accepted by the majority of the people as desirable and worthy of sacrifice.

(iii) There must be an oppressive power with which no political compromise is possible.

(iv) There must be some form of revolutionary political organization, capable of providing dedicated and consistent leadership towards the accepted goals.

(v) There must be the clear possibility or even probability of victory through generating an ever increasing support.[147]

As they stand these five points may seem highly theoretical, although Richard Tabor, from whom I have derived them, has based them upon a careful analysis of many twentieth-century revolutionary movements, summarizing the lessons to be learned from them. As reproduced, they are abstract; they have to be applied in the situation. In order to indicate how this skeleton may be clothed with flesh, I propose to attempt a brief application to the situation in Ulster, as it is at the time of writing, to examine the role of the IRA and to estimate its chances of success.

In Ulster there is certainly an unstable political situation, with sharp social divisions and a by no means buoyant economy. The various protest movements and demonstrations in support of civil rights have exposed the extent to which the system has been unjust towards the Catholic minority and favourable towards the Protestants. The first point above is then certainly a characteristic of the

Ulster situation. When we come to the second item – a political objective acceptable to the majority – we can immediately perceive that it is inapplicable. The IRA does have political goals – the unification of Ireland, possibly within a federal system – but this is not accepted by the Loyalist majority as either desirable or worthy of sacrifice. Time and again they have made this abundantly clear; they will not accept union with Eire at any price. Some Catholics too would prefer to stay independent of the south. Since then any revolutionary movement, according to Debray, 'must have the support of the masses or disappear',[148] a cool calculation of IRA chances suggests that they cannot succeed. It is questionable too whether or not the IRA objectives can be said to have a sound moral basis. There is little morality about frontiers *per se*. The divisions between the states of Africa, for example, are little more than the result of the drawing of arbitrary lines on the map by previous imperialist occupiers of those territories. The division between Ulster and Eire is no less the product of historical circumstances and the fact that both are parts of the same land mass, which has a smaller coast line than that of Africa, does not affect the issue. It is true that there has grown up a recognition of the right of a people to self-determination – but to apply this to Ulster in terms of majority decision is to know what the answer is. Hence another of the essential elements for an IRA success is lacking.

Opinions may differ as to how far Westminster, with its direct rule and its introduction of internment, constitutes an oppressive power, but few can doubt that successive British governments have sought to bring about a political compromise. To date such proposals as power sharing have proved unacceptable to both the IRA and the Protestants, but neither side is remarkable for its realism in opposing this plan and failing to come forward with a viable alternative.

The IRA is a form of revolutionary organization, although its leadership has not been notable for its consistency. However, as long as the second condition – acceptability to a majority – does not obtain, and as long as the third condition is doubtfully present, the chances of gaining increased support and therefore success in terms of the fifth item are precluded.

Since the nature of guerrilla warfare is such that it cannot be contained by any army using conventional methods and weapons, no doubt the IRA could continue as a running sore. If the Protestants refuse to surrender their absolute domination and so limit the existing injustice, the struggle could well go on in a condition of stalemate. In other words, if the IRA had made a serious analysis of the situation in Ulster and had calculated the chances of success, in accordance with the lessons to be learned from other revolutions, they would have had to recognize that their efforts were doomed to failure and they would not have launched their bloody struggle. 'Marx, correctly I believe,' observes Kai Nielsen, 'stressed the folly of trying to make a revolution before the socio-economic conditions were ripe and before the revolution had a mass base.'[149] There must then be a realistic appraisal of the situation, and while the future cannot be known with exactitude, we are not left entirely in the dark. Compare the IRA with the circumstances of the blacks in the United States – there is little doubt that an armed uprising there would lead to greater oppression and to a worsened situation. *Pace* Popper, calculation is possible and no revolution can be deemed just unless this is seriously undertaken.

It is indeed true, to quote further from Nielsen, 'that we should not let concern for certainty cripple practice, but we need not and indeed should not view ourselves as simply responding to heart-felt anguish at the spectacle of injustice and oppression and then rebelling quite independently of any calculation of our chances or of what our revolt will lead us into.'[150]

Of course revolutionary war is not just concerned with military operations. There must also be an action upon the minds of the populace (conscientization) to awaken them to their situation and to encourage them to seek a solution. It is reasonable then to think of a revolution as involving several stages, of which the first may be the coming into existence of a revolutionary group to raise the consciousness of the masses. Even if there is no immediate prospect of overthrowing a government and defeating its forces, the mere existence of such a group symbolizes the possibility of ultimate change. Revolutions can have small beginnings – witness the landing of Castro at the head of eighty-two rebels on 2 December 1956, leading to the takeover of the country by January 1959. But precisely because the conditions outlined above were present, the Batista régime fell like a rotten apple.

The Christian, then, has to steer a middle course between constant indecision, which paralyzes the nerves of action, and a fanaticism which breaks through these words of René Debray: 'For a revolutionary, failure is a spring board. As a source of theory it is richer than victory; it accumulates experience and knowledge.'[151]

To opt for revolution is not to accept the naïve belief in the universal efficacy of violence to improve the human condition. But the force of armed conflict is not the only nor the greatest evil in the world.

(*c*) I know of no better expression of the necessary relationship between the justice of revolution and the possibility of attaining its goals, than these words of the English Leveller John Lilburn.

> Knowing that in our consciences, not in the sight of God, we could not be justified, except we persevered to the fulfilling of the end; The Restauration of the Fundamental Laws and Rights of the Nation; and I especially who had spilt both my own and other men's bloods in open fight, for the attainment thereof, look'd upon my self as no other or better than a murtherer of my brethren and Country-men, if I should only by my so doing make way for raising another sort of men into power, and so enable them to trample our Laws and Liberties more under foot then ever.[152]

Lilburn had no illusions that the killing inseparable from an armed uprising would be violent and tantamount to murder unless justice and freedom were to follow. Unless the force used is a means to establish and promote freedom and happiness it falls short of justification. This implies the existence of rational criteria for determining the possibility of freedom in a specific historical situation. There must be grounds for thinking that a revolution can grasp liberty and that it is a means adequate to this end. Unless this is so, there are but two alternatives: to reject *a priori* or to endorse *a priori* every revolution. Freedom itself is not a static condition; it is a process that involves the alteration and even negation of established ways of life. The form and content of freedom change with every new stage in civilization. We always exist in relative unfreedom because of the continuing gap between actuality and possibility. But freedom presupposes liberation as a step from one state of freedom in unfreedom to a subsequent state. The probability of this advance is in proportion to the justice of the cause, the justice of the means and the likelihood of military victory. There is of course a risk, but one that has to be taken in the name of the God of freedom.

It is here that the concept of the just war in Jewish thinking is germane to Christians. To the Jew, the taking of life is sinful, no matter what the conditions. It is a reproach before God. So during the Passover Seder when the ten plagues in Egypt are recounted, each participant spills a drop of wine from the cup as they are successively mentioned. The cup symbolizes the cup of life.

> The lesson learned is that one does not enjoy a full cup because God's creatures were slaughtered in the plagues and suffered anguish; the Jew's own joy is to be diminished in his compassion for Egyptian suffering. Although Jews regard Egyptian suffering to have been justly imposed because of their hard-heartedness in not permitting the Jews their freedom, nevertheless if human beings have to be killed, whatever the reason, something is wrong. War, bloodshed, violence – these violate God's will for mankind, and we are enjoined to feel the pain of human brutality and repent.[153]

So we conclude this section with a point I have made before. Even a just revolution does not justify a Christian. The quest for the conditions of a just revolution is not a search for self-justification. Rather it is to find guide lines for conduct that can only be undertaken in the hope of forgiveness and by pursuing reconciliation and peace as the ultimate end.

Reconciliation and Peace

According to Paul, it was God 'who through Christ reconciled us to himself and gave us the ministry of reconciliation' (II Cor. 5. 18). Mindful of this, and also of Jacques Ellul's jibe that to accept a theology of revolution in place of a theology of reconciliation is to reject the incarnation,[154] we have, in this final section, to relate what has gone before to the themes of reconciliation and peace.

All revolutions are concerned with liberation, in the sense of freedom-from; and every just revolution, in achieving its goals, seeks to provide the conditions for freedom-for.[155] This distinction between the negative and positive aspects of freedom enables us to appreciate the close relationship between liberation and reconciliation. In a situation of oppressors/oppressed, both groups are dehumanized. So, as I have previously argued, love of the oppressed requires us to identify with them against the oppressors in order that they may advance to human wholeness, while love of the oppressors is shown by struggling against them to save them from themselves and from the structures they subserve. Liberation therefore has to take place before reconciliation of the two sides is possible – without liberation there is not reconciliation but conciliation. Hence, to illustrate this by reference to a specific situation, J. D. Roberts remarks that 'there can be no real reconciliation between black and white henceforth without liberation'.[156] Those who are to know the true freedom of the children of God must first be reconciled with their brethren. Liberation or freedom-from is indeed a precondition of reconciliation, which, in its turn, is an element of freedom-for. In other words, freedom-for involves reconciliation, but the latter is only possible after liberation. In this sense, a revolution, in so far as it attains the goal of liberation, is on the way to freedom, including therein reconciliation.

Reconciliation however is not to be secured without a price. This is too often forgotten and then it becomes a mere tag to sanction the *status quo*, being reduced to conciliation. Reconciliation means the bringing again into an harmonious relationship after estrangement, while conciliation refers to the gaining of good will by acts which induce friendly feeling – to conciliate can mean to placate or soothe. The result of conciliation is often that things remain more or less as they were before, apart from some minor adjustments. Reconciliation can be misinterpreted as conciliation in such a way that it always gives advantages to the powerful and not to the powerless. When reconciliation is misunderstood as conciliation then, to give an example in terms of the race issue, it is simply translated as integration, whereas the church should recognize that integration which bypasses the challenge of a Black Power movement means resurrection without the cross. Christ, after all, is our peace (Eph. 2.14) precisely because he is the crucified one. Reconciliation is no cheap option.

Often when people say they prefer reconciliation to conflict, they appear to be choosing a peaceful alternative to the use of force. But it is questionable how far it really is peaceable and how far it is always a feasible alternative to armed struggle. There is no simple way of reconciliation – reconciliation through the cross may well require the suffering of a revolutionary uprising in order to bring about that liberation that will provide its basis. A refusal to face the cost of revolution out of a profound concern for reconciliation may be no more than a shallow sentimentality that in the end will be more costly in human lives and less respectful of the human person. Reconciliation can be a pious shibboleth to justify inaction, whereas love embodied in action aimed towards reconciliation may require revolution. Reconciliation and revolution then are not necessary antitheses, since the latter may lead to the former.

There is a further mistake often made by those who persist in affirming this antithesis and that is the failure to realize that reconciliation requires identification. Jesus was the reconciler precisely because he identified himself fully with humankind – this is what the incarnation is about. As reconciler, he was no third, neutral, party mediating between two opponents. Jesus' liberating action was also his act of reconciliation because he was identified with those whom he came to set free. To this extent Jesus was partisan – as God is too. He identified with the poor and outcast, with those on the margin of society, and he attacked their oppressors, the Pharisees. Yet, at the same time, he allowed the possibility of reconciliation for these latter by remaining open towards them, sharing their table fellowship on occasion (Luke 11.37). In so doing the very one who was a reconciler became a sign of conflict, one who, in the words of Simeon, was 'set for the fall and rising of many in Israel, and for a sign that is spoken against' (Luke 2.34). Should Christians, in their true imitation of Christ, expect less? Should they not be prepared to acknowledge that their obedience to the divine will can entail their being regarded as subversives, as partisans, as signs of conflict rather than simply as ambassadors of reconciliation? But, is there any other route to reconciliation in certain circumstances of massive oppression? According to both Matthew and Luke, with slightly variant wording, Jesus declared that he did not come to bring peace but a sword or division (Matt. 10.34; Luke 12.51).

There is nothing then in a theology of revolution that sets it against a theology of reconciliation. Indeed a theology of revolution demands reconciliation as one of its themes, and in certain circumstances reconciliation, if it is to be actualized, may demand a revolution.

Reconciliation is also to be regarded as a precondition of peace. But peace too, like freedom with which it is closely connected, is to be interpreted both negatively and positively. From its negative aspect, peace is simply the absence of overt conflict; there is peace of this kind when no direct personal violence is being perpetrated. But, says Yoskiaki Iisaka, 'there is a state of peace and order in which freedom suffocates and injustice thrives'.[157] Or, in the words of John Macquarrie, ' "peace" is too often understood as simply the dampening down of conflicts which were aimed at changing the *status quo*'.[158] But a situation of oppression, where all forms of strife are held in check, is not one of positive peace. To acquiesce is not to be a peacemaker but a peace avoider. Merely to demand obedience to an established disorder, which is violent through and through, will not qualify anyone for the blessedness of which Jesus spoke when he said: 'Blessed are the peacemakers' (Vulgate, *pacifici*; Matt. 5.9). This negative peace is that which Jeremiah condemned when he upbraided his fellow countrymen, 'from the least to the greatest of them', for saying ' "Peace, peace", when there is no peace' (Jer. 6.13f.).

Positive peace is not something static; it is not a condition but a process.[159] Peace, as Owen Wingrave says in Benjamin Britten's opera of that name, is not acquiescence but searching. It is that which characterizes the Kingdom of God, which is 'righteousness and peace and joy in the Holy Spirit' (Rom. 14.17). Consequently it has an eschatological character – it is already but not yet – and this peace with God often means conflict with the world. Such conflict may take the form of revolution, which, if it is a sign of the Kingdom, is a stage on the way to peace.

The content of positive peace is indicated in the Bible in a variety of ways and it usually translates the word *shalom*. This refers to wholeness, fulness, righteousness and trust. It includes the idea of harmonious community. It denotes the exercise of mutual responsibility. It embraces, too, salvation, not in the negative sense of freedom-from but in its positive meaning of freedom-for, i.e. for growth, neighbourliness, reconciliation and hope. Such peace comprises material wellbeing (Zech. 8.12), but it is impossible without justice (Isa. 48.22). It does not exist where there is social unrighteousness (Jer. 8.11). When structural violence is overcome and replaced by social justice, then positive peace is a possibility. When revolutionary engagement takes on structural violence it is on the way to peace, and so the option of revolution must be open to Christians. This is a logical conclusion, because if in certain circumstances a just revolution can result in greater social justice, in an improvement in living conditions and in that liberation that is the condition of reconciliation, it is contributing to the creation of peace.

Is not a theology of love a theology of resistance? Is not a theology of resistance a theology of revolution and liberation? How can there be a theology of revolution that will commend itself to Christians, if it does not include a concern for reconciliation and peace? Yet, after all, is there any point in speaking of a theology of revolution unless it is also taken to imply a revolution within the church?[160]

REFERENCES

Books listed in the Bibliography are referred to by section and number

1. INTRODUCTION

1. (VII. 29), 1
2. (I. 4), 24
3. For a full account of the debate see (III. 1), 653–83.
4. T. Rentdorff in (VI. 39), 204f.
5. Antoine (VI. 4), 131f.
6. Temple (VI. 69), 21
7. Barth (I. 8), 16
8. C. Elliott in (VI. 39), 18
9. Alencar (VI. 1), 10
10. Quoted by Eppstein (I. 7), 58
11. (VII. 23), 24
12. Hence the Board for Social Responsibility of the Church of England set up a Working Party whose views were presented in the valuable report, quoted above (I. 4).

2. POLITICAL INVOLVEMENT

1. Glock and Stark (III. 6), ch. 1, specify five dimensions, adding knowledge as a distinct category, but this is identical with belief.
2. Towler (III. 11), 132–7
3. I am indebted to the Rev. Robert Hamill for the substance of this paragraph; his ideas were formulated in a sermon entitled 'God is a political God', preached in Marsh Chapel, Boston University, on 22 September 1968.
4. Robinson (VI. 64), 113
5. Temple (VI. 70), 35f.
6. (VI. 20), 67
7. Gutiérrez (VI. 34), 11
8. (I. 20), 8
9. On the subject of politics and the liturgy see the entire number of *Concilium*, 2.10.1974.
10. Metz (VI. 48), 4
11. de Clerq (VI. 21), 124
12. Bonhoeffer (I. 1), 202
13. *Joint Statement by the United Church Board for World Ministries of the United Church of Christ (USA) and the United Church of Canada Board of World Ministries.*

14. de Clerq (VI. 21), 121
15. Bonhoeffer (I. 1), 288
16. *Ibid.*
17. Rousseau (IV. 20), 4.8
18. Ellul (VI. 29), 22–5
19. Robinson (VI. 64), 16
20. Dewart (VI. 27), 55f.
21. Gutiérrez (VI. 34), 159
22. Quoted by Coste (VI. 25), 121
23. Schillebeeckx (VI. 67), 29
24. Bonhoeffer (I. 1), 115
25. Barth (VI. 9), IV. 3.2; 936
26. *Ibid.* 938
27. *Ibid.* 939. Cf. Rossel (VI. 65), 72–5
28. Wicker (VI. 72), 64
29. McCabe (VI. 47), 160
30. 39, quoted *ibid.* 160 n. 1
31. Brandon (VI. 16)
32. Cullmann (IV. 5)
33. Richardson (VI. 61), 43f.
34. Coste (VI. 25), 28
35. Micklem (VI. 49), 135
36. Herzog (VI. 36), 184f.
37. Moltmann (VI. 51), 138
38. Augustine, *Ep.* 136.2
39. Bennett (VI. 10), 3f.
40. Furnish (I. 9), 84ff., 27
41. Baillie (VI. 5), 180; cf. Davies (VI. 26), 84ff.
42. S. Esobar in Griffiths (V. 18), 98
43. M. P. Fogarty in Matthews (V. 27), 342
44. de Clerq (VI. 21), 128
45. *Ibid.* 53
46. *Ibid.* 54
47. Wicker (VI. 72), 28
48. Reamonn (VI. 60), 566
49. Miller (VI. 50), 95
50. Inge (VI. 38), 45
51. H. Naier in Peukert (VI. 57), 1–25
52. These arguments have been developed by Steeman (VI. 68), 40–7
53. *Ibid.* 45
54. (VII. 19), 8f.
55. Wicker (VI. 72), 8
56. Antoine (VI. 4), 134
57. *Ibid.* 111

58. 'Socialism and Religion', *Novaya Zhizn*, No. 28, 16 December 1905, printed in Lenin (IV. 16), 11f.

59. *Loc. cit.*

60. de Clerq (VI. 21), 53

61. Russell (VI. 66), 30

62. (VI. 45), 64

63. Moore (VI. 52), 111f.

64. (VI. 20), 110

65. (VI. 39), 146f.

66. (VI. 7), 89

67. Ramsey (I. 21), 151

68. J. H. Cone in Moore (VI. 52), 55

69. Quoted by Fanon (IV. 11), 63

70. Barth (VI. 8), 14

71. *Ibid.* 74

72. *Ibid.* 58

73. Quoted by Camara (VI. 18), 175

74. Cf. B. Blanshard in de George (I. 10), 1–23

75. Cf. J. Margolis in Held (IV. 15), 53f.

76. Downie (I. 6), 35f.

77. Echegoyen (VI. 28), 464f.

3. RESISTANCE TO THE STATE

1. Gerth and Mills (III. 5), 78

2. Rousseau (IV. 20), 4.8

3. Coste (VI. 25), 41ff.

4. Leenhardt (VI. 44), 221–36; Cullmann (IV. 5), 55ff.

5. *The Tenure of Kings and Magistrates* in Milton (IV. 17), 464

6. Bennett (VI. 10), 7

7. Bennett (IV. 2), 27

8. See the exposition of E. Wolf's ideas in Childress (I. 3), 114–23

9. H.-W. Bartsch in Bennett (I. 2), 66

10. Cullmann (IV. 5), 86

11. *Adv. Haer.* 5.23.2

12. Sabine (IV. 21), 161

13. *Ibid.* 94, 117

14. *Ibid.* 150

15. *Ibid.* 244

16. Carlyle (IV. 3), 25–35

17. *Ibid.* 458

18. *Ibid.* 99

19. *Comm. on the 'Sentences'*, ii. D.44, 2, 2

20. *Policraticus*, III. 15

21. Carlyle (IV. 3), 459

22. Allen (IV. 1), 15–34

23. *On Good Works*, XII

24. Figgis (IV. 12), 89f.

25. Tyndale (IV. 23), 90, 93

26. *Ibid*. 87ff.

27. From the edition of 1899, SPCK, 591, 609

28. Davies (IV. 6), 92

29. More and Cross (VI. 53), 691ff.

30. Ramsey (I. 22), 118ff.

31. *Instit.*, 4.20.21

32. Allen (IV. 1), 104f.

33. Knox (VI. 41), III, 223

34. *Ibid*. 225

35. 'To the Lords and others professing the truth in Scotland' (1557), in Knox (VI. 41), IV, 284f.

36. 'The Appelation to the Nobility and Estates of Scotland' (1558), *ibid*. 501

37. 'A Letter to the Commonality of Scotland' (1558), *ibid*. 523–35

38. Knox (VI. 42), I, 146

39. I am not concerned to trace the development of Knox's views in relation to the historical circumstances; for an excellent account of this see Ridley (VI. 62).

40. Knox (VI. 42), II, 16

41. *Ibid*. 122

42. *Ibid*. 126

43. *Ibid*. 129

44. *Ibid*. 117f.

45. *Ibid*. 114

46. 'The First Blast of the Trumpet against the Monstrous Regiment of Women' (1558), Knox (VI. 41), IV. 4. Zwingli included the case of Manasseh (II Kings 21. 1–9) among the examples of divine punishment being meted out because of failure to resist. Zwingli (VI. 73), 344

47. Knox (VI. 41), IV. 436

48. 'A Godly Letter to the Faithful in London, etc.' (1554), *ibid.*, III, 190

49. 'The Ungirding of the Scottish Armour' (1559) quoted by Dickinson in his introduction to Knox (VI. 42), I, 111, n. 2.

50. *Ibid*. II. 17

51. *Ibid*. 136

52. 'The Appelation to the Nobility and Estates of Scotland' (1558), Knox (VI. 41), IV. 496. For Ebedmelech see Jer. 38. 7–13; 39. 16ff.

53. Knox (VI. 42), II. 17

54. 'Letter to the Queen Regent' (revised 1558), Knox (VI. 41), IV. 441

55. Knox (VI. 42), II. 120

56. Knox (VI. 41), IV. 540

57. Verney (IV. 24), 136
58. *Pro Populo Anglicano Defensio* (1651) in Woodhouse (IV. 25), 230
59. Walzer (V. 35), 1–4
60. *Ibid.* 11
61. *Ibid.* 130. For the influence of medieval mysticism on dissent which, in a Thomas Münzer, could spill over into revolution, see Ozment (V. 31).
62. Walzer (V. 35), 148
63. Cromwell (IV. 4), I, 340, Letter LXXXV
64. *Ibid.* 341
65. *Ibid.* 342
66. *Ibid.* 343
67. *Ibid.* 344
68. *Ibid.* 343
69. *Ibid.* 344
70. *Loc. cit.*
71. *Loc. cit.*
72. *Ibid.* 345
73. *Lex, Rex* (1644), XXX, reprinted in Woodhouse (IV. 25), 211
74. *Tenure* in Milton (IV. 17), 463
75. XXVIII, *ed. cit.*, 211
76. *Ed. cit.* 491
77. *Ibid.* 451
78. *Ibid.* 456
79. *Ibid.* 470
80. In Woodhouse (IV. 25), 229
81. *Loc. cit.*
82. *The Just Defence* (1653), 2, in Haller and Davies (IV. 14), 452
83. In relation to political theory one would have to speak about the concept of sovereignty being invested in the people as a whole, of the social contract theory, etc., while the arguments in favour of resistance would involve a review, *inter alia*, of John Locke's defence of the Revolution of 1688, etc. On the last see Dunne (IV. 8), 165–86.
84. G. J. Schochet in Held (IV. 15), 185
85. In Bennett (I. 2), 51
86. Cf. Miller (VII. 17), 49ff.
87. Macquarrie (VI. 46), 48
88. For an admirable exposition of this verse see Bonnard (VI. 15), 71ff.
89. Barth (VI. 8), 37–47
90. (I. 4), 13
91. Barth (VI. 8), 76
92. Gerth and Mills (III. 5), 120

4. LAW AND ORDER

1. Devlin (II. 3), 119

2. *Div. Instit.* 6.17
3. Ruinart (III. 8), 338
4. Cadoux (VI. 17), 528
5. Quoted by Griswold (II. 7), 729
6. Sibley (I. 26), 35
7. Berman (II. 1), 89
8. Hall (I. 11), 62ff.
9. Camara (VI. 18), 45
10. Hall (I. 11), 2
11. *Pro Cluentio*, 53.146
12. Goodhart (II. 6), 5
13. Lehmann (V. 24), ch. 11, A, 240ff.
14. Herzog (VI. 36), 113
15. *Republic*, 3.1.337
16. Camara (VI. 18), 106
17. Sibley (I. 26), 28
18. Veysey (II. 8), 16
19. G. J. Schochet in Held (IV. 15), 175–96
20. Sibley (I. 26), 49
21. *De Civ. Dei*, 4.5
22. Solzhenitsyn (III. 10), *passim*
23. Golunki and Strogovich (II. 5), 370
24. *Second Treatise on Civil Government*, chs. 11, 18
25. Cf. Sibley (I. 26), 59–70
26. *Nicom. Ethics*, 5.7
27. Brunner (II. 2), 31
28. Baird (VI. 6), 40
29. Quell and Schrenck (VI. 59), 44
30. *Cf.* the parable of the labourers in the vineyard (Matt. 20. 1–16).
31. Tillich (VI. 71), 71
32. Tillich (I. 28), 39
33. *Ibid.* 15
34. *Summa Theologica, Pr. Secunda, Qu.* 96, and *Secund. Secund., Qu.* 104
35. Devlin (II. 3), 19, 23
36. Hall (I. 11), 54
37. Devlin (II. 3), 119
38. Haag (VII. 14), 22
39. Thoreau (VII. 26), 3
40. *Ibid.* 2
41. *Ibid.* 10
42. *Ibid.* 6
43. Sibley (I. 26), 36–9
44. Tillich (I. 28), 20
45. Ramsey (I. 21), 89

46. *Ibid.* 78f. While I endorse this view, it should be pointed out, in order not to misrepresent Ramsey's thought, that he has modified it in subsequent works.

47. Outka and Ramsey (I. 19), 337
48. Devlin (II. 3), 20
49. Winfield (II. 9), 429
50. Ramsey (I. 23), 11
51. Hall (I. 11), 8
52. Bonhoeffer (I. 1), 207

5.   REVOLUTION

1. Arendt (V. 2), 8
2. de George (I. 10), 134
3. Debray (V. 10), 29
4. *Ibid.* 31
5. Cf. Snoek (V. 33), 20
6. Cf. Lincoln (V. 26), 221ff.
7. Gilmore (V. 16), 40–102
8. Roussel in (VII. 13), 157
9. *Politics*, 1302n
10. Quoted Debray (V. 10), 12
11. Garcia and Calle (V. 15), 7f.
12. Hymn 573 in *Hymns Ancient and Modern*
13. Cone (VI. 23), 29
14. Merton (VII. 16), 139
15. Middleton (V. 28), 129
16. Camara (VI. 19), 73
17. A. Gully in his introduction to Fanon (IV. 10), 12
18. Ogletree (V. 55), 53
19. *Loc. cit.*
20. Cf. Cone (VI. 22), 7
21. Jackson (III. 7), 67
22. *Ibid.* 68
23. Alves (VI. 2), 10
24. Berdyaev (VI. 13), 60
25. Newfield (IV. 18), 53
26. Alves *loc. cit.*
27. *Ibid.* 15
28. Berdyaev (VI. 11), 67
29. Davies (VI. 26), ch. 1
30. Jackson (III. 7), 75
31. Coste (VI. 25), 288
32. Häring (I. 12), 78
33. Niebuhr (VI. 54), 111
34. Cone (VI. 24), 35

35. Cone (VI. 22), 47
36. Gutiérrez (VI. 35), 60
37. Freire (VI. 31), 78
38. (VII. 8), 46
39. Moltmann (V. 29), 4. For a further illuminating discussion of 'newness' see Comblin (V. 9), 216ff.
40. Dewart (VI. 27), 53f; Ogletree (VI. 56), 186, 190
41. (V. 32), 72
42. Freire (VI. 31), 20
43. (VI. 39), 144
44. Moltmann (VI. 51), 51
45. Moore (VI. 52), 145
46. So the bishop of Crateus in Brazil quoted by Fragoso (VI. 30), 14
47. Herzog (VI. 36), 72
48. van den Heuvel (VI. 37), 46
49. W. Stringfellow in Geyer and Peerman (VI. 32), 131
50. McCabe (VI. 47), 133f.
51. Boston (V. 5), 147
52. Ozment (V. 31), 72f.
53. Hayward (V. 20), 103
54. Arendt (V. 2), 25
55. Berdyaev (VI. 13), 62
56. Fanon (IV. 9), 32
57. Arendt (V. 2), 136
58. Alves (VI. 2), 126
59. McCabe (VI. 47), 156
60. Moore (VI. 52), 155f.
61. (VI. 39), 62
62. Kümmel (VI. 43), 185
63. (VI. 7), 89
64. McCabe (VI. 47), 170
65. Gruber (IV. 13), 72
66. Lehmann (V. 24), 110. My first two types are the same as his. His third category is labelled 'racism', while I prefer 'internal colonialism' as a more comprehensive category. It includes racism, but it is also applicable to white oppression of whites and black exploitation of blacks.
67. Decouflé (V. 12), 20
68. Camara (VI. 18), 42
69. Johnson (V. 22), 116
70. Gusfield (V. 19), 11
71. Quoted by J.-Y. Calvez in (VII. 13), 97
72. In his introduction to Debray (V. 10), 11
73. *Ibid.* 57. For a further discussion of whether or not revolution breaks out or is made see Comblin (V. 9), 156f.

74. Brogan (V. 7), 268
75. Brinton (V. 6), 161, 164
76. Leider and Schmidt (VII. 15), 135
77. Niebuhr (VI. 54), 109
78. Moltmann (V. 29), 29
79. Berdyaev (VI. 11), 197f.
80. Brogan (V. 7), 266
81. Garcia and Calle (V. 15), 72ff.
82. Bennett (IV. 2), 203f.
83. *Vita Const.* 3.33
84. Ellul (V. 14), 54
85. Preston (VI. 58), 145
86. Gollwitzer (VI. 33), 106
87. Ogletree (VI. 56), 202
88. Ellul (V. 24), 217–32; Giradi (V. 17), 58–64; Padilla in Griffiths (V. 18), 76–81
89. Ellul (V. 24), 218, n. 23
90. T. S. Derr in Matthews (V. 27), 302
91. Cone (VI. 22), 94
92. Ellul (V. 24), 217–21
93. Cone (VI. 24), 107

6. VIOLENCE

1. Tillich (VI. 71), 8
2. Rahner (VII. 20), 391f.
3. MacMahon (I. 15), 55
4. (VII. 19), 19
5. Ogletree (VI. 55), 54
6. Tillich (IV. 22), 118
7. Solzhenitsyn (III. 10), 147
8. *New York Times* of 31 July 1966, quoted by Gilmore (V. 16), 268
9. Tillich, *loc. cit.*
10. MacMahon (I. 15), 61–4
11. Rahner (VII. 20), 399
12. Wolff (VII. 31), 604
13. Gray (VII. 12), 14
14. (VII. 23), 6
15. Merton (VII. 16), 7f.
16. Galtung (VII. 9), 171
17. Childress (VII. 2), 10
18. Galtung (VII. 9), 168
19. *Ibid.* 171
20. *Ibid.* 175
21. van den Haag also criticizes 'institutionalized violence', but here

again his view stems from his own initial definition of violence as essentially a direct physical act (VII. 14), 65, 68.

22. Ramsey (VII. 21), 8f.
23. Fowler (III. 4), 209–12
24. Galtung (VII. 2), 183
25. Ramsey *loc. cit.*
26. On 'mere' metaphors see Smart (III. 9), 44 n.
27. (VI. 20), 115
28. Rahner (VII. 20), 399f.
29. Tillich (IV. 22), 120
30. Tillich (VI. 71), 50
31. So too Hannah Arendt understands violence primarily in terms of its instrumental character (VII. 1), 46.
32. Houlden (I. 13), 125
33. In Outka and Ramsey (I. 19), 410
34. Bonhoeffer (I. 1), 217f.
35. *Ibid.* 65f.
36. See above 84-7
37. Houlden (I. 13), 112
38. Walker (III. 12), 144
39. Marginalia to Watson's *Apology for the Bible*, 108
40. Marginalia to Thornton's *Translation of the Lord's Prayer*, iii
41. Manson (I. 17), 103
42. Robinson (I. 25), 264
43. Houlden (I. 13), 199 f.
44. Ramsey in Outka and Ramsey (I. 19), 75f.
45. Dodd (I. 5), 71
46. Ramsey (I. 21), 34
47. *Ibid.* 144
48. Outka and Ramsey (I. 19), 11
49. B. Mitchell in *ibid.* 360
50. Micklem (VI. 49), 139
51. In Outka and Ramsey (1.19), 378
52. Fletcher (I. 8)
53. Thielicke (I. 27), I, 587f.
54. *Ibid.* II, 338
55. E. J. Tinsley in Macquarrie (I. 16), 163
56. Weber (VII. 30), 20
57. Dru (III. 2), 297
58. Stein (VIII. 24), 46
59. Tillich (IV. 22), 120f.
60. Ellul (VII. 5), 127f.
61. Stein (VII. 24), *passim*
62. *Tenure of Kings* in Milton (IV. 17), 468
63. So B. Rustin in Finn (VII. 7), 336

64. So Mehl (I. 18), 32f; Tillich (I. 28), 45

65. Ramsey (I. 23), 143

66. See above 26

67. In Finn (VII. 7), 416f.

68. Le Guillou (V. 23), 13

69. He also cites Matt. 5.39–43 and interprets the verses from a standpoint of naïve biblicism.

70. *Ibid.* 47

71. *Ibid.* 49f.

72. The same view of Jesus as 'the model of the nonviolent man' is basic to the argument of Edwards (VII. 4).

73. Dussel (V. 13), 52, n. 30

74. See above 62

75. Boff (VI. 14), 82

76. Kelly (VI. 40), 120

77. Popper (VII. 18), 356

78. For a more exhaustive refutation of Popper along these lines see Edgley (VII. 3), 18–24.

79. Arendt (VII. 1), 79

80. Gasset (VII. 10), 82

81. Ferguson (VII. 6), 8

82. (I. 20), 14

83. Bonhoeffer (I. 1), 304

84. See above 66ff.

85. Lewy (V. 25), 301ff.

86. *Ibid.* 320–3

87. Niebuhr (IV. 19), 141

88. Régamey (VII. 22), 240

89. Beardslee (V. 3), 51, 32

90. See above 62

91. *Lex, Rex*, XXX in Woodhouse (IV. 25), 211

92. Freire (VI. 31), 32

93. Ellul (VII. 5), 18

94. Walzer (V. 35), 258

95. Bloch (V. 4), 147

96. Bonhoeffer (I. 1), 214

97. For once I agree with Ellul (VII. 5), 116.

98. Fanon (IV. 9), 73

99. Ellul (VII. 5), 18

100. Cromwell (IV. 4), II, 343

101. Camara (VI. 18), 109

102. In a letter to G. Trier, 18 December 1889, quoted by Macfarlane (I. 14), 30.

103. Ellul (VII. 5), 102

104. (VII. 27), 13

105. Edwards (III. 3), II, 509

106. (V. 1), 23

107. Ramsey (I. 23), 431

108. In a preparatory paper for the Cardiff Consultation.

109. Quoted by R. Coste in (VII. 13), 201

110. Quoted by de Broucher (V. 8), 542

111. Theological Issues (VII. 25), 77

112. (VII. 28), 77

113. Tooke (I. 29)

114. Ellul (VII. 5), 6

115. Stein (VII. 24), 60

116. Walzer (V. 35), 268

117. J. C. Bennett in (VI. 39), 10

118. 'The Thorough Revolutionary', in *Movement and Revolution*, Garden City, New York, 1970. I have been unable to consult a copy of this and have been dependent upon the very clear exposition given by Paul Ramsey (I. 24), 37–40.

119. *Ibid.*

120. See above 61f.

121. (I. 4), 14

122. In Matthews (V. 27), 329

123. Berdyaev (VI. 12), 267

124. Dewart (IV. 7), 271

125. Lehmann (VII. 24), 266

126. Solzhenitsyn (III. 10), 13, n. 5

127. Ellul (VII. 5), 133

128. Alves (VI. 3), 186

129. Griswold (II. 7), 730

130. Berdyaev (VI. 11), 70

131. Ramsey (I. 23), 14

132. *Prensa Latina*, No. 3054, 8 October 1868, quoted by James (V. 21), 347

133. Quoted *ibid.* 316

134. Mehl (I. 18), 10

135. Marcuse in de George (I. 10), 147, 140ff.

136. Stein (VII. 24), 56

137. Tabor (V. 35), 172

138. So J. Duquesne in (VII. 13), 146

139. Fanon (IV. 9), 203–51

140. Fanon (IV. 10), 23f.

141. Gert (VII. 11), 623

142. Quoted by Coste (VI. 25)

143. Marcuse in de George (I. 10), 141. For a statement of the extent to which past revolutions have contributed to freedom see Comblin (V. 9), 156f.

144. Nielsen in Held (IV. 15), 43f.
145. In Finn (VII. 7), 230
146. R. Darsac in (VII. 13), 66
147. Tabor (V. 35), 156
148. Debray (V. 10), 23
149. Nielsen (V. 30), 18
150. *Ibid.*
151. Debray (V. 10), 23
152. *The Just Defence* (1653), 7, in Haller and Davies (IV. 14), 459
153. A. Gilbert in Finn (VII. 7), 100
154. Ellul (VII. 5), 74
155. For these terms see above 106ff.
156. Roberts (VI. 63), 4
157. Matthews (V. 27), 329
158. Macquarrie (VI. 46), 32
159. *Ibid.* 19
160. So, very aptly, Comblin (V. 9), 215.

BIBLIOGRAPHY

(Except where otherwise stated, the place of publication is London)

I. *Ethics*

1. D. Bonhoeffer, *Ethics*, SCM Press 1955
2. J. C. Bennett (ed.), *Christian Social Ethics in a Changing World*, SCM Press 1966
3. J. F. Childress, *Civil Disobedience and Political Obligation*, Yale University Press, New Haven and London 1971
4. *Civil Strife. A Report Presented by the Board for Social Responsibility*, May 1971
5. C. H. Dodd, *Gospel and Law*, CUP, Cambridge 1951
6. R. S. Downie, *Government Action and Morality*, Macmillan 1964
7. J. Eppstein, *Does God Say Kill?*, Stacey 1972
8. J. Fletcher, *Situation Ethics. The New Morality*, SCM Press 1966
9. V. P. Furnish, *The Love Command in the New Testament*, SCM Press 1973
10. R. T. de George (ed.), *Ethics and Society*, Macmillan 1968
11. R. T. Hall, *The Morality of Civil Disobedience*, Harper & Row, New York 1971
12. B. Häring, *Morality is for Persons*, Vision Press 1972
13. J. L. Houlden, *Ethics and the New Testament*, Penguin, Harmondsworth, 1973; reissued Mowbray, 1975
14. L. J. Macfarlane, *Political Disobedience*, Macmillan 1971
15. T. MacMahon, 'The Moral Agents of Power', *Concilium*, 10.9,1973
16. J. Macquarrie (ed.), *A Dictionary of Christian Ethics*, SCM Press 1967
17. T. W. Manson, *Ethics and the Gospel*, SCM Press 1960
18. R. Mehl, *Pour une éthique sociale chrétienne*, Delachaux and Niestlé, Neuchâtel and Paris, 1967
19. G. E. Outka and P. Ramsey, *Norm and Content in Christian Ethics*, SCM Press 1969
20. *Prosperity, Responsibility, Frugality* (Lenten Pastoral 1973 of the Dutch Bishops), Secretariat of the Roman Catholic Church in the Netherlands 1973
21. P. Ramsey, *Basic Christian Ethics*, Scribner, New York, 1950
22. — *War and the Christian Conscience*, Duke University, Durham, 1961
23. — *The Just War*, Scribner, New York, 1968

24. — 'The Just Revolution', *Worldview*, October 1973
25. N. H. G. Robinson, *The Groundwork of Christian Ethics*, Collins 1971
26. M. Q. Sibley, *The Obligation to Disobey. Conscience and the Law*, Council on Religion and International Affairs, New York, 1970
27. H. Thielicke, *Theological Ethics*, A. & C. Black, 2 vols, 1968
28. P. Tillich, *Morality and Beyond*, Routledge & Kegan Paul 1964
29. J. D. Tooke, *The Just War in Aquinas and Grotius*, SPCK 1965

II. *Law*

1. H. J. Berman, *The Interaction of Law and Religion*, SCM Press 1974
2. E. Brunner, *Justice and the Social Order*, Lutterworth 1945
3. P. Devlin, *The Enforcement of Morals*, OUP 1965
4. L. L. Fuller, *The Morality of Law*, Yale University Press, New Haven and London, 1964
5. S. A. Golunki and M. S. Strogovich, 'Theory of the State and Law', *Soviet Legal Philosophy*, Harvard University Press, Harvard, 1951
6. A. L. Goodhart, *English Law and the Moral Law*, Stevens 1953
7. E. N. Griswold, 'Dissent-1968', *Tulane Law Review*, XLII, 1968
8. L. Veysey (ed.), *Law and Resistance. American Attitudes to Authority*, Harper & Row, New York, 1970
9. P. H. Winfield, *A Text-Book of the Law of Torts*, Sweet & Maxwell 1937

III. *Miscellaneous*

1. Church of England Synod, *Report of Proceedings*, 5.3, Church Information Office 1974
2. A. Dru (ed.), *The Journals of S. Kierkegaard*, OUP, Oxford, 1938
3. P. Edwards (ed.), *Encyclopedia of Philosophy*, Macmillan, New York, II, 1967
4. H. W. and F. G. Fowler, *The King's English*, Clarendon Press, Oxford, 3rd ed., 1931
5. H. H. Gerth and C. W. Mills (eds), *From Max Weber. Essays in Sociology*, Routledge & Kegan Paul, 6th imp., 1967
6. C. Y. Glock and R. Stark, *American Piety. The Nature of Religious Commitment*, University of California, Berkeley and Los Angeles, 1968
7. G. Jackson, *Soledad Brother*, Penguin, Harmondsworth 1971
8. Runiart, *Acta Primorum Maryum Sincera*, 1713
9. N. Smart, *Reason and Faith*, Routledge & Kegan Paul 1958
10. A. Solzhenitsyn, *The Gulag Archipelago*, Fontana 1974
11. R. Towler, *Homo Religiosus: Sociological Problems in the Study of Religion*, Constable 1974

12. J. L. Walker, *Body and Soul. Gestalt Therapy and Religious Experience*, Abingdon, Nashville and New York, 1971

IV. *Politics (and the State)*

1. J. W. Allen, *A History of Political Thought in the Sixteenth Century*, Methuen 1928
2. J. C. Bennett, *Christians and the State*, Scribner, New York, 1958
3. R. W. and A. J. Carlyle, *A History of Medieval Political Theory in the West*, Blackwood, Edinburgh and London, V, 1928
4. O. Cromwell, *Letters and Speeches*, (ed.), T. Carlyle, Chapman & Hall, 2 vols., 1857
5. O. Cullman, *The State in the New Testament*, SCM Press 1957
6. G. Davies, *The Early Stuarts 1603–1660*, Clarendon, Oxford, 1937
7. L. Dewart, *Cuba, Church and Crisis*, Sheed & Ward 1971
8. J. Dunne, *The Political Thought of John Locke*, CUP, Cambridge, 1969
9. F. Fanon, *The Wretched of the Earth*, Grove Press, New York, 1963
10. — *A Dying Colonialism*, Grove Press, New York, 1967
11. — *Black Skin White Masks*, Paladin 1972
12. J. N. Figgis, *The Divine Right of Kings*, CUP, Cambridge, 2nd ed., 1914
13. P. H. Gruber (ed.), *Fetters of Injustice*, WCC, Geneva, 1970
14. W. Haller and G. Davies (eds), *The Levellers Tracts, 1647–1653*, Columbia University Press, New York, 1944
15. V. Held, K. Nielsen, C. Parsons, *Philosophy and Political Action*, OUP, New York, 1972
16. V. I. Lenin, *Religion*, Lawrence and Wishart, n.d.
17. J. Milton, *Works*, Pickering, IV, 1851
18. J. Newfield, *A Prophetic Minority*, Bland 1967
19. R. Niebuhr, *On Politics*, ed. H. Davis and R. Good, Scribner, New York, 1960
20. J.-J. Rousseau, *Contrat Social*, 1762
21. G. H. Sabine, *A History of Political Theory*, Harrap, 2nd ed., 1949
22. P. Tillich, *Political Expectations*, Harper & Row, New York, 1971
23. W. Tyndale, *The Obedience of the Christian Man*, 1528. Christian Classics Series, Religious Tract Society, n.d.
24. F. P. Verney, *Memoirs of the Verney Family during the Civil War*, Longmans, II, 1892
25. A. S. P. Woodhouse (ed.), *Puritanism and Liberty*, Dent, 1938

V. *Revolution*

1. *Angola. The Independence Agreement*, Ministry of Mass Communication, Lisbon, 1975

2. H. Arendt, *On Revolution*, Faber & Faber 1963

3. W. A. Beardslee, 'New Perspectives on Revolution as a Theological Problem', *Journal of Religion*, 51, 1971

4. E. Bloch, *Thomas Münzer, Théologien de la révolution*, Les Lettres Nouvelles, Julliard, Paris, 1962

5. B. Boston, 'How are Revelation and Revolution Related?', *Theology Today*, 26, 2, 1969.

6. C. Brinton, *The Anatomy of Revolution*, Cape 1953

7. D. W. Brogan, *The Price of Revolution*, Hamilton 1951

8. J. de Broucher, 'Has the Church Opted for Revolution?', *New Blackfriars*, 49, 1967–8

9. J. Comblin, *Théologie de la révolution*, Editions universitaires, Paris, 1970

10. R. Debray, *Revolution in the Revolution?*, Monthly Review Press, New York and London, 1967

11. — *Strategy for Revolution*, Cape 1970

12. A. Decouflé, *Sociologie des révolutions*, Presses universitaires, Paris, 2nd ed., 1970

13. E. Dussel, 'Domination-Liberation. A New Approach', *Concilium*, 6.10, 1974

14. J. Ellul, *Autopsy of Revolution*, Knopf, New York, 1971

15. J. A. Garcia and C. R. Calle (eds), *Camilo Torres. Priest and Revolutionary*, Sheed & Ward 1968

16. G. S. Gilmore, *Black Religion and Black Radicalism*, Doubleday, New York, 1969

17. G. Giradi, 'The Philosophy of Revolution and Atheism', *Concilium*, 6.4, 1968

18. B. Griffiths (ed.), *Is Revolution Change?*, Inter-Varsity Press 1972

19. J. R. Gusfield (ed.), *Protest, Reform and Revolution. A Reader in Social Movements*, Wiley, New York, 1970

20. V. Hayward, *Christians and China*, Christian Journals, Belfast, 1974

21. D. James, *Che Guevara. A Biography*, Allen & Unwin 1970

22. C. Johnson, *Revolutionary Change*, University of London, 1968

23. M. J. Le Guillou, O. Clément, J. Bosc, *Evangile et révolution*, Editions du Centurion, Paris, 1968

24. P. Lehmann, *The Transfiguration of Politics Jesus Christ and the Question of Revolution*, SCM Press 1975

25. G. Lewy, *Religion and Revolution*, OUP, New York, 1974

26. C. E. Lincoln, 'The Black Revolution in Cultural Perspective', *Union Seminary Quarterly Review*, 23.3, 1968

27. Z. K. Matthews (ed.), *Responsible Government in a Revolutionary Age*, SCM Press 1966

28. N. Middleton, *The Language of Christian Revolution*, Sheed & Ward 1968

29. J. Moltmann, *Religion, Revolution and the Future*, Scribner, New York ,1969

30. K. Nielsen, 'On the Ethics of Revolution', *Radical Philosophy*, 6, 1973

31. S. E. Ozment, *Mysticism and Dissent*, Yale University Press, New Haven and London, 1973

32. 'Revolution and Desacralization', *Concilium*, 7.5, 1969

33. C. J. Snoek, 'The Third World, Revolution and Christianity', *Concilium*, 5.2, 1966

34. R. Tabor, *The War of the Flea. A Study of Guerilla Warfare, Theory and Practice*, Stuart, New York, 1972

35. M. Walzer, *The Revolution of the Saints. A Study in the Origins of Radical Politics*, Weidenfeld & Nicolson 1966

VI. (*Political*) *Theology*

1. T. de Alencar, 'The Gospel and Brazil', *New Blackfriars*, 54, 1973

2. R. Alves, *A Theology of Human Hope*, Corpus Books, Washington, Cleveland, 1969

3. — *Tomorrow's Child*, SCM Press 1972

4. C. Antoine, *Church and Power in Brazil*, Sheed & Ward 1973

5. J. Baillie, *Our Knowledge of God*, OUP 1941

6. J. A. Baird, *The Justice of God in the Teaching of Jesus*, SCM Press 1963

7. *Bangkok 1973*, WCC, Geneva, 1973

8. K. Barth, *The Church and the Political Problems of our Day*, Hodder & Stoughton 1939

9. — *Church Dogmatics*, T. & T. Clark, Edinburgh, IV, 1968

10. J. Bennett, *Christian Faith and Political Choice*, Ryerson, Toronto, 1963

11. N. Berdyaev, *Christianity and the Class War*, Sheed & Ward 1934

12. — *The Destiny of Man*, Bles 1937

13. — *Freedom and Slavery*, Bles 1943

14. L. Boff, 'Salvation in Jesus Christ and the Process of Liberation', *Concilium*, 6.10, 1974

15. P. Bonnard, *L'évangile selon Saint Matthieu*, Delachaux and Niestlé, Neuchâtel and Paris, 1963

16. S. G. F. Brandon, *Jesus and the Zealots*, Manchester University Press, Manchester, 1967

17. C. J. Cadoux, *The Early Church and the World*, T. & T. Clark, Edinburgh, 1925

18. H. Camara, *Church and Colonialism*, Sheed & Ward 1969

19. — *Race against Time*, Sheed & Ward 1971

20. *Christians in the Technical and Social Revolutions of Our Time.*

World Conference on Church and Society. Official Report, WCC, Geneva, 1967

21. B. J. de Clerq, *Religion, idéologie et politique*, Casterman, Tournai, 1968

22. J. H. Cone, *Black Theology and Black Power*, Seabury Press, New York, 1969

23. — *A Black Theology of Liberation*, Lippincott, Philadelphia and New York, 1970

24. — *The Spirituals and the Blues*, Seabury Press, New York, 1972

25. R. Coste, *Evangile et politique*, Aubier-Montaigne, Paris, 1968

26. J. G. Davies, *Every Day God. Encountering the Holy in World and Worship*, SCM Press 1973

27. L. Dewart, 'The Church and Political Conservatism', *Concilium*, 6.4, 1968

28. M. Echegoyen, 'Priests and Socialism in Chile', *New Blackfriars*, 52, 1971

29. J. Ellul, *Fausse présence au monde moderne*, Les Bergers et les Mages, Paris, 1963

30. A. Fragoso, 'Evangelio y justicia social', *Cuademos de Marcha*, 17 September 1968

31. P. Freire, *Pedagogy of the Oppressed*, Herder & Herder, New York, 1970

32. A. Geyer and D. G. Peerman (eds), *Theological Crossings*, Eerdmans, Grand Rapids, 1971

33. H. Gollwitzer, *The Christian Faith and the Marxist Criticism of Religion*, St Andrews, Edinburgh, 1970.

34. G. Gutiérrez, *A Theology of Liberation*, Orbis Books, Maryknoll, New York, 1973

35. — 'Liberation, Theology and Proclamation', *Concilium*, 6.10, 1974

36. F. Herzog, *Liberation, Theology. Liberation in the Light of the Fourth Gospel*, Seabury Press, New York, 1972

37. A. van den Heuvel, *These Rebellious Powers*, SCM Press 1966

38. W. R. Inge, *The Fall of Idols*, Putnam, 1940

39. *In Search of a Theology of Development. A Sodepax Report*, 1970

40. J. N. D. Kelly, *A Commentary on the Epistles of Peter and Jude*, A. & C. Black 1969

41. J. Knox, *Works*, ed. D. Laing, Johnstone & Hunter, Edinburgh, III, 1854; IV, 1855

42. — *History of the Reformation in Scotland*, ed. W. C. Dickinson, Nelson, 2 vols., 1949

43. W. G. Kümmel, *A Theology of the New Testament*, SCM Press 1974

44. F. J. Leenhardt, *The Epistle to the Romans. A Commentary*, Lutterworth 1961

45. *Malvern 1941: The Life of the Church and the Order of Society*, Longmans, Green, 1941

46. J. Macquarrie, *The Concept of Peace*, SCM Press 1973
47. H. McCabe, *Law, Love and Language*, Sheed & Ward 1968
48. J. B. Metz, 'The Church's Social Function in the Light of Political Theology', *Concilium*, 6.4, 1968
49. N. Micklem, *The Theology of Politics*, OUP 1941
50. A. Miller, *The Christian Significance of Karl Marx*, SCM Press 1946
51. J. Moltmann, *The Crucified God*, SCM Press 1974
52. B. Moore (ed.), *Black Theology. The South African Voice*, Hurst 1973
53. P. E. More and F. L. Cross (eds.), *Anglicanism*, SPCK 1935
54. R. Niebuhr, *Faith and Politics*, Braziller, New York, 1968
55. T. W. Ogletree, 'From Anxiety to Responsibility: The Shifting Focus of Theological Reflection', *New Theology*, 6, ed., M. E. Marty and D. G. Peerman, Macmillan, New York, 1969
56. — 'The Gospel as Power', *ibid.*, 8, 1971
57. H. Peukert (ed.), *Diskussion zur "politischen Theologie"*, Matthias-Grunewald-Verlag, Mainz, 1969
58. R. H. Preston, (ed.), *Technology and Social Justice*, SCM Press 1971
59. G. Quell and G. Schrenck, *Righteousness*, A. & C. Black 1959
60. P. Reamonn, 'Liberating Theology: Gustavo Gutiérrez', *New Blackfriars*, 54, 1973
61. A. Richardson, *The Political Christ*, SCM Press 1972
62. J. Ridley, *John Knox*, Clarendon Press, Oxford, 1968
63. J. D. Roberts, *Liberation and Reconciliation. A Black Theology*, Westminster, Philadelphia, 1971
64. J. A. T. Robinson, *On Being the Church in the World*, SCM Press 1960
65. J. Rossel, *Mission in a Dynamic Society*, SCM Press 1968
66. Letty M. Russel, *Human Liberation in a Feminist Perspective – A Theology*, Westminster, Philadelphia, 1974
67. E. Schillebeeckx, *Los catolicos holandeses*, Desclée de Brouwer, Bilbao, 1970
68. T. Steeman, 'Political Relevance of the Christian Community between Integralism and Critical Commitment,' *Concilium*, 4.9, 1973
69. W. Temple, *Essays in Christian Politics and Kindred Subjects*, Longmans, Green 1927
70. — *The Hope of the New World*, SCM Press 1941
71. P. Tillich, *Love, Power and Justice*, OUP 1967
72. B. Wicker, *First the Political Kingdom*, University of Notre Dame, Notre Dame, 1968
73. H. Zwingli, *Huldreich Zwingli's sämtliche Werke*, Leipzig, II, 1908

VII. *Violence*

1. H. Arendt, *On Violence*, Allen Lane, The Penguin Press 1970

2. J. F. Childress, 'Some Reflections on Violence and Nonviolence', WCC, Geneva, 1972

3. R. Edgley, 'Reason and Violence', *Radical Philosophy*, 4, 1973

4. G. R. Edwards, *Jesus and the Politics of Violence*, Harper & Row, New York, 1972

5. J. Ellul, *Violence, Reflections from a Christian Perspective*, SCM Press 1970

6. J. Ferguson, *The Politics of Love. The New Testament and Non-Violent Revolution*, James Clarke, Carlisle, n.d.

7. J. Finn, ed., *Protest, Pacifism and Politics*, Vintage Books, New York, 1968

8. *Force in the Modern World. A Document Prepared by the Board of Social Responsibility*, SCM 1973

9. J. Galtung, 'Violence, Peace, and Peace Research', *Journal of Peace Research*, 3, 1969

10. Ortega y Gasset, *The Revolution of the Masses*, Norton, New York, 1932

11. B. Gert, 'Justifying Violence', *Journal of Philosophy*, 66, 1969

12. J. G. Gray, *On Understanding Violence Philosophically and Other Essays*, Harper & Row, New York, 1970

13. *Guerre révolutionnaire et conscience chrétienne*, Pax Christi, Paris, 1967

14. E. van den Haag, *Political Violence and Civil Disobedience*, Harper, New York, 1972

15. C. Leider and K. M. Schmidt, *The Politics of Violence in the Modern World*, Prentice-Hall, Englewood Cliffs, 1968

16. T. Merton, *Faith and Violence*, University of Notre Dame, Notre Dame, 1968

17. W. R. Miller, *Non-violence. A Christian Interpretation*, Allen & Unwin 1964

18. K. R. Popper, *Conjectures and Reflections*, Routledge & Kegan Paul 1963

19. *Power, Powerlessness, Hope* (Lenten Pastoral 1974 of the Dutch Bishops), Secretariat van de R. K. Kerkprovincie in Nederland 1974

20. K. Rahner, *Theological Investigations*, Darton, Longman & Todd, 4, 1966

21. P. Ramsey, 'The Betrayal of Language', *Worldview*, February 1971

22. P. Régamey, *Non-violence and the Christian Conscience*, Darton, Longman & Todd 1966

23. *Report of the Consultation on 'Violence, Non-violence and the Struggle for Social Justice'*, WCC, Geneva, 1972

24. W. Stein (ed.), *Nuclear Weapons and Christian Conscience*, Methuen, 1961

25. 'Theological Issues of Church and Society', *Study Encounter*, 4.2, 1968
26. H. B. T. Thoreau, *Anti-Slavery and Reform Papers*, Haven House, Montreal, 1963
27. *Violence and Oppression. A Quaker Report*, 1973
28. *Violence in Southern Africa. A Christian Assessment*, SCM Press 1970
29. 'Violence, Nonviolence and the Struggle for Social Justice. Exploring Strategies for Radical Social Change', *Study Encounter*, 7.3, 1971
30. H.-R. Weber, 'Freedom Fighter or Prince of Peace', *Study Encounter*, 8.4, 1972
31. R. P. Wolff, 'On Violence', *Journal of Philosophy*, 66, 1969

INDEX

Absolutes (absolutize), 66f., 85,
109, 115, 117, 120f., 127, 138,
141f., 145, 148f., 151, 153, 156,
163, 173
Agag, 65
Ahab, 57
Ahimilech, 57
Algeria, 110, 177
Alves, R., 96, 107, 172
Amaziah, 57
Anderson, J. N. D., 2
Angola, 16f., 163, 165
Anscombe, G. W. M., 147, 167,
176
Anulinus, 73
Apartheid, 30, 38, 130
Aquinas, 49f., 81f., 165, 167
Arendt, H., 88, 106
Aristotle, 49, 80, 91
Assman, H., 164
Athaliah, 57
Atheism, 121, 127
Atkin, Lord, 88
Augustine, 26, 78, 165

Baillie, J., 27
Barth, K., 4, 10, 21f., 41, 69
Belem, Archbishop of, 34
Bennett, J. C., 27, 115
Berdyaev, N., 96f., 106, 113, 170,
173
Bible, 11, 56, 65f., 80, 99, 118
Blackburn, R., 111
Black Power, 95f., 185
Black Theology, 6f., 104
Blake, W., 141
Bloch, E., 160
Bolivia, 112
Bonhoeffer, D., 18, 21, 87, 127,
143, 155
Brandon, S. G. F., 23
Brazil, 3, 28, 35
Brinton, C., 112

Britten, B., 187
Brunner, E., 80
Bullinger, J. H., 54f.
Butler, C., 4

Cadoux, J. C., 73
Calvin, 50, 53ff., 68, 167
Camara, H., 75, 77, 95, 110, 161
Castro, 91, 111, 178, 182
Chiang Kai-shek, 105
Childress, J. F., 132f.
Chile, 43
China, 105, 111, 115, 148
Church, 3f., 9, 11ff., 15f., 29ff.,
41, 108f., 187
Cicero, 49, 76
de Clerq, B. J., 29, 35
Colombia, 91, 115, 178
Colonialism, 96, 165
Conciliation, 184f.
Cone, J. H., 93, 119, 121
Conscientization, 8, 101, 110f.,
169, 180, 182
Constantine, 114, 123
Corbet, J., 58
Corbett, E., 160
Coste, R., 98
Coup d'état, 89f.
Creation, 38f.
Cromwell, 44, 61ff., 70, 93, 152,
158, 161, 170
Cuba, 91, 104, 110f., 115, 178
Cullmann, O., 23, 48
Cyprus, 110
Czechoslovakia, 110

Daniel, 56, 59
Debray, R., 89f., 112, 181f.
Devlin, Lord, 72, 82, 86
Diocletian, 73
Divine Right, 51f.
Doeg, 57

Christians, Politics and Violent Revolution

J.G. Davies

The volatile situations found in Latin America, Africa, Portugal,
Lebanon and Northern Ireland make this a book of singular importance. As Professor Davies points out, he has written it in response
to a harshly real question put to him by students and theologians in
the Third World.

"We are Christians living in countries where poverty, exploitation
and suffering abound. There seems no other way to alter the
situation except by joining in violent revolution. But is it ever
possible to do this and remain a Christian?"

To this question J.G. Davies gives a carefully reasoned
theological response. Drawing an analogy between a just war and a
just revolution, he sees no theoretical objection to Christian participation in violent revolution, provided certain criteria are met.

Davies' argument is more than a dry, schematic presentation. He
cites major Protestant and Catholic statements, and deals with
South Africa, Cuba and Northern Ireland to illustrate his starting
point: that violence and revolution are on the agenda which the
world presents to the Church. His book is one of the few to deal
comprehensively with that part of the Church's agenda, even while
recognizing the Church's mission to be a creative agent of *shalom*.

J.G. DAVIES is Professor of Theology at the University of Birmingham, England. His writings encompass a wide range of subjects:
early Church architecture, liturgy and contemporary Christian spirituality.

He has lectured frequently in South East Asia, Africa and Latin
America. There he has seen close up the systems of oppression
which gave rise to this book as he tried to grapple theologically with
the issues of "Christians, politics and violent revolution."

ORBIS BOOKS

Maryknoll, New York 10545

Cover Design: Al Schreiner